# Heal Your Self,

# Heal Your World

# Heal Your Self, Heal Your World

Turn illness and suffering into health and peace
through scientifically proven methods

## Brian Rees M.D., M.P.H.

Manu Publishing
Pacific Palisades, California
1997

## Library of Congress Cataloging in Publication Data

Rees, Brian.
    Heal your self, heal your world : turn illness and suffering into
health and peace through scientifically proven methods / Brian Rees.
        p.    cm.
    Includes bibliographical references and index.
    ISBN 0-9652319-3-3
        1. Medicine, Ayurvedic. 2. Transcendental Meditation. I. Title.
R605.R435    1997
615.5'3--dc20
                                                        96-8994
                                                          CIP

Manu Publishing
P.O. Box 561
Pacific Palisades CA 90272   USA

*To my parents*

*who taught me to love*

*my wife*

*who gave me*

*my children*

*who opened my heart*

## Legal warning/Disclaimer

Please read this before buying or reading this book.

Transcendental Meditation™ (TM), Maharishi Amrit Kalash™, Maharishi Ayur-Veda™, Maharishi Vedic Science™, Maharishi's Vedic Approach to Health are all registered trademarks.

The statements and opinions in this book are those of Dr. Brian Rees, not of anyone else, nor of any organization, including but not limited to the Natural Law Party, or those teaching TM or administering any of the programs of Maharishi's Vedic Approach to Health, Maharishi Ayur-Veda or Maharishi's Vedic Science. All such statements are true and accurate to the best of the author's knowledge at the time of publication, but other persons and experts may disagree with them. No statement in this book is a claim or guarantee for any product (herbal or otherwise), program, or course of instruction.

The purpose of this book is to educate and entertain. Nothing in this book is meant to replace professional advice, medical, psychological, or otherwise. If you are sick, go to a doctor. No one should change or discontinue professional medical care because of anything written in this book.

Neither the author, publisher, nor any other person or organization cited in this book shall have liability or responsibility to any person or entity with respect to any loss or damage caused or alleged to be caused directly or indirectly by any information contained in this book. If you do not agree to release the above mentioned from such liability, you should neither buy nor read this book.

## Acknowledgments

There is an old expression: what is true is not new, and what is new is not true. It is an appropriate sentiment for the book you now hold.

Maharishi Mahesh Yogi is the inspiration for this book. Virtually everything that is of value in it has been brought to light by Maharishi, who is the leading authority in the explanation of the knowledge from the Vedic tradition. But Maharishi did not proofread this book: any errors in it are mine alone.

This book or parts of it were reviewed by about 30 experts in the field, mostly doctors and researchers. They made numerous comments and criticisms, many of which I employed to make changes, some of which I chose not to act on. I hesitate to name all these esteemed colleagues lest they be identified with any mistakes I have made here, but I do want to thank them for their insights and help.

There are a number of quotes from Maharishi herein; some came from lectures, or perhaps from a piece of paper tacked to an office wall. If the quote is not referenced, I could not confirm its accuracy.

This book was not commissioned, endorsed, or approved by any person or organization. The organizations teaching TM and Maharishi's Vedic Science are apolitical nonprofit educational organizations. Thus, the political and social views expressed here are my own. I have presented anecdotes illustrating how I try to apply this knowledge to the care of my patients. These applications and interpretations, to the degree that I have adapted them to my own clinical practice, are mine, and may be imperfect.

You the reader should thank Judith Searle of The Editorial Dept in Santa Monica California; the book was a chore to read before she cleaned it up. I want to thank Robert Howard of Howard Graphics in Boulder Colorado who did the cover design, and my very capable publicist John Raatz of the Visioneering Group in Santa Monica.

Most amorously I thank my lovely wife Atsuko whose support for me in this project has been unflagging and unconditional. I am most fortunate to have her at my side. Also I must thank and apologize to my wonderful children Matthew and Melissa who surrendered uncounted computer games so that I might sit at the computer to write. They have been gracious enough to forgive me.

# Table of Contents

## Part Three: Applications      **161**

# Part One

# The Body-Mind and Beyond

## CHAPTER ONE

# Grandpa's Veins

> A cheerful face is nearly as good for an invalid as healthy weather.
> -- Benjamin Franklin

The phone rang about three o'clock in the morning. It was the nurse in the emergency room.

"Mr. Thibodeau just arrived with chest pain. He has bad veins and we can't start an IV on him. In the past, he's required a central line. Could you come in please?"

Someone with chest pain that might be from his heart needs an *IV* (an *intravenous* line) because he may need drugs immediately if his heart rhythm destabilizes. But, if one has had a lot of IVs in the past, the veins can scar and it becomes hard to find one that will take an IV.

A central line is an IV stuck into a vein in the neck or the chest with a big needle. It can be technically difficult and risky. It's possible to poke a hole in the lining of the lung and all manner of bad things can follow, particularly if you are covering someone else's practice, as I was.

I was determined to put in a regular peripheral IV instead of a central IV if at all possible.

Mr. Thibodeau's face was flushed. The only vein I could see was a very prominent one in the middle of his forehead. He was in pain and had been poked like a pin cushion.

"You took your damn time getting here, Doc."

It didn't seem the time for pleasantries.

After a brief introduction, I put a tourniquet on his arm. The nurses were right, there wasn't much to choose from. The other arm was no better.

It was hot in Louisiana, and even though his hospital room was air conditioned I could feel a drop of perspiration trickling from my forehead down my nose, threatening to plop onto his tight, vein-less extremity.

"Doc, my chest hurts and I'm going to drop dead before you folks get any medicine in me."

Not exactly what I needed to hear.

The nurse stuck her head in the door. "Mr. Thibodeau, your daughter and grandson are here. Would you like them to come in?"

Couldn't she have asked me first?

"I hope to be done here in just a few minutes," I said.

"Come on, Doc. I want to see 'em."

Just what I needed: an audience for my fumbling ministrations.

"Of course. Have them come in."

His daughter walked in, but his attention focused on his grandson, a cute little fellow about three years old.

"There's my boy!"

The boy smiled widely and began to climb into his lap, partially disrupting my field of work. I opened my mouth to object but stopped myself. Mr. Thibodeau was wearing a big grin. He had stopped complaining and his arm felt relaxed, warm. Behold! A vein.

Without hesitation, I muttered, "You'll feel a little stick here," and zip -- in went the IV.

I stepped out of the room to get his chart and winked at the nurse.

"Thanks for sending his grandson in."

"You're welcome," she said with a confused smile.

I took Mr. Thibodeau's history and performed a physical exam, mostly with his grandson on his lap. He wasn't such a can-tankerous fellow after all. As it turned out, he required no narcotics, just a dose of loving grandson. He soon recovered and went home.

What happened here?

Perhaps his feelings for his grandson reflected the boundless love found in the natural state of a loving universe. The tightness he felt was blocking the flow of his enjoyment, and that was reflected in his body. Once that constriction was released, veins opened, blood flowed -- the procedure was successful. Whether the resolution of his chest pain was due to a similar dilatation of the arteries serving his heart, I do not know. But the overall effect was a clear demonstration to this then young physician that our emotions and attitudes can have a significant impact on our bodies for good or ill.

Another experience brought this truth even closer to home. Driving down the freeway, I looked in my side mirror and saw the car in the lane next to me approaching very fast. Too fast. He passed on my right and cut in front of me at about 80 miles per hour. Then, of course, he had to jam on his brakes because there was nowhere for him to go. The car that had been a few feet in front of me is now just inches ahead of him. I had to stand on my brake to keep from hitting this guy. My sleeping children were jostled, the baby got propelled forward in her car seat and I became livid. Horns are rarely employed on Southern California freeways for fear of return comments from assault rifles. But I leaned on my horn anyway, flashed my high beams and generally conveyed my displeasure with this guy's performance. Apparently oblivious, he changed lanes when it was possible and proceeded rapidly and unsafely down the freeway...leaving me to deal with my anger.

I don't enjoy feelings of righteous indignation. But suppressing such feelings is difficult and ineffective. Better to interpret and react to this experience differently than with my first reaction of anger.

If I'm furious with him, what becomes of that fury when its object is out of reach?

Stress hormones are percolating around in my physiology, generating considerable wear and tear. Yet the object of my fury is unscathed. Here I am, boiling inside staring maliciously at the back of this fellow's head, while he probably hasn't looked in his rear-view mirror since Carter was President. Even if he heard my horn he might well be oblivious to my presence, indifferent to my feelings. Or perhaps he has real psychopathology and loves to provoke fellow motorists and is ecstatic at getting a rise out of me. Or maybe his wife is in labor in the back seat and he's rushing to the hospital.

In any case, the take-home message for me is the same: It doesn't help to get upset. Certainly, it doesn't help to stay upset. If it did help to get upset, I'd be all for it; but it doesn't. It's best to live a life in which such stress is processed in a non-stressful fashion, effortlessly. Techniques for doing this exist. But before I discuss them, I'd like to review briefly what stress is and what it does to us.

## Stress: the modern boogie man

> You shall digest the venom of your spleen,
> Though it do split you.
> -- Shakespeare, *Julius Caesar*

Our modern understanding of stress comes from a physician and researcher named Hans Selye who was inept at handling his laboratory animals. He would drop them, lose them, chase them about and trap them. When he examined them pathologically he found changes in their immune systems and various other organs and realized that his clumsiness was making them sick. He borrowed a term from engineering -- "stress" -- and that term has stuck to this day.

Selye's work helped to define what happens to us physiologically when we become stressed. As we evolved over millennia it was advantageous to us to be able to make a simple choice: fight or flight. If we came home to the cave and found that some bear had taken up occupancy, we needed to employ one option or the other immediately. In the face of this kind of threat our adrenal and pituitary glands secrete hormones. Our sympathetic nervous system secretes neurotransmitters, all of which bring us to a state of heightened vigilance and readiness for combat or a fast exit. We shunt blood away from organs that don't need it at this moment and send it to muscles so that we can act strongly.

These days, instead of having a bear to wrestle with, we are confronted with a memo from the boss, a look from our spouse, a report on the behavior of our offspring. These stimuli usually do not provoke us into vigorous activity. Instead, they subject us to the slow burn of modern living.

There have been many attempts to measure and quantify the stress of contemporary life. Tools have been developed to measure the day-to-day minor annoyances of life which can build up and impact health.[1] Early researchers also looked at major life changes and how they affect us.[2] (See table) They observed[3] a direct relationship between the significance of life changes and the risk of health consequences.

You might want to take this test yourself. Simply add up the mean values of the experiences you've had over the last three months and see what your total is. According to researchers[4], the chance of your experiencing some illness in the near future is about 30 percent or less if your score is less than 150. It rises to about 50 percent if your score is between 150 and 299, and persons with scores of over 300 have an 80 percent chance of experiencing at least a minor illness.

## Schedule of Life Events
## and Their Relative Magnitude

| Rank | Life Event | Mean Value |
|---|---|---|
| 1 | Death of a Spouse | 100 |
| 2 | Divorce | 73 |
| 3 | Marital Separation | 65 |
| 4 | Jail Term | 63 |
| 5 | Death of Close Family Member | 63 |
| 6 | Personal Injury or Illness | 53 |
| 7 | Marriage | 50 |
| 8 | Fired at Work | 47 |
| 9 | Marital Reconciliation | 45 |
| 10 | Retirement | 45 |
| 11 | Change of Health of Family Member | 44 |
| 12 | Pregnancy | 40 |
| 13 | Sexual Difficulties | 39 |
| 14 | Gain of New Family Member | 39 |
| 15 | Business Adjustment | 39 |
| 16 | Change in Financial State | 38 |
| 17 | Death of Close Friend | 37 |
| 18 | Change or Different Line of Work | 36 |
| 19 | Change in Number of Arguments with Spouse | 35 |
| 20 | Mortgage or Loan more than $10,000 | 31 |
| 21 | Foreclosure of Mortgage or Loan | 30 |
| 22 | Change in Responsibilities at Work | 29 |
| 23 | Son or Daughter Leaving Home | 29 |
| 24 | Trouble with In-Laws | 29 |
| 25 | Outstanding Personal Achievement | 28 |
| 26 | Beginning or Stopping Work | 26 |
| 27 | Beginning or Ending School | 26 |
| 28 | Change in Living Conditions | 25 |
| 29 | Revision of Personal Habits | 24 |
| 30 | Trouble with Boss | 23 |
| 31 | Change in Work Hours or Conditions | 20 |
| 32 | Change in Residence | 20 |
| 33 | Change in School | 20 |
| 34 | Change in Recreation | 19 |
| 35 | Change in Church Activities | 19 |
| 36 | Change in Social Activities | 18 |
| 37 | Mortgage or Loan less than $10,000 | 17 |
| 38 | Change in Sleeping Habits | 16 |
| 39 | Change in Number of Family Get Togethers | 15 |
| 40 | Change in Eating Habits | 15 |
| 41 | Vacation | 13 |
| 42 | Christmas | 12 |
| 43 | Minor Violations of the Law | 11 |

## CHAPTER TWO

# How People Change

> The only time a woman really succeeds in changing a man is when he is a baby.
>
> -- Natalie Wood

Many of us resist change. Change can mean stress. We tend to stick with our current situation no matter how unsatisfactory, perhaps believing that it's better to stick with the devil we know than raise the devil we don't know. As Glen Beaman puts it, "Stubbornness does have its helpful features. You always know what you are going to be thinking tomorrow."

Psychologists estimate that we experience about 60,000 thoughts per day. This demonstrates the fertility of the source of thought which resides deep within each of us. The discouraging part of the statistic is that about 95 percent of those thoughts are the same ones we had yesterday.

Recent research[1] has identified six stages of change. Though these are most often defined in terms of quitting addictive behaviors, they apply to virtually all change.

- Stage #1 is precontemplation. In this stage we're not intending to do anything about it, whatever it is, in the foreseeable future.
- Stage #2 is contemplation. We are seriously intending to take some action at some point.
- Stage #3 is preparation. We are actually planning to take the action in the immediate future.

- Stage #4, finally, is action. We have done -- or have begun to implement our plan actually to do -- what we intend to do.
- Stage #5 is maintenance. We have done whatever it is that we've meant to do. In the context of quitting cigarettes for instance, we've been abstinent for a significant period, and we are now working toward either becoming free from the temptation to relapse or becoming free to pursue our next positive action.
- Stage #6 is termination. We are free from the temptation to engage in the addictive behavior or we have completed the particular action that we wanted to embark upon. We have changed.

How do we get ourselves into this model? It may help to ask ourselves what in our life we are looking to change or improve.

> Everybody wants to *be* somebody; nobody wants to grow.
> -- Goethe

You might try listing the areas in your life that are not perfect. This may be a long list. Then, for each of these areas, list where you are in this model. Are you in the pre-contemplation phase, really not intending to do anything about this in the foreseeable future? Or have you already done something recently and you're now in maintenance phase?

Once you've identified where you are, how do you move to the next step? You may find that you've been at one step for a while and cannot seem to progress.

There is a way of enhancing the plasticity of our nervous systems so that change can flow more readily, a technology that has been demonstrated to be more effective than anything else in the field of personal development in promoting positive change in people's lives.

In my first year of college in 1971 I had a job as a boxboy in a market. The novelty of this position lasted about half an hour. I soon began to dread going to work.

As it happened, a friend of a friend had recently learned Transcendental Meditation (TM), and recommended it. I respected his opinion, so I attended an introductory lecture. While I was primarily attracted by the message of growth of consciousness, I understood the concept of stress management. I remember having a specific expectation that this technique would allow me to bliss-out and groove to the groceries coming down the conveyor belt. I was soon instructed in TM. At first, I just noticed that the practice itself was quiet and pleasant. But instead of enjoying my job, two other unexpected developments arose.

Someone once said, "If you're not a liberal when you're twenty, you have no heart; if you're not conservative when you're forty, you have no brain." That may or may not be true, but in 1972 I was a liberal. To my mind, the world was somewhat indistinctly populated by those who sent young men to war and those who wished for peace, those who wanted to commune with Nature and those who wished to exploit Her, those who agreed with me and those who were in the Establishment. And guess who was running the world? I felt alienated and discouraged. Soon (about two weeks) after learning TM, without realizing that I had been pessimistic, I became an optimist. While my politics didn't change overnight, I found myself less opposed to just about everything. I was much less likely to attribute malevolent motives to those with whom I did not see eye-to-eye. I began to feel that the world was a friendlier place than I had thought, and that I could share a common ground with anyone.

Second, my desire for intoxication began to decrease. By today's standards I may have been fairly tame, but a significant degree of inebriation was the norm for get-togethers in my southern California surfing subcultural tidepool. To my surprise, I grew less interested in abandoning sobriety.

I was not completely thrilled with those changes at the time. I had enjoyed getting high with my friends, and there had been some comfort in viewing the world in simple Us-versus-Them terms. Leaving behind these parts of my life was inconvenient, not what I had bargained for. But I didn't experience a crisis because the changes seemed so natural and inevitable. Overall, I felt better, unmistakably better. The,e were the first of a number of changes that were nothing less than life transforming.

In another unanticipated turn of events, after about three weeks of regular practice of meditation, I left my position as a box-boy. It had become excruciatingly clear that job was not for me.

## Transcending: Is All Meditation the Same?

> Macbeth: Canst thou not minister to a mind diseas'd,
>   Pluck from the memory a rooted sorrow,
>   Raze out the written troubles of the brain,
>   And with some sweet oblivious antidote
>   Cleanse the stuff'd bosom of that perilous stuff
>   Which weighs upon the heart.
> Doctor: Therein the patient
>   Must minister to himself.
>
> -- Shakespeare, *Macbeth*

Transcendental Meditation, or TM, is a simple, natural, effortless technique practiced for 15 to 20 minutes twice a day, sitting comfortably with the eyes closed. It is easy to learn. It is not a religion or a philosophy. It doesn't involve any particular change in life-style, and in and of itself it does not require any particular code of conduct or change in values or beliefs.

TM is an integral part of the *Vedic tradition* of India. As such, it has been around for many millennia, but we know it in modern times through the efforts of Maharishi Mahesh Yogi (or simply, "Maharishi"), the man who has been teaching it around the world since the late 1950s.

The Vedic tradition derives from the Vedas, which I'll discuss later. It is the oldest tradition of knowledge in the world. While many people in the West view it as a philosophy, it is more correctly understood as a science, since it can be subjected to objective measurement as well as experiential verification, with inter-observer reproducibility.

One might reasonably ask about the qualifications of Maharishi. Some historical perspective may help. The Vedic tradition is also known as the *Shankaracharya tradition*. Shankara was a most distinguished luminary, a great teacher and author of commentaries on the Vedic literature. About 2500 years ago he established four seats in India in order to preserve this knowledge, ancient already even then. The principal seat, in the north, was recently vacant for 165 years through all the 19th century, as no one was capable of filling it. In 1941, after having been asked for 20 years, 72 year old Swami Brahmananda Saraswati (or "Guru Dev") assumed the title of Shankaracharya, the leader of this tradition. He taught an ancient meditative technique originating in the oldest Indian teachings.

Maharishi recounts first seeing Guru Dev's face in the flash of a distant car's headlights as Guru Dev sat on a dark porch. Maharishi, then a student in physics at Allahabad University, says that at that moment he knew he had seen his master, and he asked to become Guru Dev's pupil. He was told to finish college first. After graduating, he became the favored student of Guru Dev. Maharishi embarked upon a traditional educational process that could just as well have taken place many thousands of years before. The disciple surrenders completely to the master, giving up all vestiges of his limited individuality in order to attune himself to the unbounded wisdom of his teacher.

When Maharishi was asked once what Guru Dev had accomplished in his life, a life spent mostly in solitude and deep silence in the Himalayas and in the dark jungles of central India, he replied, "He made me." Maharishi regards this tradition of knowledge as supreme, and acknowledges that all of his work derives from it. Before Maharishi, Guru Dev was the living embodiment of this heritage. Whenever speaking, Maharishi has a portrait of Guru Dev above and behind him, to remind listeners that he is not speaking as an individual, but as a continuation of a long line of brilliant custodians of this wisdom. His title "Maharishi" (maha = great, rishi = seer) is often used as an eponym (e.g., Maharishi Vedic Approach to Health, Maharishi Ayur-Veda) in order to demonstrate the link between all of his activities and the tradition from whence he has come.

He attributes his own personal development to the "twelve years that flashed by" which he spent with Guru Dev before his passing in 1953. Without his master, he "was like an iron filing after the electromagnet has been switched off." He retired to a life of silence in a cave in the Himalayas. While there, he had the thought to go to a certain town in the south of India. After some years, he walked south, never anticipating not returning to his cave.

Upon seeing Maharishi, the local librarian in this town asked if he was from the Himalayas, and if he spoke. He replied, "Yes, but I do not lecture." Nonetheless, the librarian set up a series of lectures. Surprised, Maharishi acquiesced and began to speak publicly. The response was irresistible. Maharishi taught hundreds, and hundreds more, the technique of Transcendental Meditation he had learned from his master Guru Dev. After teaching TM to thousands the world over, he trained thousands of teachers of TM. Over the last four decades Maharishi has worked incessantly to make this technique available to people of all walks of life all around the globe.

The world was a fairly conservative place in the late 1950s and early 1960s. Those who learned and practiced TM found it beneficial. But it was not until the late 1960s and early 1970s, when research began to be done on TM, that it commanded the attention of scientifically minded people. The question would arise: how is Transcendental Meditation different from prayer or from other meditative techniques from the East or the West?

## Concentration and Contemplation

Most techniques involve either concentration or contemplation. TM involves neither.

Techniques involving concentration usually involve some attempt to control the mind, to keep it focused on a particular thought, a picture, a candle, or some other specific object. The downside of these techniques is that they are often rigorous and difficult, not enjoyable to perform. Few people who have practical demands on their daily lives practice techniques of concentration with any degree of regularity.

Contemplative techniques also have their value. It's pleasant to spend time thinking about God or love or one's relationships, or some positive phrase such as the aphorism from Confucius: "man is by nature good." These are uplifting pursuits, but in practicing these techniques we continue to use the same five to ten percent of the mind that psychologists tell us we access in our conscious thinking. Contemplative meditation involves swimming along pleasantly on this surface level of the mind. But it is the express purpose of TM to plumb the depths of our awareness, to experience subtler levels of thought, and to transcend that surface level of thought altogether.

## The Natural Tendency of the Mind

It is the natural tendency of the mind to seek fields of greater energy and enjoyment. If we are standing in a supermarket with our attention on the products we are about to purchase, naturally our attention tends to go to those which are more suitable and less expensive. The mind is naturally attracted to what we desire. Now, if behind us we overhear some juicy piece of gossip that interests us, our attention *effortlessly* shifts from the loaf of bread in front of us to this conversation behind us. If an attractive member of the opposite sex walks down the aisle, our attention may undergo yet another shift.

This effortless motion of the mind in the direction of greater charm is the key to the successful practice of TM. Some commentators unacquainted with TM say that the mind is like an excited monkey: always active, restless, swinging from branch to branch in an apparently purposeless display of activity. But this is not so; it only appears that way if one doesn't understand the deeper principles at work. Looking at the crowd in a train station, we may see apparently random movement; but if a track change is announced we see people change directions, revealing an underlying purposefulness to the bustle. Similarly, the mind is always moving to fields of greater enjoyment.

Thought, as we experience it on the gross conscious thinking level, is less energetic, less powerful and less charming than the subtle antecedents of thought. Therefore as in the technique of TM, if we have the mind awake but not outwardly directed, we spontaneously settle down and experience subtler and subtler values of thought. This is how we transcend the gross thinking level, and indeed can transcend the subtlest thinking level as well, to experience the field of pure unbounded awareness that is the source of thought.

## The Ends Are Not the Means

A person who is experiencing this state of transcendental consciousness appears settled. If you look at such a person, you will see that his limbs are unmoving, his breath almost imperceptible. Perhaps you can see how easily this simple technique could become lost.

Imagine thousands of years ago some students asking their master what his subjective experience was in meditation. The master might describe this quiet, settled state of the mind. But, as Maharishi points out, "The state of Reality, as described by the enlightened, cannot become a path for the seeker, any more than the description of a destination can replace the road that leads to it."[2] If the students are not very adept they might easily misinterpret what they have seen and discussed as being *means* toward an end rather than a manifestation of the end itself. They might think, *Ah! In order to have the experience that my master has had, I must still my limbs, control my breathing and try to empty my mind.* Such a misunderstanding of the relationship between the path and the end point has given rise to any number of techniques that involve rigorous discipline of the body, of breathing, and of trying to still the mind by force.

If you want to have your dog on your back porch at exactly a specific time, you could go out into the back yard with a net and a rope, capture him and drag him resisting onto the porch and tie him there. But a simpler way would be to charm the dog. All you need to do is open the back door and start rattling a can opener. Because TM uses the natural tendency of the mind to go effortlessly toward more charming experiences, and the subtler levels of the mind are increasingly charming and blissful, the practice itself is effective, effortless, and pleasant.

## A Unique State

In the late 1960s, before any significant research was published, those who disregarded TM said that the technique might indeed be restful and enjoyable but that it was in no way different from just closing the eyes, reading a book, taking a nap or any other form of relaxation. The initial research[3] was done by then Ph.D. candidate at UCLA, now Professor Robert Keith Wallace, who investigated what was called a *wakeful hypometabolic state* -- a *state of restful alertness*. Subjects reported that while they practiced TM their mind was awake and alert and having clear experience, while physiological measurements showed their body was in a deep state of rest. A number of characteristics of relaxation such as galvanic skin resistance showed a marked increase, while indicators of metabolic activity such as oxygen consumption plummeted. In fact, these early studies found that oxygen consumption dropped approximately 16 percent after just a couple of minutes of TM. Compare this with a drop of only 8 percent that one typically experiences after four to five hours of deep sleep. TM thus provides a deeper state of rest than even deep sleep[4,5,6]. TM is of course not a substitute for sleep because it differs from sleep in other ways.

Many other studies[7] have demonstrated that TM provides a style of functioning in the physiology that is different from eyes-closed rest, different from the typical waking state, different from dreaming, different from sleeping. For this reason it was characterized as a fourth major state of consciousness: Transcendental Consciousness.

At that point in the research on TM some investigators began to think they might be able to create a technique that could accomplish all TM accomplishes without the ceremony and the tradition from which TM comes. This led to the rise of a number of laboratory-generated techniques of relaxation.

## Distracted by Relaxation

Prior to the research on TM many people assumed that TM engendered a state of rest not unlike that resulting from sitting with one's eyes closed and relaxing. Research has clearly demonstrated that assumption is incorrect and that this is a unique and different state of consciousness.[3] When other relaxation techniques were studied they were found to produce some degree of relaxation in the same *direction* as TM though not of the same *magnitude*.[8]

Interestingly, the degree of discrimination employed by scientists evaluating TM was largely suspended in evaluating these other techniques. Some writers suggested that any number of techniques -- prayer, relaxation response, autogenic relaxation, progressive muscle relaxation and so forth -- would elicit a stereotypical response identical to that produced by Transcendental Meditation. It was as if TM had blazed a path, and once that path had been blazed any technique could travel along it, whether or not it actually accomplished the same results.

This hypothesis that all meditation techniques are pretty much the same is an attractive one. It saves clinicians and researchers from taking the trouble to look at actual results, and also allows them to avoid dealing with the non-western culture from which TM derives. But does this hypothesis stand up to scrutiny? Is the style of functioning in the physiology, the state of restful alertness generated in individuals practicing TM, identical to the states generated by other relaxation techniques? The answer is no.

A man from Mars might land here, meet two humans, see that each has two arms, two legs and one nose and conclude that those two people are identical. But one might be Mother Teresa and the other Charles Manson, not identical at all. Similarly, the fact that TM and other relaxation techniques produce *similar* effects does not mean they're *identical*.

In a sense, the fact that Transcendental Meditation produces a state of deep relaxation is incidental. Think about its origins, about the seers of the Vedic tradition, living in caves in the Himalayas of India many thousands of years ago. Stress management and relaxation probably were not high on the list of these people's priorities. It's unlikely that they would have spent their lives pursuing stress reduction. It's just an artifact of our culture that if you take this technique -- which really is about the process of mind-body integration, of evolution toward enlightenment -- and transplant it into the second half of the 20th century industrialized civilization, it looks like stress management and relaxation. But those are merely the gross manifestations of this meditative state. Just as the not-so-bright student many millennia ago looked at his master and saw only someone controlling his limbs and his breathing, so also nowadays we are able to see only someone experiencing a state of deep relaxation. And so a technique of great range and sophistication gets pigeonholed as a mere relaxation technique.

Relaxation is a side effect -- a salutary one, but a side effect nonetheless -- of a technique which actually involves the identification of individual mind with cosmic mind. Techniques designed simply to produce a state of relaxation, while they have their value, miss the main point: transcending is primary, relaxation an incidental spinoff of that phenomenon.

I awoke to the sound of my friend's telephone ringing. It was January of 1973; yesterday (we believed) the war in Viet Nam was formally over for the USA. Last night we had a robust celebration, and I was now finding that my friend's kitchen floor had not been that comfortable a bed. On the phone another friend told us that Maharishi was going to speak at the University of California at Santa Barbara, a couple of hours drive away, that afternoon.

The lecture hall was completely filled. We sat on the floor in the back, and I could barely see or hear anything. It was warm; I dozed. As the lecture ended, a crowd formed near the door anticipated as Maharishi's exit. There appeared to be no chance to get closer, and we were both tired, so we walked away to our car.

"It would have been great to have been closer, but that was pretty cool," we agreed.

About a hundred yards from the hall, we saw a car driving very slowly toward us along a bike path from behind the hall. We would cross the path a few moments before the car arrived. We stood on the passenger side as the car approached. The windows were down, and there in the back seat passenger side was Maharishi. When he was about eight feet from me, something extraordinary happened.

I can describe it as a wave, like the softest pillow imaginable, filled with bliss, but very palpable. I could only inhale with surprise; I felt infused with well-being. It was as good as I'd ever felt. Maharishi smiled and *seemed* to raise a knowing eyebrow. As the car moved on by, I looked over at my friend. He looked how I felt, and we both began to laugh with the purest enjoyment.

I have had the privilege of being in similar physical proximity to Maharishi a few times in the last decades, and while that is always an extremely charming experience, that day in 1973 stands out as unmistakably unique. In any case, I was impressed. This man had something very special, and I wanted more.  While I had thought before to become a teacher of TM, that clinched it.

My own bias by now should be evident.  I was trained as a teacher of TM by Maharishi in 1974 and have taught it to hundreds of people.  I use it in my clinical practice and I've seen countless beneficial effects.

But what are you to make of my experiences?  Any number of people have had unusual occurrences, and testimonials are a dime a dozen.  And as we'll see, anecdotal observations, even by trained physicians, may or may not be worthwhile.  Since you probably don't know me personally, why should any of my comments about TM be credible?

TM has a good track record.  It has been around for thousands of years and it comes from a tradition that has a profound understanding of the evolution of consciousness and of the role of consciousness in health.  Having spent a good part of my life in the study and practice of modern medicine I appreciate the value of contemporary science but I am also aware of its limitations.  When it comes to techniques that promote the growth of consciousness, I will go with the Vedic tradition over the laboratory version.

But as a practicing physician, I have an inviolable obligation to do what's best for my patients, not just indulge my own biases.  An even more compelling reason to consider the value of TM -- and one I would expect scientifically-minded individuals (and certainly health-care professionals) to take seriously -- is what the research has shown.

## CHAPTER THREE

# Meditation under the Microscope

> It ain't what we don't know that hurts, it's what we know that ain't so.
>
> -- Will Rogers

One convenient aspect of TM, from a researcher's perspective, is that approximately four million worldwide have learned it. Because they have all been trained in the same way we have a homogeneous population, in terms of the technique they practice, that we can study. Other meditative and relaxation techniques are more difficult to isolate in terms of their methodology. If you study people practicing prayer, for example, you're not exactly sure whether they are all doing the same procedure. Similarly, with relaxation techniques it can be difficult to know exactly what people are doing: many psychologists, counselors, and healers teach "relaxation" to their clients, but since they're not all teaching the same thing it's difficult to compare techniques.

Generally speaking, larger studies are better than small studies. For example, if you flip a coin a million times you'll get a clear idea that it comes up heads 50 percent of the time and tails 50 percent of the time. But if you flip a coin only eight times, it just might come up tails six of the eight tosses: your correct hypothesis that it's a fifty-fifty proposition would not be supported by your observation because your study was too small to detect the truth. So, the more subjects we can enroll in studies, the more likely it is that the information will reflect reality.

*Meta-analysis* is one way of gaining more power from groups of small studies in which researchers combine a number of different studies, done by different people in different places and at different times, that were looking at the same type of phenomenon. The researchers then pool all those data. Of course methodologies are different and it takes skilled statisticians to sort through them and discover which effects are real. But when done correctly meta-analysis is a very powerful tool.

## Anxiety

A meta-analysis was performed to compare TM, progressive muscle relaxation, and other relaxation techniques. One hundred forty-six independent outcomes were researched[1] comparing the effects of TM and other techniques on what is called *trait anxiety*, the tendency for a person to be anxious. (This is not just a moment of anxiety because someone ran in front of your car, but a general tendency to have anxiety as a trait.) Researchers found TM was approximately two and a half times more potent in reducing trait anxiety than were muscle relaxation or other relaxation techniques.

## Unique Changes in the Body

There are many findings with TM that have not been replicated in other techniques. The body is taking deep rest and requiring less blood and oxygen, yet the heart actually pumps more blood during TM.[2,3] Why? Where does this blood go? To the brain! For an average sized person about an extra quart of blood washes through the brain[4] every minute during TM. Many endocrine[5,6,7] and electro-encephalographic[8,9,10] changes also are unique to TM. There are over 500 published studies on the effects of Transcendental Meditation. Of course, it's beyond the scope of this book to go through all of them but a few high points are worth noting.

## Smoking and Drugs

During the course of learning TM, there is no instruction or admonition that deals with smoking in any way. Yet, researchers found fifty percent of the smokers who had learned TM had abstained and were still abstinent from smoking 19 months[11,12] after learning TM; drug use also declined. A typical success rate, in terms of abstinence, for smoking cessation programs which are specifically designed to facilitate quitting smoking is about 15 percent at one year. Another study demonstrated that the effect of TM on quitting smoking during a two year period was twice the rate of controls.[13]

## Psychological Health

As we'll see in the chapters to come, our attitudes and outlooks have measurable effects on our health. That can be both good and bad news; how do we go about getting a positive outlook?

Mental well-being is enhanced by TM. This technique has provided researchers with a wealth of data. Another meta-analysis[14,15] of 42 separate studies showed that the effect of TM on *self-actualization* (comprising integration and stability of personality, self regard, emotional maturity, capacity for warm interpersonal relationships, and adaptive response to challenges) was greater than that of other forms of meditation and relaxation. Virtually all parameters of human psychological health have been found to improve with TM.[14]

The results in drug abuse are more easily understood in light of TM's beneficial effects on self-confidence,[15] moral maturity,[16] increased resistance to distraction and social pressure,[17,18] even decreased dropout rate and increased self-actualization among economically deprived adolescents.[19]

Not surprisingly, this has translated into increased intelligence,[20,21] improved grades[22] in students and increased academic achievement.[23]

## Cholesterol

Cholesterol levels can be related to stress. Individuals had a significant decrease of about 17 percent in their elevated serum cholesterol after learning TM. On average it brought the cholesterol down from 234 to 201.[24,25] The control group, which did not learn TM, had no change in their serum cholesterol. The change in cholesterol was independent of any change in diet or in weight.

## Aging

There are two ways of looking at your age. One is your *chronological age,* which we can find out simply by looking at your driver's license. But your *biological age* is a different matter. Some people age prematurely, others manage to keep themselves in pretty good shape. I noticed this very clearly at my 20-year high school reunion some years ago, when some people looked great and others (particularly smokers) looked like they'd had a rough 20 years.

Biological aging slows with the practice of TM. Using a standard test for age (which measures near-point vision, auditory threshold and systolic blood pressure), persons who had been practicing TM for less than three years were approximately five years younger than their chronological age, and persons who had been practicing TM for over five years were 12 years younger biologically than they were chronologically.[26]

Another marker for biological age is the level in the blood of a tongue-twisting hormone called *dehydroepiandosterone sulfate* or DHEA-S for short. Low levels are associated with cardiovascular disease, breast cancer, and obesity. Levels are higher in youth and decline steadily with age. While it is now being marketed in health-food stores as an age-reducing agent, it is not at all clear that taking it as a supplement does any good. Certainly, it would be better to be "making it" than "taking it". DHEA-S levels were measured in TM practitioners and in controls: the meditators had levels the same as those in controls five to ten years younger.[27] That is, a 50 year old meditator would tend to have a DHEA-S level as high as a 40 to 45 year old non-meditator.

## Health Care Costs

Of great concern these days is the issue of health care and its cost. In one Blue Cross/Blue Shield affiliate in the Midwest researchers found that individuals practicing TM were hospitalized 56 percent less than those not practicing.[28] That included a 55 percent decrease in hospitalizations for cancer and *87 percent decrease in hospitalizations for cardiovascular disease,* the biggest killer in America, in those practicing TM.

Critics of this study have said, "Perhaps it's not the TM. Perhaps these people practicing TM are just sort of hippie-dippie types who don't like to go to doctors and don't allow themselves to be admitted to hospitals." Yet in the obstetric category of this study, it was found that the rates of hospitalization for childbirth were virtually identical to the rates of those persons who are not practicing TM. That tells us that there didn't seem to be an intrinsic bias in the TM group against seeking health care from doctors.

There were other criticisms: perhaps these people just started out healthier and so don't tend to go to doctors much. As part of being healthier they were interested in learning TM, and maybe if we had looked at these same people before they learned TM and prevented them from learning TM, they still would not have been hospitalized as much as the other group. This hypothesis is a plausible one and deserves to be addressed.

It has been addressed by yet another study which looked at health-care utilization patterns in Canada.[29,30] Canada has a national health service which keeps track of everyone's health-care expenditure from cradle to grave. This study looked at people who were practicing TM, viewed their health-care utilization pattern back in time *before* they had learned TM, and found it to be the same as that of the general population. The TM practitioners didn't start off healthier, using doctors less: they started off just where everyone else was. By following that pattern forward to times *after* they had learned TM, it was clear that there was a decrease in health-care utilization which eventually approximated these same findings I've already discussed, in that health-care utilization tended to drop by over half. This is powerful information that can give us hope with regard to the problems of spiraling health-care costs.

Unfortunately, most of the other meditative and relaxation techniques available have not been studied in these areas. We don't know what they might or might not be able to do. Ideally, we would want studies that have directly compared TM and other relaxation techniques to see how each performs. An ideal study would take subjects who do not select themselves -- that is, they are *randomized* -- to learn one technique or the other. Also, it would be better to conduct the study *prospectively* -- start investigating before the subjects actually learn the technique, rather than looking back in time, to minimize potential confounding factors. It would be good to have a placebo control group because as we'll see in a later chapter, *every* treatment has placebo effects. A number of excellent studies have been performed that meet these criteria.

## High Blood Pressure and Heart Disease

One recently published study looked at the effects of non-drug treatment in high blood pressure. For many reasons drug treatment of high blood pressure is not always desirable; it would be beneficial to have some other approach. This study[31] was done, not with yuppies, but with elderly inner-city African-Americans in Oakland, California. The subjects, who were identified largely through churches and community health centers, suffered from mild high blood pressure. They were recruited and randomized into one of three arms of the study: one group was to learn TM; the second group was to learn a relaxation technique; and the third group was given "usual care." Usual care meant they saw their doctor on a regular basis to have their medication and blood pressure checked and be counseled on diet and so forth, as they had been doing all along.

The study was structured so that the placebo effect, the expectations engendered, would be equal between the TM group and the relaxation group. The amount of time spent in learning the technique, the expectations that were fostered, the enthusiasm of the instructor (the instructor of the relaxation technique was a local psychologist who had her own practice and radio show and was enthusiastic about this relaxation technique), the amount of time spent in follow up and the amount of time spent practicing the technique on a daily basis were all identical between these two groups. Over the course of a couple of months, it was found that *compliance*, (actually doing what one is instructed), was excellent (over 90 percent) in both of the intervention groups.

Blood pressure reduced in the TM group about two-and-a-half times more than in the relaxation group, and TM was <u>*seven times*</u> more effective than the "usual care" regimen of diet and exercise. In fact, in the TM group, the blood pressure decreased from the mildly hypertensive range back into the normal range. It's interesting that this effect was of the same magnitude as that we saw in the meta-analysis comparing TM to other approaches with regard to anxiety. Each of these studies found the effectiveness of TM to be between two and three hundred percent that of other techniques.

The design of this study by Dr. Robert Schneider and his associates was particularly helpful in distinguishing between TM's effects and placebo effects. By having the relaxation instruction and practice as an "active control," even if all the relaxation technique benefit was due to placebo effect, we learned that TM was at least more than twice as effective as placebo.

A follow-up study looked at this same population to see if there were subgroups whose blood pressure responded differently to TM and to relaxation. Relaxation was effective only in men, only if those men were highly stressed, and then it reduced only systolic blood pressure. TM on the other hand was effective in both men and women, both high and low stress subgroups, and it reduced both systolic and diastolic blood pressure.[32]

TM also has been shown to be less expensive than drug treatment for high blood pressure.[33]

Patients with coronary artery disease and angina were taught TM and then underwent stress testing. Compared to controls, the meditating patients demonstrated greater exercise tolerance, higher maximal workload, and delay in the onset of deleterious electrocardiographic changes.[34] In contrast, the "relaxation response" did not help patients improve their exercise tolerance[35] (further evidence that these techniques are not the same).

## Survival

Another elegant study[36] looked at systolic blood pressure, aging, and cognitive function in elderly persons in nursing homes in the greater Boston area. There were 73 elderly who averaged 81 years old. They were stratified for cognitive function and gender and then were randomized to four arms: one was TM; the second was a relaxation technique; the third was a mindfulness meditation technique; and the fourth was a control group. Cognitive functioning and blood pressure were improved in the TM groups compared to the other groups. But the most intriguing finding was that after a couple of years of the study, *mortality* was decreased in the TM group.

The other groups ranged from 60 percent survival up to 83 percent survival. In the TM group, survival was 100 percent: there were no deaths in those elderly individuals in nursing homes who had learned TM over the course of this study.

Further study[37] of these elderly people revealed persistent effects in survival. After eight years, mean survival time was 65 percent higher in the TM group compared to the other groups; even after 15 years it was still 22 percent higher.

These head-to-head studies and others have clearly indicated that TM is the top of the line when compared to relaxation techniques. So superior is TM's performance that even to classify it as a relaxation technique is really too limiting.

## Common Questions about Meditation

> The acquisition of any knowledge whatever is always useful to the intellect, because it will be able to banish the useless things and retain those which are good. For nothing can be loved or hated until it is first known.
>
> -- Leonardo da Vinci

When I discuss the scientific findings with my patients, certain questions tend to arise.

Question: *Is TM then the only way one can accomplish these things?*

Answer: Transcendental Meditation can have no monopoly on transcending. Transcending is something that's part of our nature. That capability is hard wired into our DNA. We couldn't get away from the ability to transcend even if we wanted to. But we do want to have a reproducible way to transcend. There are many ways you can get to New York from Los Angeles. You can get on the Greyhound, you can drive, you can take Amtrak. But if you're interested in getting there the fastest, easiest way, you'll probably want to take a jet. TM can produce this style of functioning in the body-mind quickly, reliably, and efficiently.

Transcending is an experience that a person can have without TM. Some people are born with especially clear nervous systems, and they tend to have this experience of transcending spontaneously. Throughout history, there are accounts of saints, sages and seers who may or may not have been practicing any technique at all. But rather than wait for a breath-taking sunset, an utterly quiet moment in life or some powerful event to precipitate such a spiritual experience, it would be better if we could just create that experience on a twice daily basis, day in and day out. Also, the technique itself is effortless and enjoyable. The nature of the mind has us settle down the way we do during TM, just as the nature of gravity has us get into the swimming pool if we step off the diving board. But there are swan dives, cannonballs and belly flops. Having an instructor teach us an appropriate technique makes this experience of entering the pool from the diving board one we would want to continue experiencing day after day.

Question: *I am currently practicing another technique. Are you telling me that I need to quit doing that and learn TM?*

Answer: No. Each person will need to weigh the evidence and make his own decision. If someone is currently practicing some technique and is enjoying it and is feeling that he is gaining benefit from it, obviously he might choose to continue that technique. Could he benefit from learning TM? The available scientific data would support that.

Question: *Why didn't my counselor tell me about TM? I just learned this technique where I sit and relax for a while, but I would have liked to have known about this.*

Answer: Many published accounts of studies of relaxation techniques don't distinguish among the various techniques; so, many people in the field don't know that they are different. Also, many practitioners learn to teach one approach and then just stick with the familiar even if it's not the most effective.

It's also possible that some practitioners may have a bias against this traditional approach to meditation and prefer to teach a laboratory version.

Question: *Why does it cost (so much, too much, anything at all)? I don't think you should charge money for something spiritual.*

Answer: The simplest answer is most obvious: some fee is required in order to keep the technique available. TM Centers have rent and utility bills to pay: TM teachers have to feed themselves and their families and put gasoline in the tanks of their automobiles. One helpful way to look at it is that it's not so much the technique itself you're paying for as the mechanism to make it available. Water is free (it comes from the sky in rain), but if you want the water to come out of your tap you need the water company with all of its reservoirs and pumping stations to get the water to you. If no fees were charged, the people who are teaching TM, (except for the few who are independently wealthy) would soon be doing "real jobs" to make the money they need to live. The result of not charging a fee, paradoxically, would be that the technique would be less, not more, accessible.

The technique is subtle and personal instructions are given based on your experiences. So it can't be learned by rote from a book. The course is about a dozen hours long altogether, and each teacher has been thoroughly trained by Maharishi to teach TM in the standardized, effective, traditional way. So you can be sure when you're learning from a TM teacher in good standing with the TM organization that you're getting the genuine article.

Also, you are provided free life-long follow-up. In the medical model it's well recognized that the success of any course of treatment depends in large measure upon *compliance* -- people actually doing what's been recommended for them. Compliance degrades if follow-up is inadequate. As with health insurance, it's best if follow-up is transportable geographically, and not prohibitive economically. This is something that's usually not available with other techniques. That is, if you learn some other technique and then move from Reno to Albuquerque and want to get a refresher in the technique you've learned, your teacher back in Reno is unavailable, no one in your new town teaches exactly the same way, and you're basically on your own. If you learn TM in Los Angeles and move to Singapore, you can plug into the TM Center there and the fee you paid in Los Angeles will cover you for the rest of your life. Wherever you move, you have free follow-up forever. If only the computers and automobiles we buy came with that kind of support. This is another reason why it's best to learn the technique from the organization of qualified TM teachers.

The TM organization is a non-profit, educational organization. It has been my experience that the lifestyles of those at the head of this organization are not exorbitant by any means. For example, when I was at the International Centre for Ayur-Veda at Maharishi Nagar in India in 1987 for a course with dozens of other doctors, when we wanted to bathe, we took our buckets down to the big caldron outside in order to draw the water.

If TM were a surgical procedure we would not tolerate a second-best alternative procedure, nor would we let a fee stand in the way of our getting the best. We often consider money spent on personal development, even health, to be a luxury, while we see money spent on fixing the clutch in our car as a necessity. We may need to rearrange our priorities.

Our *time* is a far bigger investment than any course fee. This practice is something you're going to be doing for 20 minutes twice a day for the rest of your life. You don't want to save some money in the 1990s only to find out somewhere in the 21st century that it would have been wiser to have learned the appropriate technique back when you had the chance.

If the cost of learning the technique is an issue, let me just suggest that the *behavioral rasayanas* you will read about later might come into play. If you have the intention, the means will collect around that intention and in time it will become a reality.

Question: *I've read in various books that there are a number of spiritual masters who keep saying that there is no technique, that this is a path without a path, that we should not bother with techniques and we just need to learn to be. What do you say to that?*

Answer: I think some people say this out of frustration, having taken various paths and not been satisfied. For instance,

Gertrude Stein said, "There is no answer. There never has been an answer. There never will be an answer. That's the answer."

Also though, this viewpoint may seem correct to those who spontaneously have spiritual experiences. Some people are blessed with a very clear nervous system and may tend to transcend spontaneously. While that's wonderful for them, it doesn't help the rest of us much. Listening to someone describe his holiday in Hawaii may encourage me to look into it as a destination, but it is not a substitute for my own vacation. It is better to have the *experience* gained in TM, regularly twice a day, not just have an intellectual concept.

While TM by itself has been shown to have profound effects on regular practitioners, other aspects of the Vedic tradition are replete with information directly applicable to health. If biomedical research were very well done for decades and centuries to come, it might unveil a good portion of the breadth and depth of knowledge already available today from this tradition. But before delving into these details, let's look at what modern science has learned so far about the connections between mind and body. These studies show us that the physiological mechanics which are being enlivened by this ancient approach have already been documented.

**CHAPTER FOUR**

# The Boy Who Couldn't Breathe

> If we had paid no more attention to plants than we have to our
> children, we would now be living in a jungle of weeds.
> -- Luther Burbank

One night early in the second year of my family practice residency I was "on call" which meant that I was the senior pediatrician in the entire medical center, a position for which I felt ill-prepared. I'd shared in some lamentable outcomes;[1] I felt a little skittish around very sick children.

As the night wore on, a number of pediatric admissions came in, run-of-the-mill stuff. One of the admissions was an eight-year-old boy with asthma, a common problem. Asthma can be a satisfying disorder to treat because you can take people who are very sick, even on the brink of death, treat them effectively and completely resolve their acute episode. This boy had been brought to the Emergency Room by his grandmother, who had been babysitting him. Treatment in the ER had failed to clear up his breathing. He was still wheezing and somewhat short of breath, so we planned to treat him more intensely up on the ward as an inpatient. I talked to the child and did a physical examination, which revealed the typical findings of an asthmatic youngster. I was writing up my findings and writing the orders when the nurse walked by and mentioned that the boy wasn't looking at all good.

I went out to take a look, and, indeed, this patient was crashing and burning before our eyes. He was short of breath and somewhat blue. He was using his accessory muscles of respiration, which means his nostrils were flaring out, the muscles in his neck were contracting trying to lift up his collarbone and rib cage to expand his chest, and the spaces both under and over his collarbones and between his ribs were sucking in each time he would try to inhale.

We began administering more of the inhalational treatments and injected him with other medicines trying to break this acute episode. He continued to deteriorate.

I decided we should transfer him to the intensive care unit and call in the troops, the family physician who was the primary physician as well as the pediatrician senior to myself who was at home. The danger was that this boy might stop breathing altogether.

There is a certain type of test which one can draw from the blood in the artery which is a fairly good indicator of whether or not respiratory arrest is imminent. We had drawn such a test and by the time we had wheeled him down to the intensive care unit, the results had come back, indicating that indeed his demise might well be just around the corner.

The doctor who took the results over the phone called out to me, "Intubate him!" This means sticking a tube down the throat of the individual so that the airway will be open and we can control the pressure and volume of air going into the lungs.

As I began to intubate this boy he started to fight me. This was a good sign. In fact, as I was about to intubate him, I'd observed he looked a little bit more pink than blue. Apparently, in the few minutes that it took for the blood gas test to get to the laboratory and the results to be called to us, all the medications we had given him down in the pediatric ward had kicked in.

In the meantime his parents had arrived. I learned from his family physician that since his parents had separated he'd had an increasing number of these asthmatic episodes.

As I sat there at the nurses' station writing up my final notes, I looked out to see the patient lying in bed. Had I been a cartoon character, a big light bulb would have flashed over my head.

There, hovering beside the bed in tears, were his mother and his father. His illness was serving a function. Though his parents were legally separated, at that moment the family was together.

This is not to say that he had consciously manipulated himself into an asthmatic episode in order to accomplish this. But some emotional dynamics clearly were at work.

Recognition of the role of emotions and stress in asthma is a long-standing one, but of course, other disease processes and organ systems are also affected by stress. (A detailed review of the research pertaining to this mind-body connection is in Appendix F.)

## The Mind-Body Conversation

My first job as a family physician included working on the Child Protection Committee of my hospital; among the heartbreaking cases we managed was that of one two year old girl named Sally who was tiny, withdrawn, and slow to develop. Upon hospitalization, Sally blossomed: she grew rapidly and enjoyed playing with the staff and other children. After discharge, she again failed to thrive. We investigated medical causes, but discovered that her parents were not family-of-the-year material. *Psychosocial dwarfism* is a phenomenon in which children in an abusive or inhospitable home have decreased levels of growth hormone and fail to grow appropriately. Injections of growth hormone have no effect.[2] The diagnosis is confirmed by moving the child into a loving environment. The child resumes production of his own growth hormone and grows like a weed.[3]

You may have heard the terms *organic* and *functional* disorders. Organic disorders have an anatomic basis that is well recognized. Someone has a symptom, we investigate and the diagnostic tests are "positive": we find inflammation, some infection, perhaps a tumor.

Functional disorders are those for which we can find no anatomic basis. Our physical exam and diagnostic tests are "negative." This has led to the unhelpful comment from many physicians: "It's all in your head." Functional disorders account for 50 percent of all referrals to gastroenterologists.[4] Such disorders, often attributed to stress,. are windows into the mind-body connection gone awry. Some symptoms that have both organic and functional causes.[5] For example, peptic ulcer disease is twice as common among individuals who have especially stressful jobs, such as air traffic controllers.[6,7] Irritable bowel disease, or spastic colitis, and non-ulcer dyspepsia (that is indigestion and abdominal pain not associated with ulcer disease) have also been associated with stress, and with the *perception* of stress.[8]

Research has demonstrated that states of mind affect our experience of pain. I'm reminded of a scene in the movie "Lord Jim". Lord Jim has been captured by the bad guys and is about to be tortured. One of the torturers puts a knife into some red-hot embers and heats the blade, ruminating aloud about the nature of pain, his experiences in torturing people in the past, at what point they broke, and so forth. After some minutes Lord Jim is in such an exquisite frenzy of anticipation of pain that he is almost broken before any pain is actually inflicted. Many of us perhaps have had similar experiences in the waiting room of the dentist's office.

> A merry heart doeth good like a medicine.
>
> -- Proverbs 17:22

## Stress and Heart Disease

A research study followed people with heart disease for up to 14-1/2 years. The most important variable for their survival was not high blood pressure, smoking, cholesterol or any of the other commonly recognized cardiovascular risk factors, but, rather, it was the presence of a spouse or a confidant.[9] Another study showed that during the six months following a first heart attack, **loneliness** was the one significant variable among patients who suffered another heart attack or cardiac death.[10]

High **stress** in the five years after heart attack was associated with a three-fold increase in risk of death and one-and-a-half-fold increase in risk of another heart attack. In contrast, highly-stressed patients who took part in a one-year program of stress monitoring and intervention did not experience any significant long-term increase in risk.[11]

The movie "All That Jazz" which starred Roy Schneider as Bob Fosse portrayed this phenomenon. He had been admitted to the hospital for a heart attack. A man who loved to party, Fosse was enjoying his stay in the hospital and was watching television with some of his friends when a review of one his plays came on the screen. The reviewer illustrated his assessment of a play by four balloons that were next to his head. Four inflated meant a good play; three not so great; two poor; one balloon meant a real stinker. As the reviewer began to criticize Fosse's play, little beads of sweat began to emerge on the actor's face. At the end of his critique, the reviewer deflated all four balloons, one by one. Fosse's face was ashen and sweaty. "Go get the doctor" he told his friends. In the next scene he has expired.

> Every little yielding to anxiety is a step away from the natural heart of man.
> -- Japanese (Shinto) proverb

Research has consistently revealed that decreased blood flow to the heart muscle, or *ischemia*, induced by **mental stress** occurs frequently.[12] One study found that the most potent task for eliciting ischemia was simulated public speaking.[13] This means that the classic picture I was taught in medical school -- the middle-aged, out-of-shape guy who goes outside on a cold winter morning and starts shoveling snow, tries to work through this pain in his chest, gets a heart attack and drops dead -- is an incomplete if not obsolete picture. It turns out that mental stress can be much more damaging: people with *mental stress induced ischemia* have significantly higher rates of heart attacks and death than do people with "old fashioned" exercise induced ischemic heart disease without mental stress induced ischemia.[14]

Stress also affects *risk factors* for heart disease. For instance, cholesterol levels rise during stress. One study[15] reported the effects of tax return preparation on accountants. The highest serum cholesterol readings occurred right around April 15.

Stress can have lethal effects on Navy aviators[16]. Three different levels of cholesterol were associated with the type of aircraft flown and the degree of stress associated with that type of flight. The lowest levels were found in older pilots who flew transport aircraft; intermediate levels were found in land-based fighter pilots. Carrier-based fighter pilots, who must place aircraft weighing many tons flying at hundreds of miles per hour onto a postage stamp-size flight deck bouncing in the ocean in storms at midnight, had the highest levels.

**Anxiety** can make your blood pressure go up.[17] Indeed, anxiety can be fatal. One study followed almost 34,000 US male health professionals, aged 42 to 77 years, for two years. The researchers found that those who had scored higher on a test for anxiety had over six times greater risk of sudden cardiac death.[18] Another study[19] looked at 2,271 men for over 30 years, from 1961 to 1993. Here too anxiety symptoms markedly increased the odds for fatal coronary heart disease. Overall, coronary heart disease fatality increased over threefold in those men who scored high on an anxiety symptom scale, and, again, the odds of sudden death were almost six times as much.

Acute **bereavement** increases your risk of heart attack 14-fold in the first 24 hours[20] after the death of a loved one. After a month the risk is still twice normal.

Stress and anger have different flavors to them. I've heard patients say to me, "Don't worry about me, Doc. I don't get stressed, I get even. I give other people stress."

But when patients who had coronary artery disease were subjected to exercise, arithmetic, and recall of an incident that made them angry, their anger reduced the capability of the main chamber of the heart to eject blood more than exercise or even mental stress.[21] Outbursts of anger double your risk of heart attack in the next two hours.[22]

Clearly this relationship between our emotions and our heart can be a healer or a killer.

---

Heavy thoughts bring on physical maladies; when the soul is oppressed so is the body.

-- Martin Luther

---

## Has Stress Put You at Risk?

The following test was developed by researchers at Boston University Medical Center.[23] Score each statement from "1" (almost always) to "5" (never) according to how the item applies to you.

___ 1.  I eat at least one hot, balanced meal per day.

___ 2.  I get at least seven to eight hours of sleep at least four nights per week.

___ 3.  I give and receive affection regularly.

___ 4.  I have at least one relative within 50 miles on whom I can rely.

___ 5.  I exercise to the point of perspiration at least twice a week.

___ 6.  I smoke less than half a pack of cigarettes a day.

___ 7.  I take fewer than five alcoholic drinks per week.

___ 8.  I am the appropriate weight for my height.

___ 9.  I have an income adequate to meet my basic expenses.

___ 10. I get strength from my religious beliefs.

___ 11. I regularly attend club or social activities.

___ 12. I have a network of friends and acquaintances.

___ 13. I have one or more friends to confide in about personal matters.

___ 14. I am in good health (including eyesight, hearing, teeth).

___ 15. I am able to speak openly about my feelings when angry or worried.

___ 16. I have regularly conversations with the people I live with about domestic problems (chores, money, daily living issues)

___ 17. I do something for fun at least once a week.

___ 18. I am able to organize my time effectively.

___ 19. I drink fewer than three cups of coffee (or tea or cola drinks) a day.

___ 20. I take quiet time for myself during the day.

Add your scores and subtract 20. Any number over 30 indicates a vulnerability to stress. A score between 50 and 75 is a serious problem, and a score over 75 means you're a walking time-bomb.

## Stress and Immunity

The immune system *is* connected to the nervous system, the mind, and the emotions, and is affected by the events we experience. Immune functioning can be influenced for good or ill by our thoughts and emotions. (For those of us who went to medical school in the 70s or earlier, this is heresy.)

Examination stress, loneliness, bereavement, depression, and divorce, have all been found to impact immunity.

Lymphocytes, the white blood cells which are the workhorses of immunity, make substances that mediate immune function. We used to think these substances were made only by the neuroendocrine system and did not "talk to" the immune system. One elegant way of trying to figure out who is talking to whom in nervous tissue and immune tissue is to evaluate these cells for the presence of certain kinds of *receptors*. If a cell has on it a receptor designed to receive a certain molecule as a signal, then it is probably doing exactly that. Indeed, researchers have found that immune cells have receptors to neurotransmitters and *enkephalins* (which also mediate both immune response and nervous function) as well as a number of other substances.[24,25] And, these substances actually have measurable effects on immune function.[26] Leading researchers are now aware that virtually every brain receptor can also be found on large immune cells, called macrophages.[27,28]

It appears that everybody is talking to everybody else. Every time you stub your toe or have a nasty thought, your immune system, your heart, your gut, your brain -- every organ that has receptors -- is listening. These neurotransmitters are little impulses of consciousness which travel throughout the physiology and clue every system in to the status of the organism as a whole. They are messengers from innerspace.

In 1975, there was published a landmark study[29] that put the field of psychoneuroimmunology on the map, and demonstrated that the immune system can be *conditioned*.

Everyone knows the story of Dr. Pavlov's dogs, conditioned to associate being fed with his arrival in the laboratory, so that after a while his arrival alone was enough to make them salivate.

Doctors used to believe that the immune system was not influenced by conditioning. The immune system had been called the

Headless Horseman of the body, responding not to nonspecific stimuli, but only to particular organisms and antigens that it specifically identifies and then attacks.

We now know that we can take a substance which is in and of itself not a threat to us, yet via conditioning we can perceive it as a threat; indeed, our immune system and our bodies can respond to it as if it <u>were</u> a threat. An even more mind-boggling implication is that we can turn something ostensibly neutral or even negative into an experience that we process in such a way that it has a beneficial effect on the body-mind.

So Reality, to some degree, is about our *perception* of our experience rather than the experience itself. What we think of as objective reality is really a function of our processing and our perceptions of the world around us. It prompts us to ask the question: Is this the way we want to live our lives? Like conditioned animals jumping every time our boss or spouse or a traffic jam provokes us? It also prompts us to seek interventions which enhance our ability to perceive positively, and thus create a more positive individual Reality. This more positive Reality is not just psychological optimism but is physiological as well.

One topical study found that residents near the Three Mile Island Nuclear Power Plant (TMI), which had the accident some years ago, had depressed immune functioning. Different populations were studied, some within five miles, others more than 80 miles away from the nuclear power plant.[30] None of these people had been exposed to any significant radiation, but those closer to TMI had depressed immune functioning. Apparently, just the stress caused by the belief in the possibility of having been exposed to radiation was enough to lower immunity.

Another study showed that when people allow themselves to feel and express grief their immunity increases, while those who repress these feelings or are depressed, exhibit a decrease.[31] Clearly, states of mind, life events and stress affect immune functioning.

## Stress and Control

It's fairly common knowledge now that there are differences between *controllable* stress and *uncontrollable* stress. The classic (and somewhat cruel) study was of a group of mice exposed to uncomfortable electrical shocks not strong enough to cause real damage. Those who were subjected to an inescapable, uncontrollable shock had a decrease in their immune function. But those who were subjected to controllable shock -- they could learn how to escape it -- had no decrease in immune function.[32]

In humans as well as animals, the degree of stress controllability is a most significant factor in immunosuppression. For instance, students who felt that their stress was out of control had decreases in immunity, whereas those who felt in control of the stress in their lives did not experience those changes.[33]

Dr. Selye, the pioneering stress researcher, was the first to suggest that there were different types of stress: good stress and bad stress. Good stress is the type we experience if we are about to participate in an athletic event or other challenging but pleasurable activity. Bad stress is a result of things we perceive as negative and out of control: taking care of a relative facing an untimely death, or being subjected to examinations we're anxious about.

Each of us is capable of taking experiences people commonly find distressing and turning them into positive ones. Imagine yourself in a room with 17,000 people screaming at you at the top of their lungs trying to disrupt your concentration and make you fail at the task you're trying to perform. Most of us would be shattered by this experience. But, a Magic Johnson or a Michael Jordan enjoys this. As they try to make a free throw in the waning moments of a close game on an opponent's court with the fans going wild, all of the screaming serves to energize them to accomplish their task, and they report joy in hearing the crowd fall silent as they sink the winning shot.

One especially telling study[34] was performed at the United States Military Academy at West Point. Cadets in their first year at the academy were identified as being either susceptible (lack of antibody) to or immune (they already had antibody) to Epstein-Barr virus, which causes infectious mononucleosis. About one-third of the cadets lacked the antibody, and about 20 percent of them became infected at some time during the study. But only about one-fourth of those who *seroconverted* -- that is, who went from being antibody negative to antibody positive because they'd been infected by the virus -- developed symptoms of the disease. Researchers found that certain psychosocial factors significantly increased the risk of clinical infectious mononucleosis. These factors included having fathers who were over-achievers, having a high level of motivation, and doing relatively poorly academically. The combination of high motivation and poor academic performance interacted in predicting clinical infectious mononucleosis. On a level of common sense, one could almost predict that a young man going into the military academy with that load behind him and then finding himself performing poorly academically would get sick.

Nature occasionally demonstrates the flexibility of the immune system in peculiar ways. Persons with multiple personality disorder can have different immune functioning[35,36] depending on which personality happens to be running the show at the moment. One patient for instance had an allergy to orange juice; but another personality in that same patient was not allergic to orange juice. If the allergic personality came to the fore while the non-allergic personality was drinking a glass of orange juice, an allergic reaction would ensue. If the non-allergic personality then resumed control of the individual, the allergic symptoms would go away!

This amazing dynamism of responsiveness of immunity is not limited to persons with multiple personality disorder. It is the birthright of each of us.

## AIDS

> There are no such things as incurables, there are only things for which man has not found a cure.
> -- Simon Baruch

The tragic AIDS epidemic has provided a wealth of information and spurred much research on the immune system. Some of that research has explored the relationship of mind and emotions to immune functioning. The particular cell affected by the HIV or Human Immunodeficiency Virus is the CD4 Cell, a type of T-cell, a lymphocyte. HIV invades the cell and lives there, often relatively dormant for extended periods. When it becomes active and reproduces thousands more viral particles, the situation becomes dangerous. The cell can break open and spread these viruses throughout the blood, where they have the opportunity to infect other cells. Researchers found that this state where more viruses are produced can be triggered if the person is exposed to other viruses.[37]

Psychosocial or mind-body factors are associated with reactivation of latent viruses in healthy persons, and the same thing happens with persons with AIDS. Increases in stress hormones decrease number and functions of the CD4 cells.[38]

We don't need to be reminded that this population of individuals has suffered a highly disproportionate level of losses and bereavement. These are often young people whose friends and peers have been dying around them at rates which are unnatural for persons of their years. The number of bereavement losses, and the degree of distress secondary to those losses, is predictive of HIV progression.[39]

A population of men from whom we may learn something important are those who have markedly decreased T cells but do well anyway. Despite having T cell counts of less than 50, these men are and have been asymptomatic for more than six months.[40] They have some special characteristics. They tend to accept their HIV positive status but do not have the perception of a death sentence. They have a sense of control and a sense that the future holds unmet goals for them. They also have the ability to withdraw from excessive demands in order to nurture themselves. In psychological testing, they tend to score lowest on scales of meekness, bitterness and guilt. To put it simply, they know how to live.

It's not surprising that persons with HIV infection have tended to have poor outcomes for almost two decades now. I believe much of this is due to the way these people are treated. Persons with AIDS, especially earlier in the epidemic, tended to be homosexual or bisexual and/or users of intravenous drugs. Such populations are generally discriminated against in our society. All too often we take such persons, tell them they've been infected with a virus as a consequence of their own behavior, imply that they're getting what they deserve, and make sure they know that the prognosis for this infection is invariably death. And then we observe that they have poor outcomes. We've already seen how pessimism and depression affect immune functioning, health, and disease. It takes very independent and strong-willed persons to overcome all these negative messages.

> My body is sick but my mind is worse, engrossed in gazing endlessly upon its suffering.
>
> -- Ovid

A number of my patients complain that they seem to live from blood test to blood test. One young homosexual man told me: "Going into the doctor's office to have my T-cells measured feels as if I'm coming home with a sealed report card, just like I did in grammar school. If Daddy took off his belt, I knew I was going to get a whipping. That's how I learned my grades were bad. And now I feel the same way, wondering if the doctor is going to tell me my T-cells have flunked."

In general, the movement toward becoming an active participant in one's own healthcare is a sound one. Becoming knowledgeable about one's CD4 counts can be helpful if we can turn that into something positive. But while many people with AIDS feel it's their responsibility to be involved, some don't like it at all.

Many patients go into the doctor's office, have blood drawn, then walk out the door and don't even think about it: "I tell the doctor give to me a call if he needs to, but otherwise I don't want to hear about it. I'm not an AIDS patient whose life is revolving around the CD4 counts, I'm just a person who has to have some blood tests every so often, and I'm going to go enjoy my life." There's a fine line between denial and a simple change in priorities away from HIV and toward more uplifting aspects of life. Each person will need to sort out those priorities for himself.

There are many people alive today who were infected with HIV in the 1970s. They are living evidence that there is a wide range of possible outcomes open to people who become HIV positive. These long-term survivors of HIV have something special about them, but it might be something that any of us could have. According to Dr. Anthony Fauci, Director of the National Institute of Allergy and Infectious Diseases, "In some people it's clear that the virus is defective, but, in many, HIV is healthy and robust. The patients are just handling it well."[41]

My own feeling is that some time from now, be it five years or 50 years, we'll accept that even though HIV is a bad bug, individuals can peacefully coexist with HIV in much the same manner that we can peacefully coexist with other viruses such as Epstein-Barr virus, chicken pox virus and so forth -- and that a lot of what we've been seeing in terms of poor outcome has actually been generated by the hysteria and scapegoating surrounding this disease.

---

Be careful how you think; your life is shaped by your thoughts.
-- Proverbs 4:23

---

# CHAPTER FIVE

# Mind over Matter

> One of my problems is that I internalize everything. I can't express anger; I grow a tumor instead.
>
> -- Woody Allen

So far we've emphasized the effects that stress and lack of social support can have on immune functioning. Western medicine attends mostly to the downside, the bad things that can happen to our immune system as a result of this relationship between mind and body. But there is also an upside to this, despite the tendency of researchers and physicians to resist new ideas. (Not only will they tend not to believe something until all the data are in, but many of them "won't see it until they believe it", even when the data are staring them in the face.) .

A number of studies have demonstrated that positive attitudes,[1] humor,[2] and exposure to uplifting films[3] tend to strengthen our immune system. Antibody in saliva increased significantly after subjects viewed a humorous video tape and did not change significantly after they viewed a didactic or boring video tape. Students who watched a film about Mother Teresa's work had an increase regardless of whether or not they outwardly expressed approval for the type of work Mother Teresa does.

The old saying "when the going gets tough, the tough get going," is associated with what researchers call *hardiness*, a constellation of personality traits and coping skills that reflect commitment, control and challenge. Hardiness is associated with increased health[4] and also increased activity of natural killer cells ( a type of lymphocyte).

We now know that hope, faith, love, will to live, purpose, laughter and festivity help combat serious disease. Positive attitudes are correlated with significant biochemical reality.[5] Hardy patients with melanoma and colon cancer were treated with the normal chemotherapy and radiation. Half the group also received a modified form of counseling to suggest new ways of thinking about losses and encourage optimism. This cognitive therapy was supplemented with relaxation training. The control group, which got the same radiation and chemotherapy, did not receive the cognitive therapy or relaxation training. At the end of the study,[6] the cognitive therapy group was found to have sharply increased the level of natural killer cell activity compared to the patients in the other group.

This is the barest tip of the iceberg. But these data do shed light on the link between mind and body that TM (and other practical interventions we've yet to consider from this tradition) can animate not only to keep illness at bay but to establish radiant health.

## Cancer is a Two-Way Street

As all medical students do, I took courses in what's called Physical Diagnosis. In those courses we learn how to elicit the history of someone's illness and to perform a physical examination. In the course of seeing a man in the hospital, I took his history and discovered that about 20 years earlier he'd had pancreatic cancer. At the time I didn't know enough about pancreatic cancer to think much of it. In the years before I went to medical school, pancreatic cancer was a death sentence. Yet this man, while not well, was definitely alive and not suffering from pancreatic cancer.

When I learned a little more about that type of tumor I became quite excited. Obviously, if this man had had pancreatic cancer and now didn't have it, then it must be possible for people to have pancreatic cancer and later on not have it. I was naive enough at the time to think I'd stumbled on something significant.

On further investigation, I discovered there was a phenomenon called *spontaneous remission* or *spontaneous regression* of cancers. With the hindsight of the 1990s we've learned there are some cancers that sometimes tend to regress spontaneously, such as neu-

roblastoma and malignant melanoma. Pancreatic cancer is not recognized as being prone to disappearing on its own.

My teachers couldn't offer much explanation of this man's
history. The consensus was that the original diagnosis probably was
wrong and he had never actually had pancreatic cancer. But, even if
that diagnosis had been correct, this situation was just something
fluky that didn't have much to do with the practice of medicine. We
didn't look further into how that diagnosis had been made and
whether it had been confirmed. We just let the matter drop.

## The Immune Surveillance Theory

Knowledge about the possible mechanisms of spontaneous
remission of cancer came in the late 1970s. The *Immune Surveillance Theory* holds that cancer cells commonly appear as part of
normal cellular turnover, and that the immune system locates these
malignant cells, attacks them and rids the body of them before they
can establish themselves as cancers. The theory was not born of any
systematic investigation into the phenomenon of spontaneous re-
gressions of cancers, but was serendipitously uncovered as a result of
the increasing frequency of organ transplantation.[7]

Doctors observed that patients who had undergone organ
transplantation tended to fall victim to a type of cancer called lymphoma. As part of the transplantation protocol, patients are placed
on powerful drugs that suppress the immune reaction to prevent the
rejection of their newly-transplanted organ. When physicians who
were treating these transplantation patients suffering from lymphoma decided to lessen the doses of the immunosuppressant drugs,
they found that the lymphomas went away. Here was evidence that
the drugs given to suppress the rejection of the transplanted organs
were also suppressing the surveillance the immune system was performing to keep cancers from arising. When we suppressed the immune system, the lymphomas developed. So, by decreasing those
immunosuppressant drugs, we allowed the immune surveillance to
reemerge, and the lymphomas resolved.

Like all hypotheses in science, this one has undergone some
attacks. While it seems certain that virally-induced tumors are
usually killed by cytotoxic T-lymphocytes and natural killer cells, the
role of immune surveillance with other tumor types is not as clear.[8]

Nonetheless, the principle of immune modulation (of cancer) with all its attendant emotional and mental inputs is at least to some degree established.

## Emotions and Cancer

Major evidence for the association of depression with cancer death was provided by a couple of studies published in the 1980s.[9,10] In these studies, over two thousand men employed by the Western Electric Company in Chicago were given the Minnesota Multiphasic Personality Inventory (MMPI) Depression Test. These men were then followed for decades; there was a two-fold increase in the risk for death from cancer associated with higher scores on the depression scale. Depression was an independent predictor of cancer death even after the influences of cigarette smoking, family history of cancer, alcohol, age and occupational status were accounted for.

Though a number of subsequent studies[11] have questioned the role of depression in the genesis of cancer, some negative life events do seem to be associated with cancer mortality.

One hundred sixty-five women who were about to have a breast biopsy were given a life events' questionnaire prior to their diagnosis.[12] Authors of the study were able to find 37 matched pairs of subjects, one of each pair having a malignant tumor and the other benign. Twice as many diagnosed cancer patients had had a permanent loss of a first-degree relative or other emotionally important person. A possible biological basis for the activity of mind and emotions on tumors is not much of a stretch. Natural killer cell activity is an important predictor of prognosis in women with breast cancer,[13] and depression, fatigue and poor social support were associated with decreased natural killer cell activity in a three-month follow up of women being treated for breast cancer.[14,15]

One study demonstrated that patients treated with chemotherapy and psychotherapy had longer survival times than those treated with chemotherapy alone.[16] Groups of persons with malignant melanoma who underwent a six-week a program of psychiatric group therapy experienced less distress and increased lymphocytes, natural killer cells and natural killer cell activity compared to controls who did not undergo the psychological intervention.[17]

Other studies have shown that tumor growth is increased by chronic, severe stress.[18] I've already discussed the immunologic changes in residents living near Three Mile Island in 1979. Cancer rates also were examined in 69 study tracks within a 10-mile radius of the accident in relation to residential proximity to the nuclear power plant[19]. There was an increase in cancer rates, particularly in non-Hodgkin's Lymphoma among those living closer to the plant. This was not related to any increased exposure to radiation.

Understandably, over the years, attempts have been made to determine whether there is a distinctive cancer-prone personality. Certainly the incidence rates of different forms and sites of cancer are not equally distributed throughout the population and a number of factors -- including social class, occupation, environmental and lifestyle differences such as diet -- have been associated with an excess risk.

Though much of the earlier data in this area was conflicting, two main groups of factors[20] seem related to an increased risk of cancer: first, the loss of or lack of closeness or attachment to an important relative, often a parent, early in life; and, second, the inability to express hostile feelings, or more generally, the abnormal release of emotion.

We've seen the effects that stress of various types can have on immune functioning. Certainly the immune surveillance hypothesis would give us a direct channel from distress to the possible development of cancers.

## Distress and DNA

Distress can have direct effects on the ability of the body to repair DNA, which is the fundamental blueprint for the formation of all our cells. In one study, 28 newly-admitted nonpsychotic psychiatric inpatients were tested by the Minnesota Multiphasic Personality Inventory (MMPI) and divided into high and low distress subgroups. The high distress subgroup had significantly poorer DNA repair in lymphocytes exposed to x-rays than did the low distress subjects. Further, the lymphocytes from the psychiatric sample had significantly poorer DNA repair[21] than did lymphocytes from a nonpsychiatric control group. These levels of mental and emotional distress appear to be associated with significant dysfunctional differences at the molecular level which may have important implications for health, including possibly providing a direct pathway through which distress could influence the incidence of cancer.

If the cell has been damaged in certain ways, the ability of DNA to express coherent plans for our cells is adversely affected. This can result in the cells expressing the wrong message and multiplying without control. This is what cancer is.

In spite of all of the information we have discussed, conservative medical practitioners still tend to disregard the notion that mental attitude can have significant impact on disease. There had been long-standing evidence that group therapy had beneficial effects on mood and pain in cancer patients but not much evidence of effect on mortality rates. Then, in 1989 a study[22] was published which stunned many researchers in the field of cancer treatment (including the doctor who designed the study).

Women with metastatic cancer of the breast were randomly assigned to either a treatment group or a control group. The treatment group and control group were both treated the same in terms of chemotherapy and radiation, but the treatment group also met for 90 minutes weekly for one year. The meetings were to address some of the issues that we have previously seen had adverse effects on immune functioning, such as isolation, lack of social support, sense of hopelessness and lack of control.

Much to everyone's surprise there were significant beneficial effects on mortality. Survival time in the treatment group was approximately 37 months compared with only 19 months in the control group. Statistically and clinically, this was significant. Many researchers have commented that the magnitude of the effect achieved by this mental/emotional non-drug intervention is as good or better than what can be accomplished with chemotherapy and radiation, without the harmful side effects.

Obviously, it is important to take effective steps to bring about improvement in outlook and mental attitude. One recent study[23] indicates that pessimism is a risk factor for cancer patients: researchers found an association between a "pessimistic life orientation" and increased mortality rates. I've discussed the value of TM in generating optimism and improving just about any measurable parameter of mental health without straining to do so. This same tradition has a number of supplemental "attitude adjusting" interventions I'll discuss later.

These findings reinforce some important ideas which anyone with cancer -- or with a loved one or a patient with cancer -- should bear in mind. In virtually all tumor types, someone, somewhere, sometime, has recovered. It could happen to you.

Confidence and hope do be more good than physic.
-- Galen

## CHAPTER SIX

# Words that Cure,
## Words that Kill

*Hózhoojí Saad*[1]: "Talk in the Beauty Way"
-- from the Navaho

The following report was published for the first time in 1957.[2]

Mr. Wright had a generalized, far-advanced malignancy involving the lymph nodes: lymphosarcoma. Eventually, the day came when he developed resistance to all known palliative treatments. Also, his increasing anemia precluded any intensive efforts with x-rays or nitrogen mustard which might otherwise have been attempted. Huge tumor masses the size of oranges were in the neck, axillas, groin, chest and abdomen. The spleen and pancreas were enormous. The thoracic duct was obstructed and between one and two liters of milky fluid had to be drawn from his chest every other day. He was taking oxygen by mask frequently and our impression was that he was in a terminal state, untreatable, other than to give sedatives to ease him on his way.

In spite of this, Mr. Wright was not without hope even though his doctors most certainly were. The reason for this was that the new drug that he had expected to come along and save the day had already been reported in the newspapers. Its name was "Krebiozen" (subsequently shown to be a useless inert preparation). Then he heard in some way that our clinic was to be one of a hundred places chosen by the medical association for evaluation of this treatment.

We were allotted supplies of the drugs sufficient for treating 12-selected cases. Mr. Wright was not considered eligible since one stipulation was that the patient must not only be beyond the point where standard therapies could benefit but also must have a life expectancy of at least three and preferably six months. He certainly didn't qualify on the latter point and to give him a prognosis of more than two weeks seemed to be stretching things.

However, a few days later, the drug arrived and we began setting up our testing program, which, of course, did not include Mr. Wright. When he heard we were going to begin treatment with Krebiozen his enthusiasm knew no bounds and as much as I tried to dissuade him he begged so hard for this "golden opportunity" that against my better judgment and against the rules of the Krebiozen committee, I decided I would have to include him.

Injections were to be given three times weekly and I remember he received his first one on a Friday. I didn't see him again until Monday and thought, as I came to the hospital, he might be moribund or dead by that time and his supply of the drug could then be transferred to another case.

What a surprise was in store for me! I had left him febrile, gasping for air, completely bedridden. Now, here he was walking around the ward, chatting happily with the nurses and spreading his message of good cheer to any who would listen. Immediately, I hastened to see the others who had received their first injection at the same time. No change or change for the worse was noted. Only in Mr. Wright was there brilliant improvement. The tumor masses had melted like snowballs on a hot stove and, in only those few days, they were half their original size. This is, of course, far more rapid regression than the most radio-sensitive tumor could display under heavy x-ray given everyday and we already knew that his tumor was no longer sensitive to irradiation. Also, he had no other treatment outside of the single, useless "shot." This phenomenon demanded an explanation, but not only that, it almost insisted that we open our minds to learn rather than try to explain. So, the injections were given three times weekly, as planned, much to the joy of the patient but much to our bewilderment.

Within ten days (Mr. Wright) was able to be discharged from his "deathbed," practically all signs of his disease having vanished in this short time. Incredible as it sounds this "terminal" patient, gasping his last breath through an oxygen mask, was now not only breathing normally and fully active, he took off in his plane and flew at 12,000 feet with no discomfort!

This unbelievable situation occurred at the beginning of the "Krebiozen" evaluation, but, within two months, conflicting reports began to appear in the news, all the testing clinics reporting no results. At the same time, the originators of the treatment were still blindly contradicting the discouraging facts that were beginning to emerge.

This disturbed our Mr. Wright considerably as the weeks wore on. Although he had no special training, he was at times reasonably logical and scientific in his thinking. He began to lose faith in his last hope which so far had been life-saving and left nothing to be desired. As the reported results became increasingly dismal, his faith waned and after two months of practically perfect health and relapsed to his original state and became very gloomy and miserable.

But, here I saw the opportunity to double check the drug and maybe to find out how the quacks can accomplish the results that they claim (and many of their claims are well substantiated). Knowing something of my patient's innate optimism by this time, I deliberately took advantage of him. This was for purely scientific reasons in order to perform the perfect control experiment which could answer all the perplexing questions he had brought up. Furthermore, this scheme could not harm him in any way, I felt sure, and there was nothing I knew anyway that could help him.

When Mr. Wright had all but given up in despair with the recrudescence of his disease, in spite of the "wonder drug" which had worked so well at first, I decided to take the chance and play the quack. So, deliberately lying, I told him not to believe what he had read in the papers, the drug was really most promising, after all.

"What then," he asked, "was the reason for his relapse?"

"Just because the substance deteriorated on standing," I replied. "A new super-refined double-strength product is due to arrive tomorrow which can more than reproduce the great benefits derived from the original injections."

This news came as a great revelation to him and Mr. Wright, as ill as he was, became his optimistic self again, eager to start over. By delaying a couple of days before the "shipment" arrived his anticipation of salvation had reached a tremendous pitch. When I announced that the new series of injections were about to begin he was almost ecstatic and his faith was very strong.

With much fanfare and putting on quite an act (which I deemed permissible under the circumstances), I administered the first injection of the doubly-potent fresh preparation -- consisting of fresh water and nothing more. The results of this experiment were quite unbelievable to us at the time, although we must have had some suspicion of the remotely possible outcome to have even attempted it at all. Recovery from his second near-terminal state was even more dramatic than the first. Tumor masses melted, chest fluid vanished, he became ambulatory and even went back to flying again. At this time, he was certainly the picture of health. The water injections were continued since they worked such wonders. He then remained symptom free for over two months. At this time, the final AMA announcement appeared in the press -- "Nationwide tests show Krebiozen to be a worthless drug and treatment of cancer."

Within a few days of this report, Mr. Wright was readmitted to the hospital in extremis. His faith was now gone, his last hope vanished and he succumbed in less than two days.

The term placebo comes from a Latin verb which means *to please*. In modern medicine, the placebo effect is generally regarded as a nuisance. It tends to get in the way during research. A *placebo* is something done or something given that is designed to simulate therapy even though the person doing the investigating does not believe it to be a specific therapy. The *placebo effect* is a *change in the patient's illness* which is understood to be due to the symbolic importance of the treatment rather than the specific effects of the treatment.

> The efficient physician is the man who successfully amuses his patients while Nature effects a cure.
>
> -- Voltaire

Generally, there are three reasons for an improvement in a patient's condition.[3] We physicians love to take credit for the first of these, even though we really have nothing to do with it. It is called the *natural history* and/or *regression to the mean.*

Natural history is just what usually happens. Many acute and some chronic problems tend to go away on their own. So, if you go in to see the doctor when you have a cold he can give you something and that cold will be gone in seven days. Whereas, if you hadn't seen the doctor, it would have taken a week. Either way, it resolves.

Regression to the mean is a bit more complex. People with chronic conditions typically have symptoms that wax and wane -- the condition gets a little worse, it gets a little better. Such people, understandably, will seek care (and enroll in research studies) more often when their symptoms are worse than when they're better. So chances are the next change that will happen to this person will be an improvement. This tendency of extreme symptoms or findings to return toward a more typical and more benign state is known as *regression to the mean,* and it can often confound clinicians and even researchers. These phenomena have sent many a doctor's child through college.

The second general reason for clinical improvement in a patient's condition is the *specific effect* of the treatment. If a person has acute appendicitis, we perform an appendectomy and take out the appendix. That treatment has been curative and the specific effects of that treatment (the abdominal pain and disease go away) are attributable to the content of the intervention -- what we did actually worked. This is what biomedical research in Western medicine is looking for.

The third category is called *non-specific effects* of treatment. That is, the improvement is attributable to factors other than the specific active components in the drug or the surgical procedure. These factors can include physician attention, interest and concern in a healing setting; expectations on the part of both the patient and the physician; the reputation, expense and impressiveness of the treatment; and characteristics of the setting that influence patients to report improvement. Non-specific effects and placebo effects are synonymous.

> For some patients, though conscious that their condition is perilous, recover their health simply through their contentment with the goodness of the physician.
>
> -- Hippocrates

It's important to appreciate that placebo effects are real. There are misconceptions about placeboes that many physicians share. One myth is that people who respond to placebos had nothing wrong with them in the first place. That is wrong. The idea that giving a placebo is the same as doing nothing is also incorrect. Placebos can be effective and the effects they have can be persistent.

The rate of response to placebos is highly variable and can be impressive. Often more dramatic interventions seem to have stronger non-specific or placebo effects. Again, these interventions can have specific effects that are unavoidably entangled with non-specific effects.

Back in the 1950s open heart surgery and coronary artery bypass surgery, as we understand them today, were not available. The surgical approach to coronary artery disease was being explored and an operation was being performed called *internal mammary artery ligation*. The internal mammary artery is an artery which runs along the inside of the chest wall. Surgeons thought that by ligating or tying off this artery some degree of back pressure would build up which would then force its way into the arteries of the heart, improve circulation there, and help with angina. And, lo and behold, when this surgical technique was performed, it worked wonderfully! People reported improvement in their angina and decrease in their need for nitroglycerin. This surgery became quite popular and was widely practiced in the United States.

A couple of studies involving the use of a *sham operation* soon brought this to an end.[4,5] Researchers would randomize persons with angina to have either the internal mammary artery ligation surgery, or they would do skin incision only. That is, they would open the skin of the chest and then sew it back up and not do anything to the internal mammary artery. The patient would wake up with a scar on his chest, but would not know what had been done inside -- whether he had actually had the artery ligation or not.

After the internal mammary ligation, over two thirds of patients reported a 50 per cent improvement in their angina , which sounds impressive. But researchers found that when surgeons did the skin incision only, up to 100 percent of those persons reported improvement in exercise tolerance, nitroglycerin use and angina. In the first year after the sham surgery, 100 percent of the persons (who had only their skin incised!) reported over a 50 percent improvement in their angina. So just having undergone the surgery -- going into the hospital, having the anesthesia, experiencing the attention of the surgeon, going under the knife and waking up with a scar on your chest -- caused all these beneficial effects that seemed to have nothing to do with the ligation of the internal mammary artery. This surgical procedure has now fallen by the wayside.

Such experiences have prompted physicians over the years to observe as one author did[6] that "skeptics have long noted that an operation, particularly a new one, seems to bring benefit for several years until it is reevaluated and then often abandoned." Similarly, with regard to medicines, the 19th century French physician, Dr. Trousseau, commented that his colleagues would be wise "to treat as many patients as possible with the new drugs while they still have the power to heal."[7]

Interestingly enough, placebos act very much like drugs. For instance, they have demonstrable time-effect curves. That is, they work for a while and then wear off as drugs do. Their effects are cumulative.[8] They exhibit what are called dose-response effects. For instance, two placebo capsules have been shown to have more pronounced effects than one.[9] In general, larger capsules tend to be viewed as stronger; yellow capsules tend to be perceived as stimulants or antidepressants; and white capsules are appreciated as pain medicines.[10] Injections seem to produce larger effects than do pills.[9] Very big or very small tablets are perceived as being stronger than medium-sized.[11] The same drug Oxazepam, a tranquilizer, colored green, has a stronger effect than if it's colored yellow.[12]

What people have been told to expect from a treatment clearly influences their responses to those treatments. Ipecac is a drug that in certain doses causes nausea and vomiting. It can be very useful if little Johnny ingests some of grandpa's heart medicine by accident. But when subjects were told that this dose was effective in *decreasing* nausea and vomiting, it was! The expectation that this drug would settle nausea actually overrode its pharmacologic effect.[13] Asthmatics were treated with just inhaled saline and, depending on what they were told, it made their asthma either better or worse. When they were indeed given a bronchodilator drug, the drug was twice as effective if they were told they'd been given something that was going to be effective.[14]

It is clear that the healthcare provider's warmth, friendliness, interest, sympathy, empathy, prestige and positive attitude toward the patient and the treatment are associated with increasingly positive effects[15] of *both* placebos *and* active treatments.

The placebo effect is a reflection of the mechanics of creation. It is an idea that transmutes itself into a measurable medical happenstance. Mediated by neuropeptides and chemicals and immune cells, it is, in fact, consciousness coalescing into matter.

## Killer Ideas

No surprise, thought becoming biology can have a downside.

Placebos, even though they are made of inert material, can also have side effects. One study[16] described three major reactions to placebos in 31 patients enrolled in a clinical trial. One had overwhelming weakness, palpitation and nausea within 15 minutes of taking a placebo. A second patient developed a diffuse red rash that was diagnosed by a dermatologist as a dermatitis medicamentosa, which is a rash that occurs secondary to medication. A third patient had repeated reactions within ten minutes of taking the pills: pain in the abdomen, watery diarrhea, hives and swelling of the airway. Other side effects commonly associated with placebos are drowsiness, headaches, nervousness, insomnia, nausea and constipation.[17] One patient who had traveled to Miami on holiday[18] called his physician to complain that his medicine had so weakened him as to cause a near drowning in the surf. The records revealed that the patient had been taking a placebo.

There are even reports[19,20] of patients who have become addicted to placebos. Those addicted can substitute the placebo for an active drug, tend to increase the dose of the placebo and experience withdrawal when denied the placebo.

These adverse effects of placebos are sometimes referred to as "nocebo" effects. One practitioner randomly assigned his patients who had symptoms but no abnormal findings and no definitive diagnosis to either a positive or a negative encounter with him.[21] In the positive encounter, patients were given a diagnosis and told they would be better in a few days. In a negative encounter, the doctor told patients he didn't know what was wrong with them. Two weeks later, 64 percent of the positive group but only 39 percent of the negative group reported they were better. He speculated that since these minor illnesses would be expected to resolve spontaneously within those two weeks in the majority of patients, the 61 percent non-improvement rate in the negative encounter group reflected an adverse effect of the encounter.

The ability of our words to generate the nocebo effect has been recognized since antiquity. In the Bible, Acts of the Apostles, Chapter 5:36, we read, "But Peter said '... Ananias...you have lied not to men but to God.' When Ananias heard these words, he fell down and died."

It is unfortunate that we in the medical profession often tend to be unrelentingly negative. It's something we pick up in medical school that is reinforced in post-medical graduate training. So eager are we in contemporary allopathic medicine to extinguish "false" hope that we are willing to destroy all hope in order to do it. If we paint the bleakest possible picture, our patients and their families will never be disappointed in us; so they'll be less likely to sue us. While I've never heard anyone express this explicitly, I'm sure it's part of the unconscious thinking that provokes such conservatism and negativity.

I'd like to share an anecdote quoted by Norman Cousins in his book about the importance of hope.

> "As I was eating breakfast one morning, I overheard two oncologists discussing the papers they were to present that day at the National Meeting of the American Society of Clinical Oncology.
>
> One was complaining bitterly. 'You know, Bob, I just don't understand it. We use the same drugs, the same dosage, the same schedule and the same entry criteria, yet I got a 22 percent response rate and you got a 74 percent. That's unheard for metastatic lung cancer. How do you do it?'
>
> 'We're both using Etoposide, Platinol, Oncovin and Hydroxyurea. You call yours EPOH. I tell my patients I'm giving them HOPE. Sure, I tell them this is experimental and we go over the long list of side effects together, but I emphasize that we have a chance. As dismal as the statistics are for non-small cell there are always a few percent who do really well.'"[22]

Earlier, I described the study performed by Dr. David Speigel at Stanford which documented the benefit of psychosocial support for cancer patients, both in quality of life and survival. But the reactions of many health practitioners to it have been eye opening. Let me quote one such reaction:

> Human beings tend to hear what they want to hear. When someone tells them that maybe there's a small chance that this might influence the outcome of the disease, patients hear 'this is going to cure my cancer.' You cannot control people's reactions, and, therefore, it is incumbent on those of

us who work with patients *to continually reassure them that they should in no way expect support groups to impact on disease process.*[23] [Emphasis added]

Imagine being a cancer patient being *reassured* they you will die in your own sweet time and that non-standard interventions are not going to help.

I spend a lot of time in my practice trying to undo the nocebo effects that have been generated by visits my patients have with other health practitioners who treat them like a disease process that happens to have a person wrapped around it. They often get a clear message that their disease is lethal and unrelenting.

Contemporary allopathic medicine is often fear based, paternalistic and authoritarian. In the years since I began medical school a lot of these attitudes have improved but we doctors still try to scare patients into doing what we think is right for them. When they come to see me, often they have already been subjected to these negative and fearful messages and I believe this is not helpful for their healing and resolution of their disease.

He has an incurable disease who believes all he hears.
-- Arabic proverb

I spend a lot of my time discussing in depth with patients who are suffering from a diagnosis of malignancy that there is indeed hope; that virtually every tumor type that has ever been described has also been known to regress; that cancer, like AIDS and arteriosclerotic cardiovascular disease, is a two-way street.

Speaking about these issues is sometimes a delicate endeavor. On the one hand, I don't believe there is such a thing as false hope. All hope is real. When I sit across from an individual who has a particular diagnosis, I have no idea whether that person might be on the threshold of some miraculous cure, but I do believe that if I tell him such a cure is impossible, I may preclude it.

I do not know what is going to happen with that person and his cancer; perhaps it is destined to progress. But the fact that cancers *can* regress tells us that the mechanisms for healing and resolving cancers exist. Once Magellan circumnavigated the globe, he established that the old thinking, that you went to the edge and fell off, was once and for all incorrect. Similarly, the old thinking that cancer is a one-way street -- that once you get it you are certain to die -- is incorrect.

The concern that conservative practitioners have about giving people such hope is twofold. On the one hand, when people are told that cancers can go away by themselves they may delay seeking appropriate standard medical and surgical treatments or they may forego those treatments altogether. This is a legitimate concern, for such delay is often unwise. But physicians should know that when they send a fear-based message many people these days will disregard it. Many patients know that these messages are toxic and they will take *how* we physicians say what we say and wrap it with the content of *what* we say and throw out the whole thing. The beneficial effects of medical treatments are lost because of our authoritarian and inappropriate presentation of that information.

Often, I'll see people who have disregarded the advice of their oncologist or surgeon or radiation therapist, yet have fallen prey to a nocebo effect from another quarter, one from which they would anticipate support and love.

I believe in being positive, optimistic, and in empowering patients. But reliance on "positive thinking" wields a double-edged sword. People are told that the mind has the power to cure the body, that it thrives on positive thoughts, and that therefore they cannot afford the luxury of negative thoughts. This can be terribly burdensome.

People with a serious diagnosis often feel sick. Understandably, they may also feel bad about having that diagnosis. Most unfortunately, because of what they have heard from their well-meaning but misguided new-age friends, relatives or practitioners, they will feel guilty about feeling bad about having the diagnosis, believing that their blue mood is subverting their immune response. That is the triple whammy. This is the other legitimate concern conservative doctors express when they speak out against practitioners who emphasize this mind-body connection, because some do it so poorly. Patients are led to believe they should be able to think or wish their cancer away, and their failure to do so is a reflection of some mental or spiritual deficiency. I see people who have been told by their counselor, their healer, their relative who read a book once that since they have had some deterioration in their condition they don't love themselves, or they don't trust people enough, or they somehow want this cancer to spread, and that if they didn't want this to be happening the cancer wouldn't spread. What utter hogwash! These are the saddest people I see, sinking down a spiral of useless guilt and misery. If you have received such messages, don't walk, run from whomever is sending them.

Of course there is usually a kernel of truth in any errant philosophy. In this case, there is recognition of the need to resist searching for something or somebody *out there* to blame for our problems, health or otherwise. There is a regrettable tendency in our culture to overemphasize the strength and influence of factors outside ourselves. True, it is prudent to attend to inappropriate exposures to smog, pesticides, whatever. But to attend to them to the exclusion of attending to our own internal dynamics, to search incessantly for an external scapegoat is to avoid the responsibility of seeing the mote in our own eye. That is not the path to personal growth or to better health.

We've seen then that both placebo and nocebo effects are manifestations of consciousness turning into biology. This idea is still fairly novel in standard medicine. Why some people exhibit these effects and others don't are open questions. The mechanics of consciousness becoming matter are beyond the understanding of contemporary medicine.

The Vedic tradition gives us much insight into this phenomenon however. Consciousness is primary, the body is secondary. If we are told we have a terminal disease, and we have expectations consistent with that prognosis, our mind-body connection can generate influences that contribute to the creation of that reality for us.

On the other hand, there are many things that can be done to facilitate increased coherence in consciousness which in turn tends to create more orderly and healthy physiology. I've discussed plenty of data regarding TM. As we'll see, herbs, diet, adherence to appropriate routine, and many other areas of the Maharishi Vedic Approach to Health have been shown to have beneficial effects on health and longevity.

These positive outcomes are brought about by the *enlivenment of the inner intelligence* of the body, the same mechanics that create all the impressive findings discussed in this chapter. I believe that implementing the interventions of this tradition, which I elaborate upon in the coming chapters, will favor these types of marvelous responses.

Let's explore this inner intelligence, the nature of pure consciousness, the field which underlies true healing.

# Part Two

# The Unbounded

## CHAPTER SEVEN

# Through the Looking Glass

> So far as organization exists in every system from that of the atom to the universe, and from that of the single cell to the society of nations, the properties of no system can be wholly deduced from a knowledge of its isolated parts.[1]
>
> -- New England Journal of Medicine

I'd been standing in the quiet street next to my car, talking with friends. I heard the screech of the tires and looked up just in time to see the headlights of a car headed directly toward me, clearly out of control. For a moment we all stood like deer with our eyes wide open; then, the instinct for self-preservation kicked in. I jumped over my own car, hurdled the sidewalk and dove headfirst into some bushes. Behind me, I heard the sickening impact of metal on metal. As I stood and retraced my steps, I was hoping that all of my friends had gotten out of the way.

Once I'd determined that no one was injured, I walked into the street and with a curious detachment observed my own totaled car. I was in my first year of college. The car was an old junker, but it had gotten me around. I was taking physics at the time and I remember thinking, this is an illustration of force equaling mass times acceleration. (Had I appreciated at the time that for the next year and a half I'd be riding my bicycle for the 19-mile round-trip to my college classes, I probably would have felt a little less sanguine about the whole event.)

Isaac Newton was a pretty smart fellow. You recall the story of him sitting under a tree, getting conked on the head by a falling apple, and from that experience deriving the laws of gravitation. Most of what we see around us follows the rules of what we call Newtonian Physics. The conservation of mass, conservation of energy, angular momentum, electricity, magnetism -- all these physical phenomena have been fairly well known and described for centuries. Modern medicine persists, in large measure, in viewing the world from this perspective. Most of what one needs to know about orthopedic surgery and the actions of pharmaceuticals can be well understood through classical physics and chemistry. Physics, however, has moved on.

## The Trend Toward Unity

Early in the 20th century, Einstein clearly explained to us that energy and matter were interchangeable. There has been a tendency in the natural sciences, particularly in physics, to perceive more unity in what had formerly looked like diversity. Electricity and magnetism, for instance, were thought to be two different phenomena. Thanks to a 19th Century Scottish physicist named James Clerk Maxwell, we understand that they are the same.

By 1970, physicists had managed to describe four fundamental forces of nature: the nuclear force, or strong interaction, which holds the nucleus of an atom together; the electromagnetic force, which holds together atoms and molecules as well as generating the electromagnetic phenomena I've already mentioned; the weak interaction, associated with radioactive decay processes; and, gravity.

Einstein and other physicists since his time have believed that nature is fundamentally unified. He strove to generate a unified field theory that would describe all four basic forces in terms of one. The mathematics and the technology required to do this were not available in Einstein's lifetime, but contemporary researchers have made progress in these areas. The weak interaction and electromagnetic interactions were unified, theoretically, in 1974. The step taken after this unified the electro-weak forces and the strong nuclear forces in what is called a grand unification theory. In the last couple of decades a number of significant breakthroughs have culminated in the recent discovery of completely unified field theories. These described the elementary particles and forces of nature in terms of a single, self-interacting field. What is the nature of this field and how does it affect us in a practical sense?

## Quantum Reality in Your Hands

Right now you are probably sitting down, holding this book. On a superficial level, the book seems tangible and inert. From a Newtonian perspective, it has a certain amount of mass and if you threw it across the room, you could break your window. If you were to take a match and set it on fire, begin a reaction oxidizing the chemicals in the page and releasing heat and light, you would find that the book, even though it appears inert, actually contains quite a bit of chemical energy that can be released under appropriate conditions. All we're doing is moving around some electrons and changing some chemical bonds among the molecules in the book.

On an even subtler level, we find these molecules are made up of atoms. These atoms are made up of nuclei with electrons buzzing about them. The atoms themselves are largely made up of space. Perhaps you remember from your high school chemistry that atoms are structured in such a way that the nucleus is the size of a basketball sitting at the 50-yard line and the electrons are peas down in the end zone someplace: the vast majority of the atom is actually made up of space. As it turns out, the electrons and protons and neutrons themselves are actually also made up largely of space. They are just a probability that a certain particle, or wave of energy, is going to exist at a certain place at a certain time. If we deal with the material in this book on the level now of subatomic particles making up the nucleus, then we find there are immense energies that can be liberated from the nucleus of an atom. Nuclear detonations demonstrate these incredible energies.

If we look even more deeply at these subatomic particles, physics tells us that these particles are waves, fluctuations of organized energy in what is an infinite field of energy and intelligence. Just as a wave on the ocean appears to have limited individual attributes but is really a fleeting expression of the whole ocean, so each tiny piece of the universe has the entire universe contained within it.

> To see a world in a grain of sand
> And heaven in a wild flower
> Hold infinity in the palm of your hand
> And eternity in an hour.
>
> -- William Blake

The quantum field theories arose from particle physics. These particles are so small that they can never actually be seen, and they are studied indirectly in certain types of chambers in which their paths and behaviors can be traced. In these special chambers, particles can appear and disappear and energies are released. The question arises: Where or into what did they disappear and from whence did they arise? Physicists postulated this field as the source and goal of these particles.

It's fascinating that the mathematical theory which is among the most successful theories in the history of science dictates that this field is present at every point of creation and possesses an infinite quantity of potential energy. This, by itself, whether there are particles or waves or no particles or no waves, is described as being a vacuum. But it is a lively vacuum, fluctuating or vibrating constantly. The fluctuations are called *virtual*; these virtual particles are produced all the time, but most are unmanifest.

When we explore the nature of this field mathematically, reality seems turned on its head like some magical world beyond the looking glass. These processes take place on an infinitely small and quick scale -- what is called the *Planck Scale*. This realm is populated by black holes which are billions upon billions of times smaller than the diameter of the nucleus of an atom. They exist and disappear in time frames that are less than a billionth of a billionth of a billionth of a billionth of a hundred millionth of a second. Black holes, worm holes -- all possible particles and waves and states of energy and matter are infinitesimally being almost created, almost destroyed in a virtual world of all possibilities. I cannot overemphasize that this is not a fantasy arising out of some psychedelically induced hallucination. This is what the most successful theories in the history of science -- quantum physics -- dictate to us as being the ultimate reality.

What's more, this is our reality.

## You Are the Infinite

So far, we've been talking about the nature of the pages and molecules and atoms and subatomic particles of the book you hold in your lap, but we ourselves are also a part of this universe. Our liver, kidneys, brains, fingernails are made up of this same soup of energy and intelligence that has the full potential of creation in it. And it's not just our eyelids and intestines that are made of this but also our thoughts and dreams and aspirations. If they are not part of the universe, then what are they part of?

> What is Matter? Never Mind.
> What is Mind? No Matter.
> -- Thomas Hewitt Key [2]

When viewed through our particular cultural perspective, our thoughts and aspirations and emotions appear somewhat unreal. We look at automobiles and walls and furniture and kitchen utensils as being tangible and real like our kneecaps and front teeth. But all of the things I've mentioned that are man-made began as thoughts, all we have created as a species was once just a thought in someone's mind. That thought coalesced into a desire, a plan. It became action that generated some achievement and became... kitchen utensils. The thought that one might build a house turned into a house; someone had the idea that internal combustion was possible and created an internal combustion engine. All these things began as thoughts.

From one perspective, all we see around us is thought. We don't actually experience furniture and kitchen utensils and Mercedes Benz automobiles; rather, we perceive them through the agencies of our senses. We see them, hear them, touch them, taste them and smell them; our nervous system processes those experiences and then presents them to us as thoughts. So, in a sense, all any of us ever experience our whole life is thought. We never really experience anything else. In light of this, it seems almost incredible that our culture tends to view thought with suspicion and puts more faith in tangible objects.

## That Which Endures

If you see someone you haven't seen since high school, you may still be able to recognize her. When you greet her the very atoms you're feeling when you shake her hand were not there when you last saw her. Indeed, the very atoms that are in your hand were not there the last time you shook your classmate's hand.

Studies done with radioisotopes are revealing about what in our lives is enduring and what is transient. If we inject radio-labeled materials into a person, we find that these radioisotopes of carbon and nitrogen and so forth are taken up by the body, metabolized and inserted into the appropriate structures -- our proteins, cell walls, DNA and so forth. Over the course of time, we can follow these radioisotopes and watch them wash out and be replaced by other atoms.

The human body is more a process than a structure. Of the trillions of atoms that are in our bodies, the vast majority are replaced in less than a year. Certain tissues turn over more quickly: our skin, our blood cells, the lining of our gut. Others turn over more slowly: our bone and cartilage and nerve cells, for instance. But all of them are in a dynamic interplay with our environment, incessantly changing. In less than two years, about 98 percent of the atoms in our body have turned over and the rest of them have been replaced soon after.

So when you look at someone you haven't seen in a couple of years you are essentially looking at an entirely new creature. And you yourself are also an entirely new creature. Even though you may still retain the scar you got in kindergarten falling off a swing, the atoms that make up that scar have been turned over multiple times. From a purely material point of view, all that I am today was once in the interior of a star, and will in fairly short order be floating around the Santa Monica Bay. Those atoms which will be me in a couple of years are at this moment sitting in the dirt up near Monterey about to become an artichoke.

Clearly, I am more than the sum of my atoms.

What we have regarded as concrete and enduring is, in fact, transient. The blood and the guts and bones and sinew are just passing through. What endures over time is the organization, the intelligence aspect of the physiology. It is the blueprint upon which all these materials hang themselves, the grand design around which all the atoms and molecules orchestrate their behavior and alignment.

## The Mirage of Objectivity

Our Western scientific approach is based on objectivity. It's based on a presumption that we are able to stand apart from the objective world outside of ourselves, study it, break it down into smaller and smaller pieces and get to know each of them in turn. This approach serves us well on many levels.

The orthopedic surgeon who takes care of someone who has been hit by a car doesn't need to know much about quantum physics in order to appreciate that a Chevy going 40 miles an hour, striking a man in a crosswalk is going to wreak havoc on his hips and pelvis. Simple, straightforward Newtonian physics reveals virtually all we need to know about broken bones and ruptured organs and the surgical techniques used to repair them. But what's going on with that person after he has had the fractures reduced and the bone edges reapproximated? How do the bone cells know to restructure themselves? That subtle flow of intelligence and organizing power which is taking place at those bone ends is something beyond simple Newtonian physics.

Useful as our objective approach can be, it is limited and somewhat illusory. Physicists recognize that to observe is to change. Measuring the position of a subatomic particle will unpredictably change its velocity; measuring the velocity changes the position. This is known as the Heisenberg Uncertainty Principle, and is the death knell for the view that we can be outside of what we see. For ultimately, the object of our observations is made of the same stuff as the subject who's making the observation. Further, particularly when dealing with these infinitely small, infinitely energetic aspects of reality described by quantum physics, it is apparent that we cannot observe these things through our senses or even through any objective magnifier of our senses. No electron microscope is able to delve deeply enough into reality to give us reliable information at these scales.

Fortunately, since what we are looking to observe when reduced to these scales is the same as our own nature, it may be possible through our own nature to gain insight into the nature of reality as a whole. This concept has been voiced by philosophers of all times and all traditions. The Vedic seers (and some of the physicists involved in this type of work) have recognized that pure subjectivity (our inner nature) and pure objectivity (outer nature) were the same, but that insight has not been developed from the modern scientific perspective. There are non-Western traditions, though, that have used this approach with great success.

## A Field Beyond Thought

The most eminent among the Eastern approaches to understanding the nature of reality is the Vedic tradition of India. *Ved* or *Veda* is a Sanskrit term that means knowledge or science. Ultimately, it refers to this unified field from which all forms and phenomena of nature derive.

The subjective approach to knowledge was employed extensively in this tradition and has long been noted in the Vedic literature. Individuals with exceptional awareness are able to directly perceive the mechanics of nature's functioning. Since the nature of our minds and the nature of Nature is the same, we can explore all of Creation simply by clearly apprehending our own nature.

We see the earth spinning on its axis, seasons following seasons, apple trees giving rise to apples, electrons organizing themselves around nuclei and atoms -- all following these laws of nature. All nature exemplifies this beautiful, purposeful arrangement of orderliness, intelligence, and creativity, manifesting in its incessant diversity and evolution. Our thoughts have these same qualities of energy and intelligence; some creativity, some flow is there, but these impulses are not just random and undirected. The flow is in the direction of the fulfillment of our desires. By attending to the nature of thought, we can come to understand the nature of our mind, which is intelligence, and consciousness itself.

It is even more intriguing to find that the nature of this field of consciousness as defined by the Vedic tradition is identical to the unified field of all the laws of nature identified by quantum physics. It is a self-interacting field that is without boundaries, all pervading, unchanging, eternal, awake and dynamic within itself, the source of all existing forms and phenomena. This is the *inner intelligence of the body*, guiding and orchestrating the uncounted trillions of activities our physiologies perform every day.

Since it is by nature intelligent, this unified field is aware of its own existence. Long before physicists were pursuing this subject, seers (or *rishis*) directly explored within their own awareness the nature of this field and found that it contains the totality of Natural Law in seed form.

In our Western scientific approach the investigator is the subject; the frog we're dissecting or the subatomic particle we're looking at is the object; and the experiment, the process of observation, is the third leg of this triad of experience. This model applies to the subjective approach as well. Consciousness is the knower. Consciousness is also the known. So, we have the **subject** and the **object,** and it knows itself through this agency of consciousness which is the **process of knowing.**\*

I'll develop this idea further later on.

For now, it is key to recognize

- that we individual human beings are made of the unified field,
- that all the properties and qualities of the unified field are our properties,
- that all of the potential inherent in a field which contains all of Natural Law in seed form is our potential,
- that all this has the clearest utility in addressing health problems, codified and available through the Maharishi Vedic Approach to Health.

More fully enlivening this field within us tends to disallow the imbalances which are the basis of disease, and is the basis for the growth of consciousness.

---

\* Any experience, any knowledge can be recognized to contain these three components: the knower, the process of knowing; and, the known. These are known in Vedic science as *rishi, devata* and *chhandas,* respectively. The integrated undifferentiated field of wholeness is called the *samhita* of rishi, devata and chandas.

As we'll see in later chapters, ultimately all goals of health and of life can be gained by fulfilling one directive captured in a verse from the Bhagavad-Gita:

Know yourself as the field, and as the knower of the field.[3]

## CHAPTER EIGHT

# A Different Kind of Medicine

> The physician is Nature's assistant.
> -- Galen

I had the occasion in looking through my files not too long ago to come across my application for medical school. It was somewhat embarrassing in its naiveté.

My ideas about medical school were unrealistic, to say the least. Oh, I knew it would be hard work and long hours and all that, but I thought I was going to learn all about humankind. I knew I would learn about anatomy and physiology, all the organs and how they functioned and how they fell ill, but I also believed that in gastroenterology and nutritional science I would learn everything of importance about food, nutrition, and digestion. I believed that in psychiatry I would learn all that was worth knowing about the mind, emotions and spirit.

Practicing TM had probably predisposed me to seek out the more holistic and integrated aspects of health. I did not find that in medical school, but I was so busy with my studies I never really registered what was missing. Each month followed the previous one, and one year followed the next; as I was graduating I barely realized that I hadn't learned much of anything in the areas that had originally interested me most. My attention at that point was on the week or two I had free before my internship began. I was concerned mostly with surviving the residency which was to come.

Because I had become a teacher of TM, I was aware in the late 1970s that a restoration of the ancient medical tradition of Ayur-Veda had begun. Ayur-Veda, a system of prevention oriented natural medicine from India, had been around for millennia and was recognized and sponsored by the World Health Organization.

Maharishi was putting his attention on, among other things, health and health care. But during the late 70s and early 80s, while I was in my residency, I had not time to pursue training or extensive knowledge in Ayur-Veda.

But time was not the only factor. The truth is, I was reluctant to pursue Ayur-Veda. Indoctrinated by my medical school experiences, I had some trepidation about this system of medicine which wasn't mentioned in my medical education.

This attitude persisted for a few years. Because I had generated an obligation to the U.S. Army, I was not entirely free to determine the course of my career. Then an interesting thing happened. Ayurvedic doctors (or *vaidyas*; literally, "person of knowledge") were coming to the United States from India at Maharishi's request. They would go on tours and would assist licensed practitioners in various locations and see patients with them. My wife (also a physician) and I were asked if we would be able to accommodate a couple of these Ayurvedic doctors when I was stationed at Fort Ord near Monterey, California, from 1984 through 1986.

This was an eye-opening experience. The doctors came and we sat with them and saw patients (off post, in our home). I had some anxiety about this. What would they want to do in these consultations if we saw someone having a heart attack or a child with meningitis? We certainly weren't going to give them some herbs and send them on their way.

I should have known that my worries would prove to be groundless. Practicing primary care in the Army, the day-to-day content of my practice was not children with meningitis or people having heart attacks; rather, it was the people who were not sleeping well, who had poor digestion, who weren't getting along with their spouses, who weren't getting along with their bosses, who generally didn't feel well, whose back was weak and blood was tired; in short, the kinds of problems no pharmaceutical or surgical technique was designed to address. But if you don't know what to do, you do what you know. In Western medicine, we know drugs and surgery, and that's how we treat just about everything. To a child with a hammer, everything looks like a nail.

It was intriguing to watch these Ayurvedic doctors at work, for these sorts of issues were their bread and butter. Rather than ordering blood tests, x-rays and ultrasounds to rule out pathology that probably was not there, their approach was to address directly various areas in these people's lives that would bring them balance and relief. With fairly straightforward recommendations in areas such as diet and herbs, TM and adjustments in daily routine, these doctors were able to help people in ways I could not effectively address through modern medicine.

I had an opportunity to discuss the nature of Ayurvedic practice with these doctors and learned that while there are indeed means in Ayur-Veda to address the problems of men with heart attacks and kids with meningitis they have no problem in referring these people to Western doctors.

While I did not move promptly to embrace Ayur-Veda, I shared my growing excitement about this field with some of my Army medical colleagues. My coworkers were not wide-eyed with support, but neither were they cynical or difficult. Most doctors feel that the field of non-western medicines is so vast and uncontrolled and full of unproven technologies, they might not be sorted out for centuries. There was some healthy skepticism, and it helped me to sort out my feelings about this field. Why Ayur-Veda? What value did it have beyond what we were doing in Western medicine? Were there any data to support this field?

This last question led me to appreciate that there is a significant difference between 1) saying there are no data to support a certain assertion, and 2) saying that it has been studied and the data now show it is not supported. Just because something had not yet been well studied did not mean it was not of value. If we make that assumption, then virtually nothing in Western medicine was of value before the Second World War, since the studies employed then were inadequate by modern standards. Obviously, that's absurd. In fact, the British Medical Journal reported as recently as 1991 that only 15 percent of all modern medical treatments have a scientific basis. Eighty-five percent of what we do in modern medicine has not yet been demonstrated to be effective![1] Another more recent study from the Institute of Medicine[2] found that only four percent of medical decisions are based on strong evidence: 96% of the medical decisions modern doctors make have no support from clinical research studies.

So, just because every bit of Ayur-Veda had not yet, in the early 1980s, been completely studied was no reason to avoid pursuing it. In fact, that made it all the more exciting. Just to have a starting point was, I began to realize, quite helpful. And this particular starting point had many advantages:

- Ayur-Veda is time-tested. Unlike many medicines and surgeries I've previously discussed that are popular for a while until they are found to be worthless, the therapies in Ayur-Veda have been used successfully for many thousands of years.
- It is authenticated by the Ayurvedic texts.
- The Hippocratic admonition to "First, do no harm" was not threatened. The same test of time was almost certain to weed out any dangerous treatments over the many centuries.
- In the last ten to 15 years, it has been subjected to rigorous scientific investigation.

We didn't have to reinvent the wheel. We had a house that was already built that we could move right into and use, investigating it as we went along.

Still, I was inclined to drag my feet; finally, it was my wife who let me know that we were going to pursue this form of medicine. I'd like to share with you some of what we learned.

## Restoring an Ancient Science

> Only those who regard healing as the ultimate goal of their efforts can, therefore, be designated as physicians.
> -- Rudolph Virchow

Ayur-Veda comes from two Sanskrit terms: *ayu* or *ayus*, which means life or lifespan and *ved* or *veda*, which means knowledge or science. So, Ayur-Veda means the knowledge or science of life. Ayur-Veda originated in India and is the oldest natural scientific system of medicine in the world. Like TM, it is a part of the Vedic tradition. It has a written aspect many thousands of years old and an oral tradition that antedates that (but as we'll see, the knowledge of Ayur-Veda is timeless). It's the third largest system of medicine in the world in terms of the numbers of individuals who are served by it. (The other two are traditional Chinese medicine and *modern, Western, allopathic, contemporary* medicine (whichever adjective one would choose to use), that form of medicine with which we are most familiar with in the United States and the developed world.)

Vedic civilization and Ayurvedic medicine had flourished in ancient India. In the Indus Valley are ruins that date back to the third millennium before Christ and show a high degree of sophistication in hygiene and public health. Running water, flushing toilets and more were being used by these people in a city now called *Mohenjo-Daro* at a time when my European ancestors were barely out of their caves.

But these advanced civilizations came to an end and India suffered under many conquerors: the Greeks under Alexander, the Moguls, the British. Centuries of foreign rule were at best not supportive to Ayur-Veda. Those institutions necessary for the full maintenance of such knowledge declined. Prior to the advent of the printing press much information was passed down verbally from generation to generation. The long lapse of time adversely affected the fidelity of reproduction of this information in succeeding generations.

A unique collaboration that began in the late 1970s has supported the resurgence of this ancient medical tradition. At the invitation of Maharishi, three parties were involved. First, there were the Ayurvedic vaidyas. Fortunately, many pockets of this knowledge had been sustained through the centuries. The second associates in this collaboration were Western doctors and basic science researchers interested in investigating and restoring this knowledge of Ayur-Veda. The third, and most essential party to this collaboration was Maharishi himself, whose unique insight into the role of consciousness with regard to Ayur-Veda has helped restore Ayur-Veda to its completeness. His contributions so enhanced the efficacy of this science that his title Maharishi ("great seer") was added to the term; thus, "Maharishi Ayur-Veda," expressing the connection between this modern restoration and the tradition from which it derives.

The question of the validation of the approaches of Maharishi Ayur-Veda by Western scientific investigation was raised in this collaboration. Maharishi had always encouraged scientists to investigate and validate Transcendental Meditation, and in the same spirit he encouraged researchers to look into the modalities of Maharishi Ayur-Veda as well. He did this not because he was unsure of its value but rather because he understood that science is the universal language of our time.

The principles of Maharishi Ayur-Veda, timeless and true, do not rely upon scientific investigation for validation because they have been understood through the direct experience of the ancient rishis or seers on the level of their own awareness. This is sometimes difficult for us in the West to grasp. It can be particularly difficult for practitioners of modern medicine. We are so accustomed to relying exclusively upon objectively-based research that we have a problem acknowledging research borne of the subjective appreciation of our own nature.

In the last decade and a half, a great deal of modern objective research has been done on Maharishi Ayur-Veda. This research confirms the tenets of this approach, and I'll be discussing much of it in the chapters to come. Many doctors are still unaware of these findings, and of course even more of them had no idea of the value of this tradition in years past.

A few of my colleagues would say, back in the mid-1980's, that this reliance on subjectively-based research smacks of a blind reliance upon authority, like subscribing to the doctrine of papal infallibility. I submit that we're always relying on some authority. I don't know much about what goes on under the hood of my car or inside the CPU of my computer. Every time I get on a plane to fly across the country I do not personally investigate the principles of aerodynamics or even the credentials of the man flying the plane. I rely upon the authority, enlightened self-interest, and long track record of the airline. Even when reading medical studies, I rely upon the reputation and expertise of the researchers who designed and conducted the study and wrote the findings. As a clinician and not a researcher, I might not perform the study again to see if they were right, but I know that I (or someone else) could replicate their findings, just by following their protocol.

Similarly, in Maharishi Ayur-Veda the experience (and the procedures required to effect the experience) is there; it has been validated by millions of people over thousands of years. More importantly, even the subtlest aspect of this information is available for anyone to explore. Each of us who is blessed with a human nervous system has the capability to validate on the level of our own experience everything that I'm going to talk about in this book. This is not just an academic exercise. Unlike an exhaustive study of aerodynamics or biomedical research, this pursuit of pure knowledge is the ultimate therapeutic technique. Further, as I mentioned, the beneficial outcomes generated by the Maharishi Vedic Approach to Health can be and have been documented by our objective science as well.

The objectives of Maharishi Ayur-Veda include the prolongation of life, the promotion of perfect health and the complete elimination of any disease or problem from the body, mind, emotions, spirit, and environment.

---

*Ayurveda amritanam*: "Ayurveda is for immortality"

---

# Compare and Contrast:

# Maharishi Ayur-Veda and Modern Medicine

> The superior doctor prevents sickness;
> The mediocre doctor attends to impending sickness;
> The inferior doctor treats actual sickness.
>
> -- Chinese proverb

It is not my purpose to denigrate modern medicine. Though many people takes shots at contemporary medicine these days, my experience has been that most doctors are motivated by a genuine desire to help others, and that modern medicine does certain things very well: surgical technique; anesthesia; antisepsis; the control of acute infectious diseases; the eradication of smallpox. But, there are certain areas in which modern medicine has a less than stellar track record: prevention, health promotion, resolution of chronic disease. These are areas about which we do not know much or do much.

## Health versus Disease

Health comes first in Maharishi Ayur-Veda whereas in modern medicine, disease is the primary concern. In modern medicine an adversarial relationship with disease is our principal relationship. I'm sure many of you have sensed that your physician has a connection with your disease but not much of an alliance with you. How much easier for all concerned if you could just send in your knee or your liver or whatever and let the doctor deal with it and send it back to you. Psychiatrists speculate that today's physicians long to have patients as perfect as their first patient, the one who never questioned their competence, was silent, subordinate, compliant: the cadaver in their gross anatomy course.

Health is beyond the scope of what we learned in medical school. It is an abstraction, the absence of a diagnosis. Health is something we hope you have plenty of, so that after we operate on you or give you a lot of pharmaceuticals you're able to go home on time and not have too many complications or side effects. Our primary focus is on disease. We're looking to identify the bad guy: the tumor; the bacterium; the fungus; the inflammation. We get it in our sights and then blast away with drugs and surgery until we've annihilated it, controlled it, or masked it. Our world view does not encompass health and we are not trained to know much about it.

From the perspective of Maharishi Ayur-Veda, health is primary. Health is the real stuff. Diseases, symptoms, problems -- whether life threatening or merely annoying -- can all be recognized as manifestations of some incomplete expression of health in this or that area of life. So, our primary focus is on promoting health, strengthening the body's own self-repair mechanisms.

## Prevention versus Cure

When we address disease in modern medicine, our primary focus in on cure; in Maharishi Ayur-Veda, the primary focus is on prevention.

I was on active duty in the Army Medical Corps for over seven years. To my surprise, every post of any significant size had what is called a Preventive Medicine Activity. I thought this was most enlightened. While working there however, I found that the major portion of time and attention in the Preventive Medicine Activity was devoted to a couple of areas. One was hygienic and had to do more with plumbing than anything else. We would make sure that when the troops go out camping those in charge were well versed in principles such as keeping the latrines downstream and the source of the drinking water upstream. The second and sometimes the most time-consuming activity, had to do with the prevention of sexually-transmitted diseases. We made sure everyone had been followed up and everyone had gotten his shots. These are necessary activities, but they're hardly at a sophisticated level.

*Primary prevention* is an area in which modern medicine often doesn't have much to offer. Suppose, for instance, you had an uncle who suffered from rheumatoid arthritis and you went to the most distinguished rheumatologist in the land and told him, "I have no symptoms. My joints are fine but I don't want to get rheumatoid arthritis. What can I do to prevent it?" Essentially, he would have almost nothing to offer.

To some degree this is changing. Western practitioners have always understood that it's been better to prevent than to cure, and fortunately in recent years there has been a shift toward primary prevention, stopping disease before it gets started. For example allopathic medicine now recognizes that diet and dietary fats play a significant role in the genesis of heart disease. Still, by and large, our system of medicine is based on attending to diseases after they are established.

It's as if we have developed some giant mechanism, like something out of a book by Dr. Seuss, with levers and gears and long sticks with gloved hands at the end of them, leaning out over a river that is about to turn into a waterfall. It's the job of this mechanism to pluck people out of the river before they go over the falls. We spend tremendous quantities of money refining this machine and enhancing its capability to reach closer and closer to the precipice and even rescue people after they've gone over the edge and pull them back before they are dashed on the rocks below. But, we still don't give much attention to the question; Why are all these people falling in the river? Someone needs to post a sign or put up a fence or do something to prevent people from falling into the water.

It is exactly these sorts of interventions that Maharishi Ayur-Veda emphasizes. I'll be discussing some of them in detail later in this book.

## Treating Disease at the Root Cause

A third difference between modern medicine and Maharishi Ayur-Veda involves our approach to established disease. When we do find someone with a disease, we want to treat the disease at its origin, at its root cause, and not just ameliorate its symptoms or control its complications. We aspire to do that in Western medicine as well, but often are incapable of doing so. Let's look for example, at *hypertension* or high blood pressure. Most hypertension is what we call *essential* or *idiopathic* which means we don't know why it's there. In approximately 85 to 90 percent of cases, we never locate a particular cause for it.

In modern medical treatment of hypertension we make no pretense of cure, we just give drugs to control the high blood pressure. Now, this is a good idea, since it can prevent the patient from developing heart disease, retinal disease, kidney disease, vascular disease. The blood pressure goes down when we take the drugs; and it goes back up when we stop taking them. Clearly, we're not getting at the root cause.

Consider the following. Let's say someone was diagnosed as having high blood pressure on the 30th of June; and let's say just for the purposes of argument, that this was actually the first day it was elevated. Now, clearly, on the 29th of June, the day before, something was imbalanced in the physiology. There were some precursors percolating around in the body-mind complex that were about to coalesce and give rise to the phenomenon of high blood pressure.

These subtle precursors of disease are not well identified in Western medicine and not well treated. When they are adequately addressed early on, they can be made to disappear and, thus, diseases can be prevented. But even after a disease has been established, when we remove the instigating factors the natural tendency of the body-mind to heal itself can bring balance back into the system and lead to the resolution of disease. This is what we mean by treating disease at its root cause. As we'll see later, hypertension is well addressed by this approach.

There is an axiom in the Ayurvedic texts which states that prevention is also treatment. While a piecemeal approach is not recommended, it has been demonstrated that even by taking just some pieces from this tradition -- diet, meditation, yoga -- patients can not only inhibit the progression of arteriosclerotic cardiovascular disease but can actually cause regression[3] of atherosclerotic plaques in coronary arteries.

Maharishi Ayur-Veda regards health as not just the absence of a diagnosis, but as a state of balance reflecting the highest levels of integration of body, mind, emotions and spirit.

## Cost

A fourth difference between these two approaches involves cost. Like TM, the Maharishi Vedic Approach to Health need not be justified on the basis of cost containment, but this is by no means an insignificant consideration in our current political climate. I remember when I first began talking about Maharishi Ayur-Veda in the 1980s I would tell my listeners the previous year we had spent over $350 billion in health care in the United States. Now everyone in Congress and in the administration would give an arm and a leg to be able to state truthfully that last year we spent a mere $350 billion in health care costs, because the cost of health care in the United States has virtually tripled. We are now over the trillion-dollar-per-year range in health care costs.

We are both beneficiaries and victims of an attraction to high-tech, high-profile interventions in modern medicine. Doctors such as myself are trained in medical schools associated with medical centers. Our role models are specialists; the prestige of the medical centers rests in large part on how dramatic and how high tech their interventions can be. If one hospital is capable of doing heart transplants, the hospital across town or in the next state is striving to have at its disposal a heart-lung transplant team; once that is accomplished, perhaps they could manage to transplant a heart, a lung and a liver all at the same time. A large proportion of our resources is devoted to addressing in extremely expensive ways problems that could more readily be addressed earlier through preventive measures. Current treatments could be augmented and simplified with more cost-effective interventions in terms of diet, herbs, daily habits, meditation and exercise.

As I discussed earlier, one simple intervention, the practice of TM and the TM-Sidhi program (an advanced technique of TM), led to a hospitalization rate 56% lower than the norm.[4]

## Side Effects

The dramatic power of modern medicine has a non-monetary price as well. Few people realize the extent of *iatrogenic illness*: disease resulting from medical treatment. The Journal of the American Medical Association reported that 180,000 people die in the U.S. yearly in part as a result of iatrogenic injury, "the equivalent of three jumbo-jet crashes every two days."[5]  Medical misadventures account for more deaths than all other accidents combined[6] (and cost the U.S. economy $76 billion[7] in 1995).  The treatment of drug side-effects takes up 15 percent of hospital days.[8]

Natural approaches involving diet or life-style changes are virtually free of side-effects.  I am wary when I prescribe drugs, because I've seen how common adverse reactions are.  In contrast, significant problems from herbs are so rare as to be newsworthy.

Avoiding the cause is itself treatment.[9]
-- Charaka Samhita, an ancient text of Ayur-Veda

## CHAPTER NINE

# The Building Blocks of Life

> As no two faces, so no two cases are alike in all respects, and unfortunately it is not only the disease itself which is so varied, but the subjects themselves have peculiarities which modify its action.
>
> -- Sir William Osler

Taken from an ancient Ayurvedic text, this definition of a healthy person goes far beyond any criteria for health I encountered in medical school:

He whose doshas are in balance, whose appetite is good, whose bodily tissues are functioning normally, whose excretory functions are in balance and whose self, mind and senses remain full of bliss, he is called the healthy person.[1]

**Doshas** -- basic to the Ayurvedic view -- are fundamental, irreducible, governing metabolic principles which conceive and construct and become and govern all aspects of human physiology. In fact, all aspects of the world around us can be understood as elaborations of the doshas.

There are three doshas. They are called *vata, pitta* and *kapha*. In the simplest terms: vata has to do with movement; pitta with metabolism; and kapha with structure.

Most commonly, Ayurvedic practitioners understand the doshas in terms of phenomena that we evaluate diagnostically. We look at the level of balance and imbalance of the doshas, and consider which dosha(s) is/are predominant or strong in the physiology. Then, we recommend measures to restore balance among the doshas.

You've probably heard the terms ectomorph, mesomorph, en-domorph used to describe people, as well as Type A or Type B Per-sonality. While modern science has recognized the concept of bio-chemical individuality[2] since the 1950s, these attempts at recogniz-ing fundamental characteristics in people have not been particularly successful from the allopathic perspective. These models often don't seem to include many people, or seem to yield incomplete or conflict-ing information. Ultimately, they are not very clinically applicable and Western medicine tends to ignore them. In contrast, this under-standing of the doshas and their role in the human body-mind com-plex has been an integral part of Ayur-Veda for many millennia.

Everyone must have all three of these doshas to be alive. We all blink and breathe, move our bowels and our limbs -- manifesta-tions of vata, the movement principle. Similarly, we all have diges-tion, metabolic processes, enzymatic functioning -- manifestations of pitta dosha. And we all have a spine, a liver, lymphatic fluid -- struc-tures and substances that manifest kapha dosha.

An automobile might, 30 years after it was made, be perfectly maintained, buffed and tuned; have inflated tires and clean oil, and be the pride and joy of its owner. Or it could be in a junk yard. Or it could be somewhere in between, with some degree of imbalance having accumulated. Similarly, due to unsuitable influences on health we'll be considering in this book, we humans also can become imbalanced.

As we'll see in this chapter, the doshas are more fundamental than our organs and tissues. So if there is a problem in any organ, if there is a disease in any system of our body, then there must some corresponding imbalances in the doshas which are giving rise to that organ or system. By identifying those imbalances and taking appro-priate steps (many of which are the subjects of the chapters to come) to correct them, we can restore balance among the doshas. By bal-ancing the doshas, we establish the conditions that allow the organs and tissues to function optimally.

While it is axiomatic that any dosha may give rise to any symptom, there are certain common or characteristic patterns of im-balance that we tend to find when a given disease or symptom is pre-sent. Some of these are listed in Appendix D.

There is a questionnaire in Appendix C that can help you determine which dosha(s) you need to address to promote balance.

Since we're oriented toward disease in Western medicine, we are taught in medical school how to treat disease, and we often see the person wrapped around the disease as incidental. (Dealing with that person as an individual, while a noble part of Western medical tradition for many centuries, has now been relegated to what is called the Art of Medicine. The Art of Medicine is something you learn more from your parents than from medical school.) From the allopathic (contemporary) perspective, two individuals with the same diagnosis are treated in a similar if not identical fashion. Whereas, from the Ayurvedic perspective, two persons with the same diagnosis may be distinctly different; they may have arrived at their diseased state through very different pathways and have different imbalances requiring different treatments. Our primary focus is on the host, and the doshic imbalances from which that person is suffering.

> The invader is nothing; the terrain is everything.
> -- Claude Bernard, the father of modern physiology

By putting our attention on the disease rather than on the person with the disease, we lose the broader perspective. Understanding the predominance of the doshas and the degree of balance among them allows us to restore this holistic view.

Whatever our strengths may be, the doshas should be functioning optimally. This is what we mean when we talk about "balancing the doshas." We want to pacify or eliminate all imbalance to restore the natural balance. Balancing these doshas means that life is returned to, or not allowed to leave, this field of integration and wholeness. This is the recipe for perfect health.

Some people complain that having three doshas or three principles that dictate physiological phenomena is arbitrary. One commentator, John Newbern, stated that, "People can be divided into three groups: those who make things happen, those who watch things happen and those who wonder what happened." Captain Kirk in Star Trek stated that people could be divided into two categories:

those who believe in themselves and those who don't. Any dime-store philosopher can come up with any number of arbitrary attributes among people to establish whatever framework of organization he desires.

## Modern Confirmation of Ancient Insights

So, why does this tradition have three doshas? It turns out that this is not at all arbitrary. If we look at the doshas as they are understood by this Vedic tradition, we appreciate that the doshas are actually constructed of five fundamental elements.* But that just begs the question: Why five elements? Why not two? Or twenty?

These elements translated from the Sanskrit mean space, air, fire, water, and earth. It might seem that these categories of elements -- apparently far from the sophistication of modern chemistry's periodic table -- were identified by primitives too backward to appreciate that there were more than five elements in nature. But nothing could be further from the truth.

The ancient seers who cognized the laws of nature and the mechanics of creation within the silent depths of their own awareness are the ones who codified our understanding of Nature in these terms. What is it they were perceiving? Certainly not dirt and water and fire and air. On closer inspection, their scheme turns out to be a very subtle, sophisticated and complete understanding of matter and energy.

According to modern physics, all elementary particles and forces that inhabit space-time fall into five fundamental categories. These categories are distinguished by their quantum mechanical spin. I'm not a physicist and it's not my intention to make a physicist out of anyone reading this; but for those who are interested or want to pursue this further, these five fundamental categories are as follows: The Spin 2 Graviton, which is responsible for the force of gravity and which has properties and characteristics which correlate exactly with the element of space as understood in Vedic science; the

---

*The *mahabhutas* (subtle elements) are *akasha, vayu, tejas, jala* (or *apas*) and *prithivi*. The phenomona described by these terms are subtle, but for ease of reading I will use the inadequate translations into single English words: akasha means space; vayu means air; tejas means fire; jala (or apas) is interpreted as water; and, prithivi as earth.

Spin 3 halves, or 1-1/2, Gravitino, the spin which corresponds to the element of air; The Spin 1 Force Fields, which are responsible for the strong, weak and electromagnetic forces which corresponds to fire; The Spin 1/2 Matter Fields comprising quarks and leptons, corresponding to water; and the Spin 0 Higgs Fields responsible for symmetry breaking and corresponding to the element of earth.

Vedic Science holds that these five fundamental categories of matter and energy combine to form the three doshas. Space and air become vata. Fire and water become pitta. Water and earth become kapha.

In modern physics we see a clear parallel. The five fundamental spin types combine to form these more holistic entities which are the Gravity Superfield, comprising Spin 2 and Spin 3 halves, graviton and gravitino. Spin 1 Force Fields and the Spin 1/2 Matter Fields coalesce to combine into what is called the Gauge Superfield. The Spin 1/2 Matter Fields and the Spin 0 Higgs Fields serve to form the Matter Superfields.

The behavior and attributes of these fields correspond also with the three doshas. Gravity Superfield's properties correlate with vata, Gauge Superfield's with pitta, and, Matter Superfield's with kapha. I know this terminology from physics is opaque to most of us, and I raise these points only to make clear that the three doshas are not just intellectual constructs, but are fundamental to our nature. The specialist in physics should find the articles[3,4] written by Dr. John Hagelin to be intriguing.

We see then that there is no choice but to have five subtle elements and three doshas. This is not just someone's whim, this is intrinsic to the very fabric of the universe. This is the clearest way to understand it.

Since this unified field of all the laws of nature contains within it all potential states and is perfectly orderly and perfectly intelligent, the question often arises, why do we see around us any degree of disorder or disease at all? Since down to the very atoms in our bone marrow we are made up of this field of perfection, how can imperfection exist?

## Why Do We Suffer?

> I don't deserve this award, but I have arthritis and I
> don't deserve that either.
>
> -- Jack Benny

Why do bad things happen to good people? Why do children fall prey to disease? Why do wars afflict innocents? Such questions have been considered by philosophers throughout time.

To begin an understanding of this, let's return to three terms we discussed earlier: the knower; the known; and the process of knowing. The field of pure consciousness is awake within itself. Its nature is to be awake. And it knows itself. There is nothing else for it to know. It is everything. To catch a glimpse of this, just sit quietly for a moment and let all your senses be on yourself. Then you are the knower, you are the known, and you are the process of knowing. You're probably not having a clear experience of yourself as an unbounded field. Alternating transcending with activity is the recipe for that. But even this small experience can give you a taste of the three-in-one structure that is fundamental to Vedic science. There is the unified nature of consciousness, and yet, intrinsic to it, there are these three attributes.

As consciousness knows itself, there is a subtle change within the field of consciousness. It knows that it knows itself and this is yet another elaboration, another stirring within this field of pure awareness; and it knows that it knows subjectivity as itself, and objectivity, and it knows the process of knowing as itself, and so forth, on and on.

From a physical standpoint we can understand that this relationship among the three characteristics of consciousness defines a self-interacting dynamic, and this results in a full and rich spectrum of what physicists call vibrational modes. These are the mechanics by which unity sequentially unfolds itself into diversity. It is consciousness knowing itself; and every stage in this unfoldment from the unified field is an expression of the nature of consciousness in its own self-interacting dynamics.

All aspects of physics and chemistry, all aspects of biology, of mind, of intellect, of the objects of senses are expressions of this infinitely rich play and display of pure intelligence knowing itself. The entire sequential mechanics of creation exists within this field of consciousness.

So what goes wrong? How do problems arise from perfection?

As consciousness knows itself, it may be seduced into a preoccupation with its own variety. The intellect, that aspect of consciousness which is responsible for discriminating and deciding, loses sight of the essential unity which is the true nature of itself. Even though diversity being separate from unity is fundamentally a misconception, that is the way it *appears*. This apparently differentiating field of pure awareness becomes so charmed by diversity that it becomes unmindful of its own essential nature; somewhere in this sequential progression of unity to diversity the experience of unity is lost.

This misconception is called *"the mistake of the intellect."* *
It's as if a rich man falls down and hits his head and forgets that he has a million dollars in the bank and wanders the streets thinking he is penniless. When we make this mistake, the support, coherence, orderliness, bliss, integrative properties of pure consciousness are all underutilized, forgotten. It is a great paradox that they are forgotten, seemingly lost, when in fact they *cannot* be lost; these qualities are the nature of everything! Indeed, when memory is reestablished, it is clear that the ignorance and suffering were just *maya*, illusion. Think of the silly smile that comes on the face of someone who has been charging around the house looking for his glasses, only to have it pointed out to him that he is wearing them.

If the awareness is sufficiently established in its own unified nature and the sequential unfoldment of pure consciousness from unity to diversity is understood and experienced as an expression of the play of unity, disease has no ground on which to establish itself,

---

* **pragya aparadha;** literally, "the mistake of the intellect," which is the ultimate source of all suffering.

for the mistake of the intellect is eliminated as is the basis for all suffering in life. Again, one establishes one's awareness in its own nature by regularly transcending, experiencing pure consciousness at the source of thought, then coming out into activity to ground and sustain that experience.

> The Sanskrit term for health is *swasthya*: literally, "established in the Self."

I'll be discussing in a later chapter what happens in the evolution of consciousness and growth of higher states of consciousness, but for now it's essential to note that it is not helpful to try to maintain the idea "I am infinite" or impose some mood of blissfulness when you feel miserable. That is not your reality at that time. However, there are some helpful things we can do to manage our thoughts and emotions.

## CHAPTER TEN

# Behavior for Immortality

> The art of behavior influences not only the surface values of
> life, making people happier and better in every way, but
> also touches the inner core of life and advances it to the
> higher levels of evolution.[1]
>
> -- Maharishi Mahesh Yogi

As the ancient seers of the Vedic tradition plumbed the
depths of their own awareness they discovered and developed some
practical principles that have important applications to our lives today.

Among these approaches is one called behavioral rasayana
(*achar rasayana*). *Rasayana* in a broad sense is just about anything
that strengthens our body functions.   (Most rasayanas are substances we ingest, such as herbal preparations.) *Behavioral* rasayanas then, are behaviors, mindsets, and attitudes known to promote
health.

Specifically, rasayana is something which enhances the value
or the flow of *ojas*. Ojas is a substance which is as much consciousness as it is matter: it is the finest aspect of the material physiology,
the junction point between consciousness and matter.  Ojas is the
substrate from which healthy tissues are born.  It is a material expression of the self-interacting dynamics of consciousness.  A primary purpose of all that we do in the field of health is to promote the
quantity and flow of ojas.  The more there is and the more readily it
flows through the physiology, the better your health.

I mentioned earlier that the body can be seen as being a series of channels (called *srotas* in the Ayurvedic tradition).  From the

time we were an embryo, we began to form channels upon channels in the physiology that became the gut, airways, blood vessels, lymphatic channels, even the interstices between cells and the channels within the walls of the cells themselves. The entire physiology can be appreciated as being channels and through these channels flow substances, some obvious like blood and air, but the subtlest of which is ojas. It is a material form of this flow of pure organizing power and intelligence that upholds the orderliness of the entire body-mind complex, from our immune functioning to our enjoyment of life. Visibly, ojas gives luster to hair, glow to the skin, brightness to the eyes; we experience it as bliss. The <u>Charaka Samhita</u>, an ancient Ayurvedic text, describes ojas as a fluid which is located primarily in the heart and secondarily circulating throughout the entire body.[2]

Everything we eat, obviously, has effects on the quality of the tissues we are able to construct. And not only everything we eat, but also everything we see, hear, feel, smell and taste we ingest in just a real a way as we ingest foods. So all of these objects of our senses may increase or decrease ojas.

By the same token, every time we have a thought or a feeling, we generate neurochemicals and neuropeptides which are the physiological correlates of these internal mental and emotional experiences. Neurotransmitters and hormones and chemicals are extremely powerful and can have profound effects. We need to know what we're doing when we generate these hormones and chemicals. Though our brain is the primary source of these neurotransmitters and hormones, our immune system and other organs can also generate and receive their messages.

## Ojas and Your Heart

Perhaps the easiest effect to appreciate is that on the heart. Since I've already quoted scientific data documenting the effects of mind and emotions on the heart, it's intriguing to note that this information was known in great detail many millennia ago. Long before the first randomized placebo-controlled clinical trial was ever considered, Vedic seers had already realized the fruit of all scientific study by directly cognizing the effects of mind and emotion on our organs and physiology. The Chakara Samhita states, "One who wants to protect the heart, the great vessels and the ojas, should avoid particularly the causes of the affliction of mind. Over and above he should regularly take the measures which are helpful to heart and ojas, cleansing of srotas [channels] through regular panchakarma [rejuvenation and purification] and also make efforts for serenity of mind and knowledge." (We'll discuss *panchakarma* in a later chapter.)

"Those who eat heavy, cold, too unctuous [fatty or oily] and in excessive quantity and do excessive mental work suffer from the morbidity of *rasa vaha srotas*." That sounds like a stressful day at the office followed by a meaty American dinner. *Rasa vaha srotas* are described elsewhere in the Sushruta Samhita[3], another of the Ayurvedic texts, as being the channels of nourishment within the heart. Their descriptions parallel the modern understanding and anatomy of the coronary arteries, the arteries which supply blood and oxygen to the heart muscle itself: "Enhanced flow or obstruction or formation of nodules and flow of contents in wrong direction, these are symptoms of morbidity in srotas." Clearly, this text is describing coronary artery disease which is currently epidemic in the United States (thousands of years before modern science had figured out that the heart pumps blood!). It has identified measures that we should take that are helpful to the heart and ojas and things to avoid, both dietary and psychological.

In psychological terms, one can identify four general categories of attitudes and mindsets which are most enhancing to our health.

The first of these is **love**. Obviously, this is positive. That's why we have photographs of our children on our desk at work. Looking at these photographs refreshes and kindles that feeling of love. Our heart swells, we smile. We feel that sense of unity. Love mimics the ultimately unified value of creation. We feel boundaries dropping away between us and our beloved. We are sold out to our beloved. What is ours is also our beloved's. Blockages on this level of the heart are dissolved by the flow of love. But straining to feel love when love is not comfortably available is not healthy or helpful.

The second of these emotions, then, is **friendliness**. When the unrestrained, unconditionally positive nature of love is not available or appropriate with someone, friendliness, that uplifting predisposition to help and to enjoy the company of another is a good second. Some boundaries remain between us and our friend, but we feel some boundaries falling away.

The third of these attitudes is **compassion**. What if we just don't seem to like this particular person? He's ornery or whining, demanding, hostile, malodorous. He's asked us for spare change, holding out nicotine-stained fingers, and cursed us when we decline. Love is out of the question, perhaps, and even friendliness would be a strain. One way to look at compassion is to contemplate how uncomfortable you are being with this person after only a few minutes. Now, imagine what it would be like to live inside that person's skin day after day, your whole life long. Now perhaps this guy is just having a bad day. All the more reason to cut him some slack and intend to experience compassion rather than rejection.

> Look upon the errors of others in sorrow, not anger.
> -- Henry Wadsworth Longfellow

But if even compassion is not available, what then? Intellectually, perhaps I can understand the forces that shape the lives of a Hitler or a Stalin. Perhaps if I walked a mile in the shoes of terrorists I could understand (though not condone) their actions. If one can't muster love, friendliness or compassion, then **indifference** is optimum.

Indifference does not mean passivity. It does not mean that we can't pursue legal remedies or fight in wars or speak out clearly to make known that evil exists and must be addressed. But should we culture an adversarial relationship within our hearts? No. As Maharishi commented, "We either enjoy, or we just don't mind". In common usage "don't mind" means: don't let it bother us. But also it means, don't dwell on it, don't give this person or phenomenon rent-free occupancy between your ears. These may seem to be contradictory perspectives but they are not.

Similarly, there are three areas that are particularly damaging in relationship to an experience or a person. These are **Disappointment**, **Doubt**, and **Rejecting**.

All grief and regret we can understand in terms of disappointment. Of course, we shouldn't try to suppress these feelings; if anything, that only tends to make them stronger. But our experience of them is evidence that there is room for improvement in the way in which we're processing our experience. Just because these emotions are common doesn't mean they are necessary.

All fear and anxiety arises from doubt; doubt about our experience, doubt about the propriety of our action, doubt about the reliability of others. Maharishi has stated that "doubt is the dry rot of life." Why doubt and disappointment come and how to get rid of them will become clearer when we talk about the growth of consciousness.

The third point is rejecting. When we are rejecting, we are not just being subjected to some unhelpful influence from someone else rejecting us, but we are actually creating the effect throughout our own intellect and emotions and heart and body. We are infusing the entire body-mind complex with this emotion or attitude of rejecting in order to project that experience onto some other person or phenomenon. This doesn't mean we must embrace dictators, nuclear weapons or heroin. But when we reject anything we reject an expression of the unified field which is our own nature. Ultimately, all rejecting is rejection of our own Self.

There is another principle that may seem a little opaque: the **Need to Choose**. This can be understood to underlie the other three. Maharishi has made clear that "the hurt is in the 'or'": the impression that we must choose between two options, that the possibility of having both, of having our cake and eating it too, is not available to us. We can either have our cake **or** we can eat it, but we can't have both. On the one hand, our nature is holistic, integrated and all-inclusive, and yet we find that there is some aspect of our fulfillment which is blocked. This apparent contradiction decreases the flow of ojas. It is born of the illusion of the predominance of diversity, arising from the mistake of the intellect, and resolves with the reestablishment of the memory of Unity.

What is the value of attending to these attitudes? The Chakara Samhita identifies the benefits:

> From promotive treatment (rasayana) one attains longevity, memory, intelligence, freedom from disorders, youthful age, excellence of luster, complexion and voice, optimum strength of physique and sense organs, successful words, respectability and brilliance. Rasayana (promotive treatment) means the way for attaining excellent dhatus (tissues).

How do we get these benefits? There is a single paragraph in the Charaka Samhita that is laden with information about behavioral rasayanas.

> The person who is truthful, free from anger, abstaining from alcoholic beverages and immoderate behavior, non-violent, non-exerting, calm, sweet-spoken, engaged in transcending, observing cleanliness, perseverant, observing charity, worshipping God, showing respect for elders and teachers, devoted to love and compassion, observing vigil and sleep in balance, using regularly ghee extracted from milk, knowing the measure of place and time with propriety, unconceited, well-behaved, simple, having the senses attending to spiritual development, keeping the company of elders, being positive, self-controlled and devoted to holy scriptures should be regarded as using the rasayana forever. That who endowed with all these qualities, uses rasayana, attains all the aforesaid fruits of the same.

This paragraph contains at least 19 separate admonitions of how to obtain the value of rasayana. Let's look closely at each of these points.

Behavioral Rasayanas

1) Be truthful
2) Be free from anger
3 Abstain from alcohol and non-moderate behavior
4) Be nonviolent, nonexerting and calm
5) Be sweet-spoken
6) Be engaged in transcending
      (this is achieved in Transcendental Meditation)
7) Observe cleanliness
8) Be perserverant
9) Be charitable
10) Worship God according to religion
11) Be respectful to teachers and elders
12) Be loving and compassionate
13) Use regularly ghee extracted from milk
14) Know the measure of place and time with propriety
      (that is, observe regularity in daily routine)
15) Be unconceited, well-mannered and simple in behavior
16) Be devoted to the development of higher states of
      consciousness
17) Keep the company of elders
18) Be positive in outlook
19) Be self-controlled and follow the precepts of your
      religious beliefs.


(The admonitions to observe cleanliness and observe regularity in daily routine will be discussed later in the chapter on daily habits. The point to use ghee, we'll discuss when we talk about digestion and diet.)

In this chapter and the next three chapters, let's consider these points more or less in turn. They can serve as a framework for discussing a wealth of wisdom found in the Maharishi Vedic Approach to Health.

## Be Truthful
## Be Sweet-Spoken

Truth is now becoming popular even in the dog-eat-dog world of business. Books and tapes inform us that if candor and ethics weren't already part of our culture, we would need to invent them in order to support business. But truthfulness is good not only for business but for anything we do. The Charaka Samhita states that *cunning* blocks the flow of ojas. It makes sense. Being untruthful requires us to be think a few steps ahead. My mother has often quoted the saying, "What a tangled web we weave when first we practice to deceive." (In a cynical sense, life is easier if we tell the truth because that way we have to remember only one thing.)

Nature herself is unified, free from duality or contradiction, truthful and simple. As we are a part of Nature, Truth is a part of us. Being untruthful is contrary to our nature; it is a basis for ill health.

> This above all, -- to thine own self be true;
> And it must follow, as the night the day,
> Thou canst not then be false to any man.
>
> -- Shakespeare, *Hamlet*

But doesn't being truthful conflict with being sweet-spoken? If we are truthful all the time, aren't we committed to speak like Howard Stern since tact may lead us to dissemble? Maharishi said, "When a man speaks ill of others he partakes of the sins of those of whom he speaks. Such a man then draws more and more bad influence to himself."[4]

This combination of being truthful yet also sweet-spoken is captured in the expression, "Speak the sweet truth." This means simply that though we always speak the truth we never speak it in a harsh or hurtful manner. The purpose of speech is to uplift the listener. Another favorite expression of my mom: "If you don't have something nice to say about someone, don't say anything at all."

I must emphasize that this need not keep us from being assertive. It is perfectly possible to give commands and make demands in such a way that the person affected is eager to comply.

## Be Unconceited, Well-Mannered and Simple in Behavior

Simplicity is desirable. But this doesn't mean we have to behave like Forest Gump. His charm derived from the innocence of his heart, but we don't have to be a simpleton in order to be simple. Simple in our behavior, according to Maharishi, "Means that right or wrong, virtue or sin should be the primary consideration when deciding upon the validity of an action. It should not be decided on the basis of loss or gain."[5]

Just as being truthful and sweet-spoken keeps us from engaging in rejecting, so also does being simple in behavior, well-mannered and unconceited. When we are unconceited and simple we will be nonjudgmental. We won't be rigidly attached to a particular point of view because we will have relinquished the need to judge. Further, we'll tend not to be judgmental of ourselves. This doesn't mean we lose the capacity to discriminate between healthy and unhealthy pursuits, or can't give ourselves or others a swift kick in the pants when needed. But we should proceed with simplicity and compassion. Doubt, fear, and anxiety, which grow out of judging oneself unworthy and inappropriate, become less of an issue. This means guilt and regret, which are so often worthless, will not arise at all.

Some psychologists suggest that the vast majority of our worries are pointless. Approximately 40 percent of our worries are about things in the past about which we can do absolutely nothing. Another 40 percent are about things in the future that never actually come to pass. About 20 percent are about things in the present and of that 20 percent, 16 percent are about things over which we have no control. That leaves about four percent of our worries being about things that we can actually do something about. And in my view worrying about even those four percent doesn't help us deal with our actual problems.

> We have an infinite number of reasons to be happy and a serious responsibility not to be serious.
>
> -- Maharishi Mahesh Yogi

The value of simplicity in our behavior is illustrated by the fact that we keep pets or "dumb animals," as they are called. But dumb is a pejorative; simple might be a better term for these creatures. They are present in 60 percent of American households and they tend to get more affection than anyone (else) in the family. One study actually counted the number of touches and strokes family members gave to one another, and the family dog received by far the most. It's not completely clear if the frenzied greeting we get from our pet at the end of a day's work is a manifestation of affection or of the fact that we control the can opener, but we are often irresistibly drawn to this picture of innocence.

Some 80 percent of American men say they at least sometimes feel that they are to some degree impostors. Their roles as fathers, spouses, workers are not reflective of their true selves. They live a lack of simplicity and feel they're wearing masks. Boris Pasternak encapsulated this phenomenon in a paragraph is his novel Dr. Zhivago. Zhivago is describing his cardiac difficulties to an old friend:

> "It's a typical modern disease," Zhivago says, "I think its causes are of a moral order. The great majority of us are required to live a life of constant systematic duplicity. Your health is bound to be affected if day after day you say the opposite of what you feel, if you grovel before what you dislike and rejoice at what brings you nothing but misfortune. Our nervous system isn't just a fiction, it's a part of our physical body and our soul exists in space and is inside us like the teeth in our mouth. It can't be forever violated with impunity."

Perhaps this sense of living a life of duplicity is less today in the United States than in post-revolutionary Russia, but it is certainly not absent, and the health consequences are significant.

## Be Free from Anger

> ...it is anger...all consuming and most evil. Know this to be the enemy here on earth.
>
> -- Bhagavad Gita (chapter 3, verse 37)

Several behavioral factors such as Type A behavior, hostility, low social status, and social isolation, in conjunction with increased levels of stress,[6] can lead to cardiovascular disease.

Type A people exhibit hostility, competitiveness, a sense of time urgency and overall aggressiveness.[7] The National Heart, Lung and Blood Institute sponsored a review panel which concluded, not surprisingly, that Type A behavior is a risk factor for coronary artery disease.[8]

There is increasing evidence these days that hostility and anger are among the most important of these pathogenic behaviors.

• One hundred eighteen lawyers given the Minnesota Multiphasic Personality Inventory who were followed for a number of years demonstrated that there was an association between hostility and increased mortality rates.[9]

• Two hundred twenty-five physicians were followed for 25 years; higher hostility resulted in four times more heart disease and six times more death.[10]

• Hostility more than doubles the rate at which the coronary arteries clog up again after they've been opened with the angioplasty balloon.[11]

• Outbursts of anger double your risk of heart attack in the next two hours.[12]

An explanation from Maharishi: "When the flow of a particular desire is obstructed by another flow, energy is produced at the point of collision and this flares up as anger which disturbs, confuses and destroys the harmony and smooth flow of the desire. Thus, confusion is created...and the...expansion of happiness is marred; the very purpose of creation is thwarted."[13]

Of course, we have all experienced the "flow of a particular desire" being obstructed at times. It seems that if we could just remove all those things that are frustrating our desires, life would be all that we would want it to be. But the problem lies not with the blockages *out there*. As Maharishi notes, "Anger arises from weakness or inability to fulfill one's desires although it is generally attributed to obstacles in the way of such fulfillment."[14] Once again we see the locus of control is internal, not environmental.

What about bad desires? When we are fully conscious and attuned to our own Nature, life-damaging desires tend not to arise. Powerful evil people are examples of lack of balance and integration in the development of their capabilities in life. Great strength in leadership or in the ability to manipulate people, without wisdom and compassion, may give rise to a Hitler or a Stalin.

Some philosophers and popular thinkers have maintained that anger is an asset. If we look at anger as being a signal that something is wrong, we may be able to turn it into an impetus to some positive effect. But, in general, again from Maharishi, "anger is a great enemy; it reduces one's strength."[15]

We tend to think of anger and rage giving us great strength. But in fields that require strength and are prone to the provocation of anger, such as the military or in athletics, it is axiomatic that anger more frequently degrades than augments performance. The expression in athletics, "he's playing angry", connotes someone who is aggressive but not necessarily intelligent. While a lot of activity may be taking place, not much is being achieved toward winning the game.

"He who is able, even here, before liberation from the body, to resist the excitement born of desire and anger, is united with the divine. He is a happy man,"[16] states an ancient text. Much has been written over the centuries particularly in Eastern philosophy, about the need to be free from desire. It is one of the most misinterpreted aspects of the Vedic tradition and Vedic literature.

From Maharishi:

Life flows through desire. As long as desire is present, the possibility of anger will always exist, and, therefore, the stir produced by desire and anger is an essential feature of life. This ... does not advocate the elimination of desire but only says that it is necessary to create a situation in which "the excitement born of desire and anger" is automatically resisted in the sense that it does not overpower life.[17]

## Be Non-Violent, Non-Exerting and Calm

Being nonviolent is not just abstaining from the performance of violent acts. Indeed, one could be a soldier or a policeman and practice nonviolence more completely than someone who harbors violent thoughts or desires. Nonviolence refers to the lack of the intention to harm another; as we've seen, the intention to harm primarily harms the intender.

The expression "non-exerting" does not mean that we never act rigorously. It means only that we should not strain. Athletes may appear to be performing almost superhuman feats, yet they may later report that it all felt effortless, they were "in the zone." Straining is rarely if ever as productive as using one's intelligence to find a way of fulfilling the particular desire in a non-stressful manner.

The term "calm" is in counterpoint to the sense of time urgency that has been identified specifically in the Chakara Samhita as diminishing the flow of ojas. When you feel you're always running late you know you're not being non-exerting and calm. Time urgency is born of the need to choose, the fourth of the main blocks to the flow of enjoyment I mentioned earlier. When you're time pressured, you need to choose between what you need to do now and what you needed to do five minutes ago, neither of which you seem to have time to do at all. The hurt, then, is in the *or*. I can either do this *or* I can do that, but I can't do both.

We need to change our perception of this experience by developing a style of functioning in the nervous system that can maintain the awareness of our unified Nature even in the midst of diverse demands. By alternating transcending and activity, we culture the physiology to be able to do just that.

Remaining calm or free from anger does not mean straining to make a mood of calmness, nor does it mean we ignore or repress the distress we might feel. Researchers have found that the risk of cardiac death is four times higher in persons with so-called "Type D" personality, compared to non-Type D.[18] Type D persons tend chronically to suppress emotional distress.

You may by now think, "This is just great. I can have an outburst of anger and double my risk of cardiac death in the next two hours, or I can suppress my emotional distress and quadruple my long term risk of cardiac death. I'm 'damned if I do and damned if I don't.' What good is this information?"

Escape from this dilemma lies again in transcending and acting. Regular practice leads to less emotional distress, and the increased self-actualization and integration of personality makes us better able to process, and less likely to repress, what distress we do experience.

Further, we promote the development of higher states of consciousness, as we'll see later.

## CHAPTER ELEVEN

# Smoking and Bad Habits

> A custom loathesome to the eye, hateful to the nose, harmful to the brain, dangerous to the lungs, and in the black, stinking fumes thereof, nearest resembling the horrible Stygian smoke of the pit that is bottomless.
>
> -- King James of England, circa 1604

## Be Self-Controlled
## Abstain from Alcohol and Non-Moderate Behavior
## Be Perserverant

Let's consider bad habits such as smoking within the context of the above behavioral rasayanas. The Charaka Samhita says:

> The wise should not suppress the impending urges of urine, feces, semen, flatus, vomiting, sneezing, eructation [belching], yawning, hunger, thirst, tears, sleep and breathing after exertion.

We are notoriously inattentive to these natural urges in our culture. If you are at a movie or in a business meeting and the urge to urinate arises, often you'll just sit there with your legs crossed as long as possible despite discomfort and an imbalancing effect on the body. Similarly, when we are tired we often ignore our fatigue and have a cup of coffee. We disregard hunger that doesn't fit into our daily routine and suppress sneezes in church.

But there are some urges which are "unnatural" in that they are borne of some imbalance, and should not be acted upon. They also are enumerated in Chakara:

> One desirous of well being here and hereafter should hold up the urges of evil ventures relating to thought, speech and action. The urges of greed, grief, fear, anger, vanity and also of shamelessness, envy, excessive attachment and desire of taking another's property should be held up by the wise. One should check the impending urge of speech which is harsh, betraying, untrue and untimely used. Whatever bodily action causes pain to others like adultery, theft and violence should be checked in its impending urges. The virtuous named person, because of having thought, speech and action free from vices, is really happy and enjoys and earns virtue, wealth and desire.

Attending to these urges in the manner described would certainly exhibit **self-control**. But how does one deal with bad habits and addictions? The urge to drink the coffee or smoke the cigarette or inject the heroin may be overpowering. To exert control at that moment would certainly be a strain, but we've been instructed to avoid straining. How do we reconcile these two apparently opposed instructions?

The programs of Maharishi Ayur-Veda advocate the fulfillment of desires, not the frustration of desires. Frustrated desires merely sow the seeds of future cravings and imbalances.

## Smoking

The smoking habit can serve as a helpful illustration of some of the principles of Maharishi Ayur-Veda.

About a fifth of all deaths in the United States can be attributed to the use of tobacco, the number one preventable cause of disease in the U.S.A. It is an abhorrent habit whose damaging effects have been well documented. Yet telling people to quit smoking is often by itself not very effective. Further, the failure rates for the nicotine-containing chewing gums or nicotine-containing skin patches are quite high.

There are some steps we can take. While we don't want to strain, we do want to **be perserverant**. These approaches of Maharishi Ayur-Veda do not require a lot of self-discipline and deprivation. They are not difficult. But they may not be spontaneous: they do require attention.

Among the first steps in conquering any addiction or bad habit involves our *intention*, our desire. It is a function of the intellect to discriminate between what we are doing and what we wish we were doing. Our intention is an aspect of ourselves we can project into the future. Do I want to be a smoker? Five weeks from now, five years from now, five months from now -- will I be smoking or shall I become a non-smoker? This is an essential step: basically nothing good is going to happen regarding your behavior until you've taken this step and decided that at some point you want to be free of this habit. We cannot expect Nature to support our desires if we are not clear about what we want.

If our intention is our grand strategy, we need some tactics to implement it. The foot soldiers of our *intention* are the powers of our *attention*. It is our attention, assiduously applied and reapplied to this issue, day in and day out, that has organizing power. It is this organizing power that enlivens the healing response both in our physical body and in our behaviors.

Some people decide to quit smoking, put down their cigarettes, and effortlessly abstain from smoking forever. If you can do that, do it. But for many, the story is different.

A woman in my practice was smoking two packs of cigarettes per day. In the course of the evaluation and a follow-up visit, we addressed this and went through this litany. What about this smoking? What was she thinking about it? She knew it was bad for her, but so many areas of her life involved smoking that she had not considered the possibility of stopping. We worked with that and I asked her not to strain but to culture the intention, to consider herself at some point in the future becoming a non-smoker, to realize that it was within her capability to get there, to desire explicitly to stop smoking. Now, many people are reluctant to do this because they associate discontinuing smoking with a lot of discomfort. Perhaps they've tried it before and were miserable. I asked her not to deal with all that. Nothing we were going to do in this program was going to involve any pain or strain; so if it could be done painlessly and without straining, would this be something she wanted to do? Of course! So that was the first step for her. We'd established that she wanted to become a non-smoker if it could be done without driving her crazy.

"If you're smoking two packs a day, that's 40 cigarettes. Of these 40 cigarettes a day, some of them -- maybe two, maybe 36 -- you probably don't have a desire for. They just sort of happen automatically." She gave me an uncertain look. I knew she was an Arnold Schwarzeneggar fan. I asked her to recall one of the scenes in "The Terminator" when the police lieutenant was distracted and distressed by his homicide investigation and asked his colleague to give him a cigarette. When the lieutenant reached for the cigarette the hand he reached with was already holding a lit cigarette! He was so habituated that when that type of situation arose he would light a cigarette without even thinking about it. Obviously, he wasn't thinking much about it because he already had a cigarette in his hand and didn't even notice it. She began to nod vigorously and recounted times she had been on the telephone on a stressful business call to someone in New York and at the end of a phone conversation of 20 minutes or so, she saw in the ashtray before her three cigarette butts freshly smoldering, clear evidence that she had lit and smoked three cigarettes. Yet she had no specific memory of having done so and certainly did not enjoy them at all.

"These automatic, unconscious cigarettes we can eliminate because there is no strong desire to smoke them. So the next step is just to pay attention. Each time the impulse to smoke arises, check and see: is the desire to smoke really there? If the answer is uncertain or the answer is no, then we defer that particular cigarette at that particular moment. We're just not going to smoke that cigarette right now."

She wrinkled her brow. "But how many cigarettes am I supposed to decrease?"

"For the moment, don't worry about numbers," I said. "Already you see we're mobilizing our attention. Perhaps just by this simple maneuver of paying attention you go from 40 cigarettes a day down to 36. Some people have reported that just by paying attention they're able to decrease from 40 cigarettes a day down to half a pack."

"But I know that sometimes I really am going to want a smoke. What then?"

"Let's presume, realistically", I told her, "that five minutes after you have deferred the cigarette the impulse arises again. And when that impulse arises and you check to see, 'Do I really have a desire for this cigarette?' the answer is an unequivocal, 'Yes. I want to smoke this cigarette and I want to smoke it now.' That's fine. Again, as I mentioned, in this program we do not believe in frustrating desires, and if omitting that cigarette would be a strain we don't advocate straining. In someone who has not yet quit, if the desire to smoke arises and it's very strong, then go ahead and fulfill that desire. But if you are going to smoke, do nothing but smoke. Go outside, or into a special designated room that's used for smoking and do nothing but smoke. You shouldn't be distracted by conversation, by television, by reading, by any kind of work, by anything at all. Your primary focus of attention should be on the cigarette and on your body and how it makes you feel with each puff. Whatever it is that the body-mind is telling you it wants to get out of this cigarette, you should get it 110 percent.

"Often people will report that instead of smoking three cigarettes, they'll smoke one, or, instead of smoking one, they'll take three or four puffs and feel they really don't want any more of the cigarette and they'll put it out. Again, we're not looking for that particular experience. You want to be 'simple in your behavior', so you're just being innocent. You're just smoking the cigarette and witnessing the experience as if you were a fly on the wall seeing what happens when one smokes a cigarette."

This woman also began practicing TM. We've seen that TM by itself facilitates quitting smoking, and I believe the process I just described is much more successful in meditators because the quality of applied attention is more coherent. She was able to dismiss smoking from her life.

This procedure offers an excellent beginning to the end of cigarettes. By having our attention incessantly on this phenomenon day in and day out, the inner intelligence of the body is more fully enlivened and the difference between how we feel when we don't smoke and how we feel when we begin smoking becomes clearer. At first that rush and whatever it is we are getting out of the cigarette will be predominant. Over the course of time, particularly when we also use all the other programs of Maharishi Ayur-Veda I'll be discussing in this book, we begin to notice that we feel better when we're not smoking. At that point, we are on our way to becoming a non-smoker, which is distinctly different than being a person who has managed to quit despite the continuous emergence of desires to smoke.

In being self-controlled we employ what is called in this tradition "restraint of the senses," or even better, "balance" of the senses. We use our senses to nourish ourselves. Ideally, we would be as aware of our Self as of the world around us. We do not want to get lost in the object of our attention. But this should not be interpreted as being a mood that we create of paying attention to ourselves as much as we are paying attention to what we're doing. That is a recipe for dividing the mind and weakening our attention and our action.

While we are wise to read through these behavioral rasayanas on a daily basis and keep their principles lively in our awareness, it's not practical to try to concentrate on them or strain to implement them. The problem is, we're most likely to violate the tenets put forth in these behavioral rasayanas when we are most stressed, which is of course just when we need them the most. It's seems a Catch-22. These points can be especially difficult to attend to when our attention is unsettled. Here particularly TM is helpful. We need to create a style of functioning in our physiology that gives these ideas fertile soil to grow in.

## CHAPTER TWELVE

# The Evolution

# of Consciousness

> This is the greatest danger to life: that one lives life, time
> goes by, without any progress on the path of evolution.[1]
>
> -- Maharishi Mahesh Yogi

It is perfectly possible to understand the growth of higher states of consciousness in reliable, verifiable, even left-brained scientific terms without robbing the phenomenon of its mystic beauty.

There are seven distinct major states of consciousness. All humans experience three of them: waking, sleeping, and dreaming. By transcending via TM one can experience the fourth -- the transcendental state. To reach that state, one begins in the waking state of consciousness and experiences subtler and subtler levels of thought. One can transcend gross thinking and ultimately transcend thought altogether to experience directly the field from which thought arises. This is the unified field of all the laws of nature. Other common names for this state are: pure consciousness, pure awareness, Being, the Absolute, *sat-chit-ananda* (being-awareness-bliss). There are many scientific studies documenting the uniqueness of this state and its differentiation from waking, dreaming, and sleeping.[2]

After meditation one engages in activity. Over the course of time, having had repeated experiences of this fourth major state of consciousness (called *transcendental consciousness*) alternating with activity, one begins to develop a style of functioning in the physiology which incorporates the qualities of transcendental consciousness. So once we have established awareness of this field of pure consciousness, we maintain the awareness of this unbounded field even in the midst of our waking state, dream state and sleep state. This then is the fifth major state of consciousness. Since it includes all of the other four, it is called *cosmic consciousness*, which means all inclusive.

I discussed earlier the need for us to be able to "create a situation in which 'the excitement born of desire and anger' is automatically resisted." The mechanism for this is elucidated by Maharishi's commentary:

> This situation is created by culturing both the mental and physical aspects of life through the practice of Transcendental Meditation which produces the necessary refinement in the mind and the nervous system simultaneously. In the state of cosmic consciousness, which is the state described by "united with the divine," this refinement is such that it does not allow the excitement of desire and anger to arise .... "Before liberation," before gaining cosmic consciousness .... the knowledge that the Self is divine in its nature and is completely unattached to the field of activity grows as the practice of gaining transcendental consciousness advances. So that long before a man has actually gained cosmic consciousness the infusion of Being into the nature of the mind becomes intense enough to give him the ability to resist "the excitement born of desire and anger." The need for resisting this excitement arises only when there is a chance for the excitement to arise. This happens only before cosmic consciousness is actually gained.[3]

The field of activity then has a two-fold value. One is subtle: it helps to ground and establish what is gained by transcending. The second value is obvious: it is the field in which things are accomplished.

A person in cosmic consciousness then continues to meditate and act. In practicing TM such a person can still experience pure consciousness -- transcendental consciousness -- by itself. Coming out of this state and continuing to act while in the state of cosmic consciousness leads to a further refinement of perception. Just as we experienced subtler and finer of levels of thought on our way to transcending during the technique of TM, in the midst of activity we can experience, as the objects of our sensory perception, finer and finer levels of creation. Ultimately refined perception (or *celestial vision*) results: this is the sixth major state of consciousness, called *God consciousness*. [Note: God consciousness is not the same as having God's consciousness.]

Finally, just as in TM we are able to transcend all the relative states of creation to experience transcendental consciousness, it is also possible to refine our sensory perception to perceive all of the forms and phenomena about us as manifestations of this field of all the laws of nature, which is our own nature. This is not just an intellectual construct; we have direct sensory experience of it. Thus, when we hear sounds and see objects, we see that each object is, in fact, the unified field of all the laws of nature. That object is composed of pure consciousness just we ourselves are. This is the experience described in the Upanishads: "I am That, thou art That, all this is nothing but That." It is the experience of *unity consciousness* in which object and subject are now unified and recognized as being one. This is the seventh major state of consciousness. It refines from *I am that*, which is cosmic consciousness, *thou art that*, which is unity consciousness, to an even finer state of expanded unity, recognizing that *all this is nothing but that*: all of creation is defined in terms of the Self.[4]

Now, how long does all this take? It's impossible to say. I'm reminded of Woody Allen in the movie "Sleeper," who awoke centuries in the future and said that if he had continued with psychoanalysis, "I'd be normal by now." I doubt we would have to wait that long. Fortunately, it's not necessary to think of unity consciousness as an end point so much as a path of growth. Cervantes said, "The road is better than the inn." In growth to Unity, the road becomes increasingly marvelous, but the inn is indeed even better. So it is essential that we do not lose sight of our goal and pursue some lesser state.

It's important to appreciate that a person's behavior in higher states of consciousness is a function of that level of consciousness. Trying to behave as you anticipate you would if you were in a higher state of consciousness can sometimes lead to strain. From the Bhagavad-Gita:

> Creatures follow their own nature. Even the enlightened man acts according to his own nature. What can restraint accomplish?[5]

The whole point of going through these behavioral rasayanas is to avoid contradictions in the mind and strain in the physiology. A person in cosmic consciousness or unity consciousness may spontaneously be able to be loving and compassionate, but for us to strain to do so might create contradictions in the mind and so inhibit the very outcome which we are trying to gain.

There are a couple of expressions in the Vedic literature which are of fundamental importance for this issue. One says:

**Knowledge is structured in consciousness**.

In other words, what you know as Truth is a function of your level of consciousness. The other expression is:

**Reality is different in different states of consciousness**.

Now, it's interesting that it doesn't say reality *seems* different in different states of consciousness. Your reality *is* the one you're experiencing; to take someone who is either suffering or in ignorance and try to convince him that what he's experiencing is not real is likely to be a futile endeavor. Also, it's not really true. Each of us has his own reality. While it's helpful to have the understanding elucidated in this book of what the deeper physical reality of the universe is, that which you experience is your reality. In other words, to look at an automobile as a collection of waves of energy and intelligence might encourage an ignorant person to stand in front of a Chevrolet as it moves down the street at 40 miles an hour. That is not a helpful approach.

Mixing reality from different states of consciousness can be problematic. In other words, for someone to say that a patient has 'created his cancer' -- well, on one level perhaps that is true. After all, that patient is a manifestation of the unified field of all the laws of nature, and that unified field is the source of all forms and phenomena in Creation including that person's malignancy. So in a sense he did create that cancer. But mixing different states of consciousness and applying logic results in nonsense.[6] That person is not living the reality that he is the unified field and therefore the source of everything. Selectively to say, "You're the source of this problem," is about as useful as saying that I, the author of this book, am the source of hydrogen bombs and all the leukemias in the state of Nebraska. On one level, it's true, but it's obviously silly. I, the individual, did not do any of those things. The flip side of this nonsense would be the New Age version of "the devil made me do it": the unified field robbed the bank, not me; that was two years ago, I'm a completely new creature now with new atoms and I bear no responsibility. Sorry, my friend, off to jail.

## Duty and Sin

> I slept, and dreamed that life was joy.
> I awoke, and saw that life was duty.
> I acted, and behold: Duty was joy.
> -- Rabindranath Tagore

This brings us to the concept of *dharma*. Often translated as *duty*, dharma actually refers to that path of action which is most appropriate for you in your own growth. From Maharishi's commentary on the Bhagavad-Gita:

> Life has different stages of evolution. For the process of evolution to advance it is necessary that one stage should give rise to the next and in this process each successive stage is of vital importance....

There are people at various levels of evolution and each level has a guiding principle, a standard of its own. The guiding principle or dharma of a higher level will be suitable and practical for that level but will not be so for men of lesser development...so far as the process of evolution of life is concerned, one's own dharma is the most suitable although it may appear "lesser in merit" when compared with the dharma of another. The true merit of dharma lies in its usefulness in promoting evolution in the most effective manner.

Life at one stage, when promoted by the dharma of that stage to a higher stage, begins to be governed by the dharma of that higher stage. This is how stage by stage life evolves through the dharma of different stages of evolution. The comparative merit of the dharma of one's present state may be less than the dharma of a higher state but its merit in its own place is greater by far. The first English reader is certainly inferior to Milton's "Paradise" but it is more valuable for the student of the first grade because it is more suited to him.[7]

This gives us a new insight into the concept of following the precepts of our religious beliefs and the mechanics of sin. Again from the Gita: "Now, if you do not engage in this...which is in accord with dharma then casting away your own dharma...you will incur sin."[8] "Casting away your dharma means falling out of the path of evolution and that in itself is a positive sin. *Sin is that through which a man strays from the path of evolution. It results in suffering.*"[9] [*italics added*]

Right thoughts and actions must arise from our own awareness and intelligence. There is no code of conduct which any particular tradition or religion can develop which will be complex and refined enough to be applicable to all possible situations given the different dharmas of all the individuals who may encounter those situations, because as is pointed out in the Bhagavad-Gita, "Unfathomable is the course of action."[10]

There is much confusion about dharma in today's society. Traditional values are often questioned, sometimes for good reason. Those who lived through the 1960s will recall the slogan "do your own thing." And we all need to find our own dharma and act accordingly. But to dismiss all knowledge and values accumulated through tradition is, of course, foolish.

## Working Women

Many women today feel burdened by conflicting messages. On the one hand, many denigrate the traditional role of the homemaker. Women who participate exclusively in that role may sometimes unfortunately be subjected to a message that they are not living up to their full potential. Professional women on the other hand, often feel they are missing out on the pleasures of motherhood and being at home. Many women try to do both, which for some women may be wonderful. But we see coronary artery disease is becoming more prevalent among women.

At the lowest risk for coronary artery disease are single women who enjoy their work and who are rewarded both monetarily and emotionally in jobs over which they have some control.[11] In contrast, female clerical workers who are not readily recognized, whose bosses are not supportive and who feel trapped in their jobs are at an increased risk for this disease. This risk is increased if they add to their workplace role domestic chores and primary responsibility for raising young children.

Studies of working couples show that when husbands come home, their pulse rates and blood pressure decrease. They have left their job and are coming to relax in the bosom of their family. Whereas their wives leave their jobs and begin their second shift at home: their pulses and blood pressures rise! Women* who work exclusively in the home are at intermediate risk for coronary artery disease; those who supervise small children are at high risk for depression.[12] This may be a result of the absence of the extended family to dilute the intensity of these child-rearing duties. For these women, part-time work can actually reduce their risk.[13]

---

* For a deeper consideration of women's issues from the perspective of Maharishi Ayur-Veda, read *A Woman's Best Medicine* by Nancy Lonsdorf M.D., Veronica Butler M.D., and Melanie Brown Ph.D. (New York, Jeremy P. Tarcher/Putnam; 1993).

By being devoted to the development of higher states of consciousness, being regular in our practice of transcending, gaining the attributes of intelligence and integration we can see more clearly our own dharma. By behaving in accord with our dharma, unfettered by the bonds of ignorance and limitations on our vision, maintaining that level of awareness which is unbounded at all times we can be assured that we not perform wrong action. Our thoughts, desires and behaviors will be in accord with natural law, since the source of natural law is lively on the level of our awareness at all times.

## Karma

Every thought we think, every action we perform has far-ranging effects which reflect back upon us. We understand this phenomenon in our Western tradition as the law of cause and effect, action and reaction. What goes around comes around. In this Vedic tradition it is called *karma*. Karma simply means action.

This concept of karma is often poorly understood in both East and West. One common misinterpretation is that our fate is predetermined. Whatever happens to us is our karma and there's nothing we can do about it. This belief has led to generations of suffering, particularly in India, where many who are stricken by poverty have the mistaken idea that they should not strive to do anything about it, even that such striving is futile and against the will of God. But such misunderstandings occur not only in the East. Christ's admonition that the lilies of the field toil not and yet appear beautiful could be interpreted as instructing us not to strive. My own view is that we are being urged not to over-exert ourselves to the point of strain.

> God will not shoo flies from a tailless cow.
> -- West African proverb

I played football at a Catholic high school. Fortunately we realized that it was not quite appropriate to go to God and pray for victory, particularly since we were playing another Catholic high school, presumably just as worthy as we were. Nonetheless, we would go to church before every game. The message was actually appropriate. The priest would say 'we should pray, but if you want to win the game, you still have to go out there and block your man'.

Our karma, then, is firmly in our own hands. And what about the question of predestination vs. free will: since God knows everything, is everything already set and am I just spinning my wheels trying to influence events? This has been clarified to my satisfaction by the following analogy:[14] If you want to travel, you can go to the airport, look up at the board listing all the destinations, and walk up to the ticket window. In this action you have virtually unlimited free will. You can pick any destination and get on the plane to, say, Bangkok and take off. Once you get on the plane, however, your destination is fairly well predetermined. You're probably going to end up in Bangkok. You have made a decision, performed an action and now the consequences of that action are going to be visited upon you.

So we need to be sure that the actions that we perform are appropriate. If we've acted unwisely in the past, some effect from those actions may come back to us. What can we do about this "bad karma"?

The first step is to stop generating bad karma. There is nothing we can do about the past, but we are continuously creating our present and sowing the seeds of our future.

We should do what we can to make amends: write the IRS, confess we lost our buddy's playoff tickets, replace the borrowed lawn mower we trashed last week.

Also, we need to strengthen ourselves. If we mailed ourself a real doozey in the past and the cosmic postman is going to nail us, we want to be in good shape when he knocks. This means attending to our mental and physical health.

Sometimes there may not be clear steps to take to remedy the situation. We may not even have insight into what precipitated the negative conditions we're experiencing. Maharishi Jyotish is a discipline used to calculate the effects of the cycles and rhythms of nature in order to identify influences that might otherwise go unperceived and unattended. Maharishi Yagya (also called *Vedic engineering*) is a technology to generate specific effects in the environment to help modify those potentially negative influences we may otherwise encounter. I'll discuss in a later chapter in greater detail the other applications of the Maharishi Vedic Approach to Health.

Rare is the situation that can't be salvaged, problem that can't be fixed, relationship that can't be renewed, illness that can't be improved, hurt that can't be healed, offense that can't be forgiven, desire that can't be fulfilled. Every desire we experience is an impulse from the unified field and, as such, contains within it the organizing power to fulfill that desire. The capability for fulfillment comes in the package of desire.

## Keeping the Faith

Several of the Behavioral Rasayanas relate to charity, kindness, and religious practice. The essence of these precepts can be located in virtually all religious traditions. When I was a medical student, we were not taught to address the spiritual or religious dimensions of our patients. Nurses might inquire as to whether an inpatient wished to see a clergyman, but we doctors were outside that loop. Now it is becoming standard practice to inquire about these issues with our patients, as even Western medicine begins to recognize their impact on health.

## Be Charitable
## Be Loving and Compassionate

"Philanthropy leads to longevity." Our understanding of quantum physics and the identification of ourself with that infinite, unbounded field of consciousness confirms that all charity is directed toward the Self. We know that our entire physiology must mobilize to produce hormones and neurochemicals in order to generate any particular thought or feeling. If our lives are manifesting love and compassion, we must be incessantly bathing ourselves in the biochemistry of love and compassion.

> The house which is not opened for charity will be opened to the physician.
>
> -- The Talmud

I don't pick up hitchhikers anymore, but while driving to work one cold winter morning on a lonely highway in Iowa I gave a middle-aged man a ride. He was on his way from Washington state to Georgia to visit his adult daughter. He'd been laid off months before and was broke. The previous year, his wife of thirty years had died after a bout with cancer. After an hour's conversation, we arrived at my hospital. With genuine reluctance, he accepted all the cash I had on me, and went on his way. Yet, I almost never give money to panhandlers. What's my story?

Charity, like non-violence, begins in our hearts. I'm not convinced that giving money to panhandlers actually helps anything. Does it just perpetuate their dependence upon such handouts? I'm discouraged if approached by someone asking for money when that person is smoking a cigarette and has alcohol on his breath. But by lumping all panhandlers together, I know I miss some people I would be glad to help if I knew them better, like I came to know the man in Iowa. Clearly there are many people "just like us" who have fallen upon hard times and are trying to make the best of their lives. There are many people whom we would regard as "innocent": children, women with dependent children whose partner has left them in the lurch, those who are trying to escape an abusive situation. Those are the sorts of folks for whom even the least philanthropic members of society feel that charity is appropriate.

Whatever our individual approach is to this type of situation, it's most desirable that we have established in our own body-mind-emotional-spiritual complex enough purity and stability that we are able to regard these people with something other than resentment, contempt and disregard. If that is what we're feeling when we are witnessing a skid row bum or an aggressive panhandler, then we are experiencing the internal dynamics of rejecting, which again block the flow of ojas. While they may need a meal or a job, we need to experience charity in our hearts.

## Be Respectful to Teachers and Elders
## Keep The Company of Elders

The aged in our society are often disregarded. Those individuals with the greatest wisdom, the greatest accumulated experience are often dismissed from their employment at age 65, which is of course a completely arbitrary age. The message for the elders at that point is that they have no further function in society and I think it contributes in large measure to the decline in health we see in our older population. As a society and as individuals we need to be respectful to our teachers and elders -- both for their benefit and our own.

There is a part of the Chakara Samhita which discusses what persons are suitable and unsuitable company to keep.

Individuals suitable as company: Those who have attained maturity of virtue of wisdom, learning, age, conduct, patience, memory and meditation; those who maintain the company of mature persons; those who are acquainted with human nature; those who are devoid of all anxieties; those who are well behaved with everybody; those who are peaceful; those who follow a righteous course of action; those who advocate good conduct; and those whose very name and sight are auspicious. Individuals unsuitable as company: Such wretched human beings who are of sinful conduct, speech and mind; back biters; those who are quarrelsome by nature; those who indulge in sarcastic remarks about others; the greedy; those who envy the prosperity of others; the cruel; the fickle minded; those who serve the enemy; those devoid of compassion; and those who do not follow the virtuous course of life.

All of us occasionally find ourselves in the company of unsuitable individuals. Some people's profession actually require it; for instance, the police, and to some extent soldiers, physicians, nurses. Friedrich Nietzsche said, "Whoever fights monsters should see to it that he does not become a monster himself. And, when you look into the abyss it also looks into you." We respect persons in those professions when they execute their duties appropriately because we recognize that this requires integrity and strength of character. An individual must be living in his dharma if he is to deal with criminals on a daily basis and yet not become a criminal. So must the physician or nurse who can deal with sick and dying people on a day-to-day basis and not become sick, enmeshed, or unfeeling. Soldiers who protect us and uphold order in society while maintaining their professionalism are worthy of the highest respect. One can only admire the strength of character and compassion required by those who become social workers or teachers in tough schools and remain free of burnout.

## Follow The Precepts of Your Religious Beliefs
## Worship God According to Religion

Modern medicine has generally been less than cordial toward the spiritual dimensions of health. Sigmund Freud himself called religion "a universal obsessional neurosis" and referred to mystical experience as "infantile helplessness ... a regression to primary narcissism."[15] As recently as 1984 the National Academy of Sciences stated: "Religion and science are mutually exclusive realms of human thought whose presentation in the same context leads to misunderstanding of both scientific theory and religious belief."

While the domains of science and religion have many important distinctions, the rigid thinking reflected in the above quote has become obsolete. A number of studies demonstrate that there are health-promoting effects associated with attending church or synagogue on a regular basis.[16]

There are many ways the worship of God according to our particular religion could positively influence our health. Many belief systems require certain behaviors with regard to food, hygiene and abstinence from alcohol that have documented health benefits. Most religions provide social support that also promotes immune functioning and health. And we should not underestimate faith as a generator of the placebo effect (remember, the placebo effect is real). Also, religious beliefs and rituals can trigger any number of positive physiological changes.[17] Feasting or fasting or other types of ascetic behavior, which people may undergo prior to healing-type religious activities may in and of themselves be health promoting.

An overwhelming proportion of studies that investigated participation in religious ceremonies, social support, prayer and enhanced relationship with God showed benefits for physical and mental health.[18,19]

For most of us, our worship will be in the religion of our parents. Confusion sometimes arises because the information I'm discussing comes from India, and because Maharishi Mahesh Yogi himself is a Hindu monk. But the tradition of Vedic science predates Hinduism, and Maharishi has made it clear that it is neither necessary nor desirable for us westerners to try to act like Hindus. After learning TM, many people experience a renewed interest in the religion of their family of origin.

Many of you reading this book may not feel particularly religious, may even be estranged from the religion of your birth. If that is the case, you would perhaps be wise to speak with a member of your religion's clergy, because the absence of a religious and/or spiritual dimension to your life can legitimately be considered a risk to your health. Others of you may know that your religion clearly has the answers for you, but it is difficult to make your devotion to God a constant living reality. I think we can all have a more abundant life to look forward to. As valuable and fulfilling as religion may currently be for us, an even greater appreciation for, and most productive application of, religion may be found when we are in cosmic consciousness.

You will recall that cosmic consciousness is that state of consciousness when the Self is experienced as separate from activity. Transcendental consciousness, a state of unbounded awareness unaffected by the ever-changing phenomenal field in which we appear to live is experienced and maintained at all times along with each one of the three relative states of consciousness: waking, dreaming and sleeping. This may seem a paradox: the ultimate reality of the universe is one of unity, but here we are saying that the growth of consciousness is involving duality: the Self separate from activity.

Naturally, as one begins to perceive what is called celestial vision, the ability to perceive the divine in that around us, an appreciation grows for the Creator of this universe. That is why this sixth state of consciousness has been termed God consciousness.

The state of cosmic consciousness provides the basis for the development of the state of perfected Yoga in God-consciousness. The development of cosmic consciousness into God-consciousness requires that the separation found to exist between the Self and activity be transformed into a fusion of these two separate identities, resulting in the eternal Unity of God-consciousness.

This transformation of the state of separation takes place by virtue of the most refined activity of all, the activity of devotion to God....

The activity of devotion comprises the feelings of service, reverence and love, which are the most refined qualities of feeling. It is through the activity of devotion that cosmic consciousness develops into God-consciousness.[20]

It seems clear then, that religion or devotion to God will become a part of the life of each fully evolving person.

Fortunate are they who live in Union with God. They are man's guides on earth, furthering the evolution of all creation. [21]

-- Maharishi

## CHAPTER THIRTEEN

# "Be Positive in Outlook"

*Hózhoojí Nitsihakees*[1]: "think in the Beauty Way"
-- from the Navaho

A number of caveats come to mind regarding the instruction to be positive in outlook. It might be helpful to differentiate between having a positive attitude and being in a positive mood.

Positive attitude is more a long-term trait than a momentary state of mind. It is a perspective that one may cultivate. It is more readily generated by regular transcending than it is result of attempts to engage in "positive thinking." The stable, spontaneous consequence of integration of pure bliss consciousness into the body-mind flowing from our own reservoir of positivity within leads not surprisingly to a more positive outlook.

A positive mood, by contrast, tends to be transient. Straining to create a positive mood may "take more tread off the tire" than just allowing a bad mood to run its course. On the other hand, bad moods may sometimes be simply a bad habit, and therefore we should always challenge them when they arise to see if they reflect our true feelings in a particular situation.

The bottom line then is that in order to have a positive attitude and think positively, we should pursue enlightenment and the growth of consciousness through the means we've already discussed. Affirmations, pep talks, positive thinking, inspiring discourses, all may be somewhat uplifting, but are still acting on that fairly limited five to ten percent of our minds that psychologists tell us we routinely access. But if we are covering that base by meditating regularly, if we understand that the admonition to "be positive in outlook" is meant to augment regular transcending, not to substitute for it, this tradition recognizes the value of paying attention to our perspective. Because in attending to our outlook, we employ the *organizing power* that modern Measurement Theory tells us is inherent in our attention.

"Enjoy your life and be happy," Maharishi says. "Being happy is of the utmost importance. Success in anything is through happiness. More support of nature comes from being happy. Under all circumstances be happy, even if you have to force it a bit to change some long-standing habits. Just think of any negativity that comes at you as a raindrop falling into the ocean of your bliss. You may not always have an ocean of bliss, but think that way anyway and it will help it come. Doubting is not blissful and does not create happiness. Be happy, healthy, and let all that love flow through your heart."

## Denial or Rational Optimism?

Relatives, physicians and well-meaning friends sometimes attack us for displaying a positive attitude. If we try to maintain a positive attitude in the face of a serious diagnosis some may accuse us of being in *denial*. Having a positive attitude is distinctly different from denying to your physician in the coronary care unit that you have had a heart attack when the physician has absolute proof to the contrary.

Denial in the coronary care unit can actually be a functional defense mechanism. Those individuals who initially deny the heart attack they have had tend to have better outcomes than those who are not in denial.[2] Unfortunately, many physicians don't know this, and will try to break through the patient's denial even though they may do more harm than good.

In an otherwise mentally healthy individual, denial eventually will give way to an appropriate recognition of the gravity of the situation. I say "appropriate" guardedly because we in our culture are somewhat conditioned to believe that certain *prognoses* or outcomes inevitably follow a given diagnosis.

Mr. Hayes was a retired master sergeant with a long and distinguished service record; by anyone's definition, he was a brave man. He was under my care and had become anxious to the point of hypochondriasis about a number of nonspecific symptoms. One evening I saw him in the Emergency Room for chest pain, and as fate would have it, he was indeed suffering from a myocardial infarction (heart attack).

I knew he would not handle that news well, so while I planned to educate him further later, I told him truthfully that he had a circulatory problem that was now stabilized, it was something we see quite commonly, he'll be monitored in the hospital for a few days but he shouldn't worry about it. He seemed OK so I sat to write up my paperwork. A few minutes later, I looked up to see a newly arrived staff member talking with him when he exclaimed, "You mean I've had a heart attack?!" As I approached him I could almost see the skull and crossbones rising over his countenance. It took a lot of time and conversation to undo the link, in Mr. Hayes' mind, between the dreaded "heart attack" and the feared outcome of death.

Unfortunately, we physicians often reinforce if not create this kind of thinking. I spend a lot of time counseling patients to accept the diagnosis but challenge the prognosis. When we discuss the prognosis with a patient we are talking about anecdotal experience (which may be in part a result of placebo or nocebo effects) and/or informing the patient of the results of scientific studies. The trouble is that the statistics derived from scientific studies apply to *populations,* not individuals.

In studying, for instance, survival times in a population of persons with a given cancer, we'll probably see a *bell-shaped curve* with a big bulge in the middle and two tail ends at either side. One end would represent people who succumb quickly, the big bulge in the middle is full of folks with "average" survival times, and the other tail has folks who live longer than average. Physicians sitting across from a given individual generally have no idea where that person fits in the bell-shaped curve. Since we are often surprised by what happens, it is only fair to give every patient the benefit of the doubt.

In addition, data derived from these studies are not always applicable to persons outside the study. A study from rural Finland

151

may be minimally applicable to urban African-Americans. You may be very different from the group studied in ways researchers do not currently control for, such as optimism, spiritual outlook, and/or doshic imbalances, all of which may have profound influences unrecognized today.

If you are concerned enough about your health and the health of the world to be reading this book, I believe you might differ in many salient characteristics from the subjects in a given scientific experiment. So this whole bell-shaped curve may not apply to you with any degree of reliability.

"Six years ago, my oncologist gave me six months to live," a patient once told me. "So I asked him, 'If I make it to seven months, can I have your Mercedes?' My life expectancy increased immediately."

Some people have a positive attitude based upon faith or an emotional attachment to a certain world view. Many would like to have a positive attitude but are so indoctrinated by the negativity which floats around, particularly in the medical model, that they don't see much rational basis for it.

## Must We Suffer?

John came to me nearly a decade ago with a complaint of back pain. We discussed a number of Ayurvedic interventions. When he returned in a month, I asked how he was doing.

"I've done all the things we talked about, including the meditation." And his pain? "My back pain hasn't changed." I was surprised; he didn't look as distressed as someone complaining of no results.

"Well, you look better," I replied lamely.

"Oh yes," he said. "I feel much better. My back pain doesn't bother me nearly as much."

While John went on to have improvement in his pain as well, it took me a couple more years of hearing comments like his before I understood them. *Pain* and *suffering* are not the same thing. The marathon runner about to win his race may be experiencing all manner of pain in his legs, lungs and chest, yet he is exhilarated at the prospect of capturing a gold medal. Similarly, a woman in labor is having what you or I might experience as terrible pain, but within that context it does not feel like suffering. In a study of men wounded in battle[3] the investigator was surprised to find that of over 200 seriously-wounded men, only a quarter had enough suffering to accept the offer of a narcotic. In the civilian world where the injury was a surgical wound made under anesthesia, more than 80 percent wanted narcotics. The wounded soldiers were on the Anzio beachhead in World War II where the shelling had been continuous for months. For them a wound meant that the torment of living on that beachhead, fearing death, was about to end. In that context, the wound was painful, but did not provoke suffering: it was a ticket home.

The mind has power to affect and to adapt to any prognosis. German soldiers in World War I who were subjected to what was then called "shell shock" were retired from the front lines, moved to the rear areas and hospitalized. They were not expected to recover and they didn't. Many were still hospitalized when World War II broke out twenty years later, and hardly any of them ever recovered any function or were gainfully employed for the rest of their lives.

Our understanding of this type of battle fatigue or battle stress, as it is called, has evolved over the years. Now, soldiers who are subjected to battle stress injury and who are unable to function are relieved from the front line but are taken to clearing stations close to their unit of origin. They are given a change of uniform, a shower, a hot meal, a good night's sleep, and are briefly counseled, with the expectation that they will be returning to their unit in 24 to 72 hours. Over 90 percent of these men are able to recharge their batteries, go back with their unit and function completely adequately.

## The Fulfillment of Desire

I've already discussed the problems that can arise if taking responsibility for one's health is somehow converted into guilt. One helpful approach is to arrange the rules of the game in such a way that we cannot fail. For instance, some people tell themselves that any day above ground is a good day. Most of us, however, presume that certain outcomes connote failure: worsening of disease, spreading of a malignancy, death. Physicians especially tend to view death of the physical body as failure, which can make for a pretty dismal professional outlook, since that fate awaits us all. But if we don't insist on that interpretation, then we don't have to live with failure.

We could interpret any unfulfilled desire as a failure and respond with frustration and anger. But in the Vedic tradition it is axiomatic that no desire remains unfulfilled forever. The basis for such a statement is twofold. Since our individual desire is just an impulse, a wave on the larger ocean of consciousness, it has intrinsic to it all the properties of the ocean from which it arose. And that ocean, latent with intelligence, organizing power and awareness, is the self-referral matrix for the fulfillment of all possible desires. So the desire contains within itself the mechanisms for its own fulfillment. From this viewpoint, all desires can be fulfilled. Yet sometimes, they don't seem to be. What's going on here?

From one perspective, they may simply be *delayed*, and by continuing with our appropriate application of intention and attention our desire is eventually fulfilled. Or the desire itself may *change*. Think back, for example, to when you were 15 years old and perhaps all your friends had fancy bicycles, while you had an old clunker. It was not much fun to ride and you felt embarrassed to be seen on it. You had a strong desire for a bike like the ones your friends had. So you got a paper route and began cutting lawns and doing chores and saving money for this bicycle. But in the meantime, you got your learner's permit, learned to drive and arrived at your 16th birthday. At that point, your desire probably changed: "Forget the bicycle, I want a Corvette." Now, the desire for the bicycle was never fulfilled; yet, it was not an unfulfilled desire because your desire had evolved into something different and was no longer a source of frustration.

In cases of spontaneous remission of cancer there does not seem to be any particular formula in terms of visualization or prayer or desire. But one common denominator among the case histories of these events was that the people with spontaneous remissions were *nonattached to that particular outcome*.[4] Perhaps they still wanted the outcome and probably they did, but they seemed to have surrendered to whatever happened. (Obviously, straining to be nonattached is not productive.) If they addressed the cancer at all, it was merely to recognize that they put their attention on improving the quality of life rather than trying to delay the end of it, and, in so doing the end was indeed delayed, in some cases, for many decades. It was also common for these people to report genuine spiritual enlivenment. Perhaps they were beginning to sense themselves as being the unbounded field of life I've previously discussed. As described in the Bhagavad-Gita:

> He is never born, nor does he die; nor once having been, does he cease to be. Unborn, eternal, everlasting, ancient, he is not slain when the body is slain....
> Weapons cannot cleave him, nor fire burn him; water cannot wet him, nor wind dry him away.
> He is uncleavable; he cannot be burned; he cannot be wetted, nor yet can he be dried. He is eternal, all-pervading, stable, immovable, ever the same.
> He is declared to be unmanifest, unthinkable, unchangeable; therefore knowing him as such you should not grieve.[5]

Faced with a terminal prognosis, one confronts one's mortality. If perception of Reality is clear enough, the above quoted verses are alive, and one knows that it is mortality that is unreal. Such a realization leads to faith, surrender, peace of mind. In such a state of body and emotions, when the outcome of cure is no longer so imperative, ironically, cure may occur. But cure is often incidental to the healing of spirit that preceded it.

Maharishi's advice speaks to the essence of this attitude:

"Keep your desire turning back within and be patient. Allow the fulfillment to come to you ... be simple, be kind, stay rested. Attend to your own inner health and happiness. Happiness radiates like a fragrance from a flower and draws all good things toward you. Allow your love to nourish yourself as well as others. Do not strain after your needs of life....In this way life proceeds more naturally, effortlessly. Life is here to enjoy."

## The Illusion of Control

"You have control over action alone, never over its fruits,"[6] says the Bhagavad-Gita. This may sound somehow like an impotent reality, in which the universe pitches and we catch, and we don't get to call the signals. But in fact it is a liberating reality: all we can do is the best that we can do. As T.S. Eliot put it, "For us there is only the trying. The rest is not our business."

Stress often arises from the illusion that we can control outcomes. I recall times working in an emergency room without any physician back up when things would get crazy. I would have one man with chest pain, someone else with asthma, someone else with abdominal pain along with miscellaneous other cases. Then the obstetric floor upstairs would call to say that a precipitous delivery was occurring, the attending physician was not yet in the hospital, and could I come up right away, at the same time the man with the chest pain would go into cardiac arrest, and an ambulance would pull up with two victims of a car crash down the street. At that point, all possibility of control evaporated, and, actually I was less stressed than I had been a half hour earlier when I was still laboring under the delusion that I could control all the outcomes, write perfect notes in all the charts and keep everyone happy and healthy. Now all I could do was yell for help, prioritize, and do my best, recognizing that some people were going to go unattended until my back-up arrived.

Having control over our action alone and not over its fruits does not mean that we don't *influence* the fruits of the action. In fact, our actions influence the fruits of the action more than anything else does. But it is sobering to recognize that life is like an archery contest on a windy day. You can be the best archer, with the best preparation and the best equipment, but a gust of wind can take your arrow off course and give you a poor reward for all your abilities. On the other hand, a gust of wind could also take a shot of yours that was off target and move it into the bullseye. Those sorts of things are born of the unfathomable depths of action. We cannot control them, and we really shouldn't sweat it.

When I was just out of my residency, I was put in charge of a cardiac rehabilitation program for individuals who had suffered heart attacks and had recovered enough to be discharged from the hospital but who would not be ready to go back to work or full activity for a couple of months. During that transition time, we would rehabilitate these people to some degree of exertion. We would have them walk around the gymnasium, and we would measure their heart rates and make sure they were not having chest pain. On the gymnasium wall was a placard that listed the two rules of the cardiac rehab program:

Number one: Don't sweat the small stuff;

Number two: It's all small stuff.

Facetious as this might seem, it was helpful to these people. They had just had their lives turned upside down and had all the problems that you and I have plus months of lost income, fear in their families, and a prognosis that was guarded. They were in danger of being overwhelmed, of allowing their stress to further poison their lives. An attitude of not sweating anything allows us to relax while doing what we can.

## Karma Revisited

How can we justify a positive attitude with all the apparently awful goings-on in the world? Why do bad things happen to good people? To answer these questions we need to explore further the concept of karma. Karma, you'll recall, is action, and in this context it refers to the fruits of actions we have previously performed. By definition, everything in the field of action is a result of action or karma. Sometimes the relationship of action to outcome is clear: a man who has a heart attack has been eating cheeseburgers and smoking three packs a day for the last 40 years. But sometimes cause and effect are not so easily seen.

There is a moment in the Bible when the apostles see a blind man. They ask Jesus, "Master, who did sin, this man or his parents, that he was born blind?" Jesus replies, "Neither hath this man sinned nor his parents: but that the works of God should be made manifest in him."[7] Perhaps in some way this fate is appropriate for this person even though he committed no sin, no action that took him off the path of his evolution. (Of course, the possibility that it is the result of some wrong activity or "bad karma" exists also.)

157

We often define illness as something negative, and, in general, I would agree that we certainly do not want to pursue illness. Obviously, who would want to become blind? Yet would Helen Keller or Stevie Wonder have been able to demonstrate their special gifts if they had been born sighted? We'll never know. But clearly it is not helpful to be judgmental, to see a diagnosis as a sign of spiritual bankruptcy, to feel guilty about falling ill. When I ask people with cancer about their experience, many tell me they would not trade having lived with cancer for anything because that disease has been such a catalyst for transformation in their lives. They may have renewed relationships with estranged children, or found a new spiritual dimension to their lives.

I would hold that the transformation is available to us without the disease as a catalyst. While it is not prudent to desire any type of disease, the reports of these patients do give us insight that even pain and suffering may have accompanying gifts.

One doctor and author recounted[8] his own experience of a ruptured disc in his back. He was bedridden for an extended period and was subjected to all manner of healing from alternative healers with whom he had become acquainted over the years. He reveled in that for some time but then felt the need just to be alone with his illness and process it. At that point, he really didn't want to snap his fingers and have it go away. There was something to the illness that he didn't want to encourage but he did need to experience. Subsequent to that, he required surgery and presumably has done fine since then, but that illness for him was a catalyst for some of the most prolific writing he had ever done.

Every situation we experience as negative seems so because our reality is contingent upon our state of consciousness. Reality is different in different states of consciousness, because our consciousness structures our knowledge. No matter how awful a situation may be there is always some perspective, which may not be open to us at the time, from which the situation does not appear awful. Maharishi tells a story that illustrates this idea:

> There is a story in India about a wise man living in Benares, the seat of learning in Northern India. He would always admire others and no one had ever heard him speak

ill of anyone. People were astonished that this man could see good in everything in creation. He would only admire, he would never allow his mind and heart to become impure from seeing bad in anything or anyone. One day a mischievous man thought he would find something that was all bad and show it to the wise man so that he would certainly be unable to see any good in it. He found a dead and rotting dog lying in the street, and having invited the wise man to have dinner with him, he took him along the street where the rotting dog lay. A bad smell was coming from it, and it was an obnoxious sight. When they reached it the mischief-maker pointed to it and remarked: "What a horror to come across in the street". But the wise man exclaimed: "Look at the clean white teeth, how they sparkle like pearls". As he praised the sparkling whiteness of the dog's teeth the mischievous man fell at his feet, and the wise man said: "If we do not wish to ignore it we will find some good in everything in the kingdom of God". This world is the garden of almighty God and He has made the flowers in all their variety. You may pick the one you like but you have no right to say another is bad. Even if you do not like that flower, God created it for someone who can admire it and who will be happy to see it. Do not always go about lost in your own taste; admire the great variety in the garden of God.[9]

Every form and phenomenon we behold can be seen on its subtler level as latent with energy and intelligence and indeed made up ultimately of pure consciousness. This field of pure consciousness is characterized in the Vedic literature as sat-chit-ananda, which means being-awareness-bliss. Since everything about the situation we're in is actually composed of bliss and intelligence, somehow there must be a way that can be appreciated. And, indeed, if we had the broadest perspective we could appreciate it that way, though often, we don't.

There is an allegedly true story about a worker in a factory that manufactured helicopters. A new design had come along and the specifications dictated that certain bolts be placed in what looked like an upside-down position. This man had been working in this factory for a number of years and he saw this change and assumed something was wrong here. He continued to place the bolts in the former upright position, which was not appropriate for this new design. His performance was not checked, and his incorrect placement of the bolts resulted in a couple of fatal accidents. Had this man had broader perspective, he would have seen that, even though it seemed he was being asked to put them in upside down, that was exactly the way they were supposed to be.

If we could see how the entire universe hangs together we would see that every aspect of our lives is appropriate at this moment. This doesn't mean that we should not seek to fulfill our desires and act dynamically to change those things we want to change. But if our desire is not promptly fulfilled, there may be a good reason for it. The next time you read of a plane crash, consider the person who was fuming with frustration in the airport because he had just missed that flight. Nature may be protecting us from ourselves. Often times, we gain this insight just with the passage of time.

> If God had granted all the silly prayers I've made in my life. where should I be now?
>
> -- C. S. Lewis

# Part Three

# Applications

CHAPTER FOURTEEN

# The Source of Disease

> I have formerly said that there was but one fever in the world. Be not startled, Gentlemen, follow me and I will say there is but one disease in the world.[1]
>
> -- Benjamin Rush

Where does disease begin?  Maharishi Ayur-Veda has much to say on the subject.  The Charaka Samhita sums up the causes this way:

> Wrong understanding by the intellect and wrong actions accordingly should be known as intellectual error which is committed by mind.  Perverted, negative and excessive use of time, intelligence and sense objects is the three-fold cause of both psychic and somatic disorders.[2]

Let's take each of these areas -- mind, senses, and time -- in turn.

"Wrong understanding by the intellect," according to Charaka, is the root cause of all disease.  When the mind forgets its true nature (the "mistake of the intellect" discussed earlier) it loses its appreciation of unified wholeness and diversity predominates.  Because of this loss of memory, our recognition of Natural Law is incomplete, and so we proceed to violate the laws of nature through our thought, speech and action.  As discussed earlier, this is the primary cause of all disease, and is the basis for the other subordinate causes discussed in this chapter.

The second area involves unwholesome contact between the senses and their objects.* Chakara describes this further:

> There are three causes of disorders: *excessive; negative*; and *perverted* uses of sense objects, actions and time. Such as excessive gazing at the over-brilliant object is excessive use, avoiding looking altogether is negative use and seeing too near, too distant, fierce, frightful, wonderful, disliked, disgusting, deformed and terrifying objects is perverted use of visual objects. Likewise, to hear too much the loud sound of clouds, drums, cries, etc. is excessive use; not at all hearing is negative use; and hearing of harsh and frightful words and those which indicate death of dear ones, loss, humiliation, etc. is perverted use of auditory objects. Too much smelling of too sharp, intense and congestant odors is excessive use, not at all smelling is negative use and smelling of fetid, disliked, impure, decomposed, poisoned air, cadaveracious odor, etc. is perverted use of olfactory objects. Likewise, too much intake of taste is excessive use, not at all taking is negative use of gustatory objects. Perverted use of those will be described in the chapter dealing with the methods of eating except the quantity. Too much indulgence in very hot and very cool objects and also in bath, massage, anointing, etc. is excessive use of tactile objects.[2] [emphasis added]

I will discuss the "perverted use" of taste at more length in a later chapter.

The third area involves the transformations of time.** This includes both the actions of the cycles of nature such as daily rhythms and seasonal rhythms, and the quality of time as a result of past actions (already considered in our discussion of karma).

---

* The Sanskrit term is *asatmya indrya artha samyoga.*
** This also has a Sanskrit term associated with it: *kala parinama.*

In a practical sense these three causes of disease appear in our daily lives as mistakes in three areas. The first of these is called *manas*, which refers to the mind and has to do with thinking and the initiation of speech and action. The second is called *ahara*, which has to do with the ingestion of food and any other sensory experience. The third is called *vihara* or regimen, which has to do with the quality of our daily and seasonal routines. (I'll discuss these routines in some depth in a later chapter.)

As the Charaka Samhita succinctly puts it: "Avoiding the cause is itself treatment."

If we can attend to these three areas of life (sometimes called the pillars of Ayur-Veda), we will have addressed the causes of disease and no disease process will readily be able to establish itself. If some disease process is already established, it may not be able to persist in the face of appropriate attention to these three areas.

Thus, if we can move toward eliminating the "mistake of the intellect," regularly meditate so that our thinking and initiation of speech and action are proper; if we can attend to our food intake, our diet and digestion and sensory experience and make sure that no weakening influences arise there; and, lastly, if we can attend to our regimen and daily routine to make sure our activities are not in conflict with the rhythms and cycles of nature, we are well on our way both to preventing any problem from arising and disposing of any problem that is already present.

This is no doubt what the ancient physicians meant by the saying, "The physician treats but nature heals." Our main role in curing disease, preventing disease and promoting health is basically just to get out of the way. If we can give the inner intelligence of our body-mind complex the raw materials to build itself appropriately and if we can refrain from damaging it with inappropriate input from our mind, our senses and our routine, then we're doing our part.

This does not require of us any rigorous control of the senses or sensory deprivation. As Maharishi tells us, negative uses of the senses or underuse of the senses are also inappropriate:

Wrong interpretations ... have led many genuine seekers of truth to undertake rigorous and unnatural practices in order to control the senses, thus wasting their lives and benefiting neither themselves nor others. Mastery of the senses is gained only through the state of established intellect, for in this state where man is established in awareness of the Self as separate from activity, his behavior is quite naturally unaffected by the otherwise overpowering influence of the senses....when behavior in the sensory field does not in any way disturb the state of established intellect, and established intellect behaves as master of the senses, the highest state of human evolution has been reached.[3]

Research has documented the effects of sensory input. If the hospital room window has a nice view, hospitalization is shorter. Exposure to noise decreases wound healing in rats.[4] Also, noise affects sleep in humans and also affects their cognitive functioning.[5,6] When recordings of noise collected in a coronary care unit were played for healthy volunteers throughout the night, the volunteers had increased heart rates and decreased sleep.[7] More analgesics or pain medicines are administered when the noise level in the recovery room was high and less when the noise level was low.[8] Noise has been shown to increase stress hormones and decrease growth hormone and lymphocyte proliferation and measures of immune function.[9,10] Also, sound, specifically music, has been shown to have effects on the fetus in utero.[11,12]

The quality and nature of our sensory experience -- and the way we interpret it -- structures our universe. An experiment[13] was done with kittens, exposing some from the time of birth to an environment with only horizontal stimuli, while exposing others to an environment with only vertical stimuli. After some months, the brains and visual systems of these kittens had developed in relation to their environment. Those who had been exposed only to horizontal stimuli could now see only horizontal objects even if they were placed in a room that contained vertical objects as well. This gave rise to the spectacle of these kittens being able to jump onto chairs and tables (horizontal surfaces), yet bumping into the table legs and chair legs (vertical objects) they literally were not able to see. The other kittens could climb up vertical table legs but were unable to perceive tabletops and seats of chairs.

So attending to our own sensory exposure would be appropriate. Studies have demonstrated that exposure to the thousands of murders a child sees on television has a stressful and desensitizing effect on children. I recall, to this day, feeling acutely poisoned after walking out of the movie *The Exorcist* back in 1973. Even though the film was technically excellent, I felt as though I had eaten some spoiled food. What we see and hear we ingest and process. We metabolize our experience in just as real a way as we metabolize food, for good or ill.

There is an intriguing representation that was reported by the Associated Press in an article about the research of Shisumu Onnu, who won the Emory Prize in 1981 from the American Academy of Arts and Sciences for his work in reproductive genetics.

While searching for the chemical origins of life, Shisumu Onnu found something unexpected: a waltz. Bored with tedious mathematical equations, the geneticist decided to convert chemical formulas for living cells into musical notes. He figured listening to the complex genetic codes, rather than staring at them, would make elusive patterns easier to detect. In the process, Onnu, who works at the Beatman Research Institute in Diwate, discovered genes not only carry the blueprint of life, but they also carry a tune. The tunes he found were not just the interesting random notes which other scientists had predicted. Although there is no practical musical use for his research, Onnu found genuine music, like music of baroque and romantic eras, classical and structured, sometimes with an uncanny similarity to the works of great composers.

Translated into sheet music and performed on the piano, a portion of mouse RNA, a complex messenger substance, sounds like a lively waltz. Except for its quicker tempo, parts of the mouse RNA Waltz are dead ringers for passages in Frederick Chopin's "Nocturnal Opus 55."

· "More than anyone ever expected," said Onnu, "art imitates life. It is not surprising," he said, "nature follows certain physical laws. The universe obeys them as does the process of life. Music follows the same patterns as well." Onnu suggests this genetic well spring for music offers an explanation for the origins of music in man and nature and also might explain why certain melodies seem sad and others seem happy. "Possibly," he said, "because we are genetically predisposed to hear them that way."

The musical score within a cancer-causing oncogene sounds somber and funereal, while the gene responsible for bestowing transparency to the lens of the eye is filled with trills and flourishes -- airy and light. Reversing the process, converting music to chemistry works as well. When Onnu translated a funeral march by Chopin from notes to chemical equations, "entire passages appear identical to a cancer gene found in humans," he said. "Because of periodicity, the same patterns which govern the movement of planets and galaxies also appear in genes and in music," Onnu said.

This knowledge can serve as a firm basis for our understanding of why we should attend to what influences our senses. It is necessary to strengthen ourselves internally so that whatever we perceive does not generate stress within us, and also to be selective about what we expose ourselves to. Thus, watching slasher movies, listening to heavy metal that's cranked up to 90 decibels, or absorbing the input from people in toxic relationships can adversely resonate with molecular processes within ourselves and lead to disease.

But the primary way we ingest our environment is through eating.

## CHAPTER FIFTEEN

# Bringing Balance to Life with Food

> Food and drinks...produce energy in mind, constitution of tissues, strength, complexion and clarity of sense organs if taken properly; otherwise they become harmful.[1]
>
> -- the Charaka Samhita

The three doshas, you will recall, are fundamental metabolic principles that govern all aspects of human physiology: vata, pitta and kapha. Vata has to do with all motion and movement. Pitta has to do with heat, metabolism and digestion. Kapha has to do with structure, substance and fluid balance. *Balance* in life involves balancing the doshas.

*Vata* dosha is predominantly cold, light, minute, moving, hard, strong, invisible, unsteady and quick. It tends to take on the qualities of surrounding circumstances. It is the *leading dosha* since it primarily has the quality of motion. The seat of vata is in the colon (although all of the doshas are located everywhere in the physiology).

*Pitta* dosha, in contrast, is warm, slightly oily, sharp, fluid, acidic, laxative; it has a hot taste. It is located primarily just under the diaphragm, and also in the spleen, pancreas, stomach, liver, blood, small bowel and heart.

*Kapha* dosha is heavy, cold, soft, unctuous, sweet, steady, sticky, earthy, moist, semi-solid and slow. It is located primarily in the chest and head, but, like the other doshas, also is ubiquitous.

(See Appendices C and D for more information on the doshas).

Everyone has to have all three of these doshas in order to be alive. We all have vata dosha, which has control over expiration and inspiration, is responsible for evacuation of feces and urine, and activates the mind, speech and body, including all of the senses. We all have some pitta dosha, which controls heat, metabolism and digestion as well as sight, appetite and thirst. And we all have kapha, which has to do with all cohesion in the physiology, fat, body fluids, and the lubrication of joints.

In terms of personality, vata dosha is responsible for quickness, spontaneity, exhilaration, and liveliness. Pitta is more responsible for efficiency and ambition as well as chivalry and joy. Kapha has to do more with stability, strength, courage, and forgiveness.

## Disease and Food

I discussed the source of disease in the previous chapter. Before considering food specifically, let's look at how disease develops.

Ayur-Veda recognizes six stages in the growth of disease. These are subtler than what I was taught in medical school, but any western physician will be able to recognize the modern understanding of the pathogenesis of a number of diseases in the descriptions that follow.

The first stage is called **accumulation**. That is where these doshas tend to accumulate in their own place. For instance, vata may accumulate in the mind due to stress or in the gut due to eating while distressed or anxious.

The second stage is called **aggravation**. This involves a qualitative change in the doshas which tends to precipitate their spread.

The third stage is **dissemination**, where these spoiled doshas do indeed spread to other parts of the body.

The fourth stage is **localization**. Here, the doshas which have been sort of percolating around through the physiology will stick to *ama*, a heavy toxic byproduct of incomplete digestion, in a particular tissue or organ where the *srotas*, the channels, have been damaged.

The fifth stage then is **manifestation** and this is finally where we actually have something to take to the doctor. The symptom becomes manifest and the disease becomes apparent.

The sixth stage is called **disruption**. In this stage, the disease moves from an acute situation where there is some manifestation of disease to a more complex situation where the disease becomes chronic or some complication begins to develop.

These first four stages are often imperceptible except perhaps in some subtle way, depending on the level of attunement that we have to the physiology. Very attuned people can perhaps perceive these subtle imbalances beginning to accumulate and deal with them. But often, particularly in our culture, the first four stages are ignored. Once stage five or six develops, the person is usually inspired to take some step such as going to the doctor. In Maharishi Ayur-Veda, we want to address stages one, two and three because the later stages are more difficult to treat.

The fourth point, localization, occurs in part due to some injury to the *srotas*. There are a number of factors that can damage these body channels, contributing to the cascade above. Some of these are identified in the Charaka Samhita as:

> over eating, eating before the previous meal is digested, unwholesome food, incompatible food, sleeping after meals, too much exercise, too little exercise, *agnimandya* or weak or dull agni [digestive fire], suppression of natural urges, excessive heat or cold, concussion or shock and excessive worries....
>
> Food and regimen that aggravate the doshas and are contrary to the well being of the *dhatus* (or tissues) vitiate the srotas or channels.[2]

Not only inappropriate food, but a number of factors can aggravate the doshas. A dosha will accumulate and aggravate when we are exposed to imbalancing influences which are similar in quality to the attributes of that particular dosha. See if you can recognize errors in mind, senses and regimen among the following examples.

Vata is disturbed by cold dry wind, staying up late at night (active, moving at an improper time), a noisy chaotic environment, irregularity in routine, irregularity in mealtimes, roller coasters, overstimulation of any kind, such as TV at night.

Pitta is disturbed by heat, straining at intense competitive exercise (if it's blissful, if you're "in the zone," then you're probably not straining), time pressures, workaholism, lack of moderation in the application of the person's natural ambition and dynamism, skipping meals, coffee and alcohol, any impure ingestion (air, water, food), non-natural settings (urban decay, beholding metal and asphalt instead of alpine lakes).

Kapha imbalance arises from daytime sleep (anytime between dawn and dusk), lack of exercise and activity, cold wet weather, dull surroundings, going outside with wet hair.

> One should not use food articles from either attachment or ignorance. Rather, he should use wholesome ones after due examination because the body is a product of food.[3]
>
> -- Charaka Samhita

"The body is a product of food." Food (like everything else) is essentially intelligence. Food is an expression of the field of pure consciousness, organized into packets of intelligence (atoms and molecules into carbohydrates, fats, proteins, vitamins etc.) suitable for ingestion and digestion. It is the job of our digestive *agni* to transform the food we eat into the tissues that will become us. Thus diet and digestion play a fundamental role in the Maharishi Vedic Approach to Health.

Food then has certain qualities. The taste of food is indicative of those qualities. We tend to disregard taste in modern nutritional science as being something quite irrelevant, but, in fact, it is integral. Taste can tell us how the body will be influenced by a particular food. Animals know what and how much to eat based upon the taste and smell of the plant or food they are about to eat. Ayur-

Veda recognizes six tastes (or *rasas*), as well as six major qualities of food. These are listed in the following two tables, along with some examples.

| Table 1: EXAMPLES OF THE SIX TASTES | |
|---|---|
| Sweet | milk, ghee, butter, rice, breads, dates, raisins, figs, sugar, coconut |
| Sour | yogurt, lemon & other citrus, vinegar, aged cheese, cooked tomatoes |
| Salty | salt |
| Pungent | spicy, radish, pepper, ginger, cumin, clove, onions, chills |
| Bitter | leafy greens (spinach), olives, chicory, turmeric, fenugreek |
| Astringent | leafy greens, beans, lentils, sprouts, lettuce, walnuts, turmeric, pomegranate |

| Table 2: EXAMPLES OF THE SIX MAJOR FOOD QUALITIES | |
|---|---|
| Heavy | cheese, carrots, yogurt, nuts, banana, wheat, oats, dates, honey |
| Light | spices, apples, barley, corn, millet, mung beans, many vegetables |
| Unctuous | dairy, ghee, butter, oils, coconut, nuts |
| Dry | barley, corn, millet, rye, buckwheat, potato, beans, honey, many spices and vegetables |
| Warm | warm food & drink |
| Cold | cold food & drink |

These tastes and qualities of food have specific effects on the three doshas. That is why people who have particular doshas stronger in their physiologies are well advised to favor certain tastes and textures. One can appreciate the internal coherence and consistency of this system if you recall the *mahabhutas* or subtle elements that make up everything, including the doshas and the tastes. Akasha (space) and vayu (air) become vata. Tejas (fire) and jala (water) become pitta. Jala (water) and prithivi (earth) become kapha. The tastes and qualities of foods and how they affect the doshas are listed in the next two tables. Remember, imbalances of the doshas are typically accumulations or increases, so therapeutically we look to decrease or *pacify* the doshas.

| Table 3: EFFECTS OF TASTES (RASAS) ON THE DOSHAS | | | |
|---|---|---|---|
| **TASTE** | **SUBTLE ELEMENT** | **DECREASES** | **INCREASES** |
| Sweet | Earth & water | Vata & Pitta | Kapha |
| Sour | Earth & fire | Vata | Pitta & Kapha |
| Salty | Water & fire | Vata | Pitta & Kapha |
| Pungent | Air & fire | Kapha | Vata & Pitta |
| Bitter | Air & space | Pitta & Kapha | Vata |
| Astringent | Air & earth | Pitta & Kapha | Vata |

If you consider the subtle elements that make up a given dosha, then look at which elements make up a given taste, you will quickly see why the taste has the listed effect on that dosha.

Another perspective on this information is in table 4:

| Table 4: EFFECTS OF TASTES ON THE DOSHAS | |
|---|---|
| Sweet, sour, salty | Decrease VATA, Increase KAPHA |
| Pungent, bitter, astringent | Decrease KAPHA, Increase VATA |
| Sweet, bitter, astringent | Decrease PITTA |
| Sour, salty, pungent | Increase PITTA |

Since vata and kapha are opposite in every way (except that they're both cold), they have opposite reactions to tastes.

Let's look next at the food qualities:

| Table 5: EFFECTS OF FOOD QUALITIES ON THE DOSHAS | | | |
|---|---|---|---|
| QUALITY | Effect on VATA | Effect on PITTA | Effect on KAPHA |
| Heavy | Decreases | Decreases | Increases |
| Light | Increases | Increases | Decreases |
| Unctuous | Decreases | Decreases | Increases |
| Dry | Increases | Increases | Decreases |
| Warm | Decreases | Increases | Decreases |
| Cold | Increases | Decreases | Increases |

While it is helpful to appreciate how these tastes and textures affect the doshas, it may be difficult to translate that into specific dietary recommendations. Many foods have more than one taste and/or they have different types of after-tastes and potencies that are recognized in this tradition but not in modern nutritional science. Appendix C lists certain foods that tend to *decrease* or *pacify* an accumulation of the dosha after which the diet is named. Also in the appendix is a brief questionnaire that will help you discover which doshas are more active in you now. In the next chapter I'll discuss how these diets (with some variations) can be tailored to address doshic imbalances, or seasons of the year.

Since the questionnaires are simple tools with limited value, the best way to determine your most beneficial diet would be to have a consultation with a doctor trained in Maharishi Ayur-Veda. A course on diet is offered by the Maharishi Ayur-Veda Schools, nationwide.

It is interesting that these ancient seers, who had no specific knowledge of proteins, fats, carbohydrates, vitamins and minerals, put together dietary recommendations that are completely in line with those of modern nutritional science. But while a balanced Ayurvedic diet is a balanced modern diet, the reverse, sadly, is not true. A diet balanced from the perspective of the major food groups might not be a healthy diet from the Ayurvedic perspective.

> The typical American will consume over the course of his life 15 cows, 24 hogs, 12 sheep, 900 chickens and 1,000 pounds of assorted beasts.

## The Three Gunas

Food also has effects on our mind. The three *gunas*, which help describe these effects, also are fundamental principles of nature: *sattva, rajas* and *tamas*. Sattva has to do with creation and purity, rajas has to do with activity and motion, and tamas has to do with destruction. All three are necessary. Maharishi describes the interactions of the gunas this way:

> Activity needs raja guna to create a spur and it needs sato-guna and tamo-guna to uphold the direction of the movement.
>
> The nature of tamo-guna is to check or retard but it should not be thought that when the movement is upwards, tamo-guna is absent. For any process to continue, there have to be stages in that process and each stage, however small in time and space, needs a force to maintain it and another force to develop it into a new stage. The force that develops it into a new stage is sato-guna, while tamo-guna is that which checks or retards the process in order to maintain the state already produced so that it may form the basis for the next stage.[4]

Foods can be classified according to sattva, rajas and tamas.

- Sattvic food is that which connotes lifespan, purity, virtue, truth, strength, resistance toward imbalances, freedom from disease, happiness, satisfaction and pleasure. This food is savory, pleasant, comfortable, tasty, unctuous, moist, stable, firm, giving strength, pleasing to the heart and enlivening to bliss.

- Rajasic food causes misery, unhappiness, sorrow, grief, disease, sickness and creates ama. This type of food is predominantly pungent, sour, and salty; too hot, too sharp, too dry, too rough; it causes a burning sensation.

- Tamasic food is food that is stale, leftovers, spoiled, unappealing. It is tasteless, its nourishment value gone. It's putrid, having decayed smell, rejected by others, impure or foul.

Sattvic foods include: milk, ghee (clarified butter), rice, honey, almonds, food that is fresh, pure water, mung dahl (a type of legume), barley, dates and figs, fruits and fruit juices.

## Dispelling Confusion about Food

It is easy to get confused about food. The information we read in popular magazines seems to contradict itself every other year. Even the tables reproduced in this book could lead to confusion.

There are two stories that may dispel the confusion a bit.

One involves a student of Ayur-Veda who learned of vata, pitta and kapha and decided he was going to go shopping for the family. So he went into the store and was about to buy some nice sweet cake when he thought: *Wait. This will be aggravating to kapha. I shouldn't buy it.* So he moved on to some nice spicy soup that had been prepared and he thought: *Wait. This is hot and spicy. It'll be aggravating to pitta. I shouldn't buy that.* He began to buy some cabbage and thought: *Wait. This will be aggravating to vata. I shouldn't buy this, either.* He continued in this way and finally returned home with an empty bag. His family was disappointed, and his teacher disciplined him for his poor grasp of his lessons in Ayur-Veda.

Everyone should have all six tastes -- if not at every meal, then every day. We also need all the textures, but in balanced and judicious portions.

If we look at every food only in terms of what it might aggravate, we can become paralyzed and not be able to eat anything. That's why the diets say, "reduce or avoid," not "thou shalt not eat." And "favoring" certain foods doesn't mean you must eat them. You need to eat what you enjoy. As your imbalance grows less over time, you will tend more and more to enjoy those foods that are most balancing for you. But there is no list, book, doctor, diet or program that can completely keep up with the dynamism of your internal milieu which is changing not just from season to season but from day to day, meal to meal, minute to minute, on an ongoing basis. Among our goals is to become so balanced that we spontaneously desire the right quantity of the correct food; thus we should not in the process disregard the signals our body sends us. These diets are not meant to be followed slavishly, rather, they should confirm our own experience. Of course, some people are totally out of touch with how food makes them feel. And if you are ill, particular foods may be prescribed medicinally, and it may be necessary to follow that prescription meticulously for some time.

The second story involves three students of Ayur-Veda who were told by their master that they should go out and find something that was of no medicinal value in Ayur-Veda and bring it back to him. The first student returned in about 10 minutes with a rock and said, "Master, I found this rock. It appears worthless." The master nodded and took the rock from him. The second student returned in a couple of hours and said, "Master, I found this stick and I can't think of any use for this stick in Ayur-Veda." The master again nodded and took the stick from him. Years later, the third student returned and said, "Master, I have looked far and wide and I can't find anything that can't be used in Ayur-Veda." To this the master replied, "You are the master Ayurvedic vaidya; I am retiring and you shall take over my duties."

Everything in nature has some value because everything is, after all, a manifestation of pure consciousness. Some manifestations are more useful than others, but virtually any food or beverage might possibly be appropriate for a given person at some time.

## CHAPTER SIXTEEN

# Natural Weight Loss and

# Digestive Fire

> Food is the vital breath of living beings.[1]
> -- Charaka Samhita

The National Institutes of Health estimates that 40% of women and 25% of men in the U.S. are on a diet at any given moment, and that within five years 90% to 95% of them regain the weight they have lost, two-thirds of them regaining their lost weight within the first year.

Mary was 21 years old, overweight, distressed by it. "When I get real angry or upset about something, I'll tend to eat," she told me. "It sort of settles me down. But then after I eat I feel terrible about it and I'll get angry at myself and then I'll eat some more. It's become sort of a habit and I can't seem to break it."

I inquired about her pattern of eating. Mary had a rushed breakfast of a doughnut and a cup of coffee in her car. Lunch sometimes would be okay when she went out to eat, but more commonly she would sit at her desk and work while eating. Often she would be interrupted by phone calls, and frequently her boss would ask her to do some other work during her lunch hour since everyone else was gone. When that happened she would take some food with her and eat on the run. Having her lunch interrupted didn't bother her too much; there was usually some snack food stashed around the office by her co-workers, and she would graze on that during the afternoon.

She would have low-fat yogurt and would often bring some diet food to put in the microwave at work. While she didn't seem to be eating many calories, she couldn't seem to lose much weight, didn't have much energy and certainly didn't feel like doing much exercise.

Weight normalization is a result of increasing balance. The more balanced we are, the more our desires for foods will tend spontaneously to be in accord with our nutritional needs. The nice thing about this is that it doesn't involve a lot of deprivation and will-power.

"Have you ever been on a diet?" I asked Mary. She nodded vigorously, an unhappy smile on her face.

Diets are difficult. They're difficult because they're unnatural. They're unnatural because they command us not to eat even if we're hungry. The rubber meets the road in a diet when your body is demanding food yet you've already eaten all your allotted calories for the day. Unfortunately, this has a number of effects which undermine the goal of weight loss.

If we don't eat when we're hungry, our body goes through a number of changes, many of them unhealthy. Hunger is our ally. Hunger is the sign our body-mind sends that tells us our digestive fire is enkindled and ready to combust the food we are craving. If we diet, sooner or later we find ourselves faced with a situation in which we're hungry but don't get to eat. Our body responds: *Where's the food? I'm hungry but I'm not getting anything to eat. There's something seriously wrong here.*

Right after air and water, food is near the top of the list of priorities that nature has plugged into the nucleus of every cell in our body. And if hunger -- which is more important than shelter, more important than sex, more important than job security -- is not satisfied, the body will take certain steps. It will anticipate that the next meal may be paltry or absent. It will decide: *I should turn down the thermostat and stop burning up as many calories. Everything I ingest I should try to hang onto -- store as much fat as I can to preserve myself through these lean times.*

But when we turn down the thermostat and decrease our caloric expenditure and metabolic rate, our energy drops. We don't feel like exercising. We have less muscle mass and we tend to turn more into fat. None of these changes are helpful.

When hunger is present, that's the sign that we *should* eat. If we don't eat at that time, we are sowing the seed of some future craving or imbalance that will blindside us sometime down the line. Diets often end that way. We've been so good for so long, yet find that we're not losing much weight and certainly not feeling good. When we leave the diet, we leave it in a binge precipitated by the sight of potato chips or a box of candies.

Here are some of the principles from Maharishi Ayur-Veda I discussed with Mary about how we ought to behave with regard to food:

First, we should eat when we're hungry. Hunger is *not* just the desire to eat or the impulse to eat or the reaction we feel when we see food, but rather, hunger is a physical sensation. This may seem obvious, but I've been surprised to learn how many people are completely out of touch with the experience of hunger. Hunger is a sensation of warmth and emptiness which is located in the left or middle, upper abdomen. It's a sensation which is diminished when we eat and which tends to grow more intense and eventually becomes very uncomfortable if we do not eat.

Obversely, in the absence of a signal of hunger, we should not eat. We may want a raise, or a hug, or a day off -- something that's not readily available -- and we may try to feed that desire with food -- which *is* readily available -- as inappropriate and ultimately unsatisfying as the food may be.

Unfortunately, and insidiously, it can seem to work...for a while. If we're feeling anxious or frustrated, the body-mind is sending us a signal of discomfort. If we can't readily see a productive way of addressing and resolving this discomfort then we'll take a nonproductive way of resolving it.

If we eat when we're not hungry, the food is poorly combusted and tends to form *ama*. This toxic debris gets in the way and clogs the channels through which the body-mind has been sending us distress signals. At that point, we will actually have a less clear experience of distress: that is the insidious nature of this phenomenon of overeating (and/or other toxic ingestions). We feel less uncomfortable because, in effect, we have shot the messenger.

Feeling less distressed comes at the price of feeling less altogether -- because we don't just clog this channel, we clog all the channels. This increases dullness and causes mind-body *dis*integration.

> Complexion, cheerfulness, good voice, life, imagination, happiness, contentment, corpulence, strength, intellect -- all these are dependent on food.[2]
>
> -- Charaka

When we are hungry, we don't have to eat immediately. But if we wait until we become famished, we tend to be less discriminating about what we eat. We go into the line in the cafeteria and anything that's slower than we are is going to find its way onto our tray. Once it's on the tray, there may be inappropriate scripts from our past that drive us to consume everything we've taken. So we want to eat when we're hungry and avoid eating when we're not hungry.

How do we know when it's time to stop eating?

In my practice, many people have told me it's helpful to see ideas in the form of a simple graph.

The horizontal axis of the graph below shows the quantity of food we're eating. The vertical axis shows the level of fulfillment we're experiencing. Initially, the relationship between these two is a direct one: if we eat some food, we have some degree of fulfillment. If we eat more, we have more fulfillment. Eventually though, we reach the point of being fulfilled, and at that point, the line stops rising and flattens out. We don't become more fulfilled, we just get more filled.

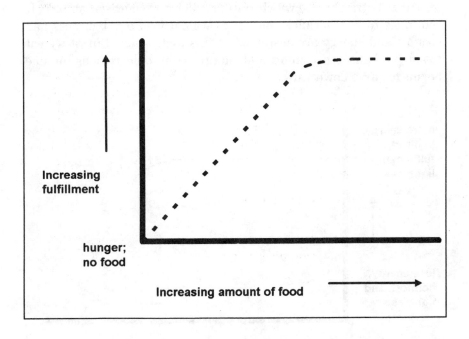

Increasing fulfillment

hunger; no food

Increasing amount of food

GRAPH # 1

We should be fulfilled. If you're interested in losing weight there are programs that recommend that you always end a meal a little bit hungry. There are worse ways to live, I imagine, but I can't think of one off hand. Lack of fulfillment creates more problems. Fulfillment means hunger is taken care of, we still feel light and comfortable and energetic, and if no more food is available, that's fine. We aren't inspired to go in search of any more.

There is -- in addition to fulfillment -- another issue related to our body's level of comfort and that is the degree of *lightness* and *energy* we experience as we're eating. In graph #2 the horizontal axis again represents the quantity of food we're eating, but the vertical axis represents our level of lightness and energy and comfort. At the beginning of a meal, presuming that we have not allowed ourselves to become so famished that we are weak with hunger, our lightness, comfort and energy are maximum. They are optimum before we begin to eat. As we eat, this line is at the top of the vertical axis, it is a straight line which runs parallel to the horizontal axis. It continues to run parallel, that is, as we eat food our lightness and comfort and energy are sustained at this high level. But, if we eat too much, lightness, comfort and energy begin to degrade as the line begins to curve downward.

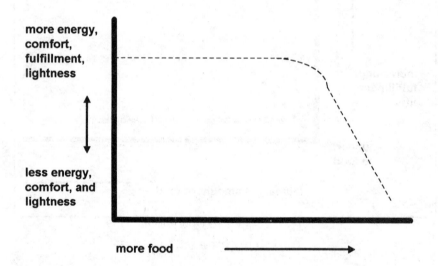

GRAPH # 2

By overlapping these curves in graph #3, we can see that the first line (thick dashes representing fulfillment) plateaus before the second line (skinny dashes representing levels of lightness, comfort and energy) begins to degrade. At that point, within a fairly narrow range, we are completely fulfilled, yet feeling no degradation of our lightness and comfort and energy. That is our ideal point of balance at the end of a meal.

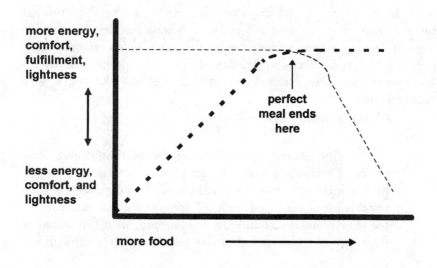

GRAPH # 3

If we continue to eat at that point, we regret it. If we're watching TV or reading the paper and not paying attention, we may not realize until 20 or 30 minutes after the meal how heavy we feel. Many of us use the experience of fullness as our cue to stop eating. We make such comments as "I can't eat another bite." By the time we have that feeling, unfortunately, the horse is out of the barn and long gone, and we are long past the ideal balance of fulfillment and lightness. All the food we eat beyond the point of being fulfilled is poorly combusted. This forms ama, further clogs our channels and perpetuates the vicious cycle I've described.

Not only is what we eat important, how we process what we eat and what we turn it into after we've ingested it is integral to our health. The relationship between our digestion and our general health is an area largely neglected in modern nutritional science, but is given close attention in Maharishi Ayur-Veda.

## Agni: Energy of Transformation

Charaka has identified a number of factors which derange *agni*, in this context, the digestive fire. Among these factors are fasting, over eating, eating before the previous meal is digested, irregular eating, eating during indigestion, unwholesome food, suppression of natural urges, emaciation due to some disease, faulty adaptation of place, climate and season and emotions like anger, worries and sorrow.[1]

Charaka further instructs us:

> One should take wholesome food timely and regularly. Further, one should eat warm, unctuous [food] in proper quantity after the previous meal is digested ... in favorable place equipped with all accessories, not too fast, not too slowly, not while talking or laughing, with full attention (presence of mind) and after due consideration to the Self.[3]

Many of us in our culture do not eat with full attention, and do eat while talking and performing other activities. Anything that divides the mind can weaken digestion and ultimately lead to disease.

You will recall that vata, one of the three doshas, has to do with motion and movement. It is composed of the subtle elements of space and air. If the mind is divided between two activities, this motion and movement in the mind is aggravating to vata. And if vata is aggravated while we're eating, we tend to generate this influence of vata (space and air) in our gut. This is why many people experience gas and bloating after a meal that has been eaten in an unsettled environment. We should eat in a quiet place, without distractions, with our primary focus of attention on the food we are about to eat.

186

Our food should be on a plate, the plate should be on the table and our bottom should be on a chair.

I was eating breakfast during a 60 hour weekend emergency room shift in rural Louisiana. The ER nurse strolled over and sat opposite me.

"I thought I should let you know about a call we just got," he drawled easily. "They won't be here for another 20 minutes or so, but some kid got ahold of his dad's rifle and shot his little brother."

A gunshot wound to a child! The bite of toast I'd been chewing instantly felt like clay inside my mouth.

As he left, he called over his shoulder, "Well, you enjoy your breakfast, and I'll see you in the ER in a few minutes." Not very likely that I would eat any more breakfast! My digestive agni was extinguished by the prospect of attending to this boy.

The ambulance soon arrived. Two brothers thought the rifle wasn't loaded (an all too common story), and the seven year old was shot in his left arm. It was a terrible injury, with a huge exit wound defect; his X-ray showed about two inches of his humerus, the upper arm bone, disintegrated into tiny particles. Amazingly, his nerves and circulation were intact. This child underwent bone grafting and extensive rehabilitation, and eventually he recovered fully, an example of a modern medicine success story.

By lunchtime, I was hungry again.

It is worthwhile to have a moment of silence before meals. Many people follow the practice of saying a prayer before a meal. But even if that's not your habit, it would still be good to close your eyes for half a minute or so before you eat, just to allow the body-mind to settle down. Many of us carry into our midday meal all the tensions of the morning and let them poison our food. It's better if we just settle down and let go of all that has happened earlier. We'll be better able to deal with it in the afternoon if we have had a settled and enjoyable meal at lunchtime. Then at the end of the meal it is also good to sit, ideally for 15 minutes after a meal just to allow digestion to proceed before we get up and go about our business. If we could do that even for five minutes, it would still be worthwhile.

The food we eat should be fulfilling. It should be of the appropriate taste and texture according to our doshic predominance and imbalance. We could readily envision a meal that is composed entirely of carrots. This meal we could eat until our stomach was sticking out like a basketball, yet we would never reach the level of fulfillment I discussed earlier in the graphs because there is not enough variety in the taste and textures of the food we're eating.

Appropriate variety in our diet is essential. Ideally, the food would be fresh and of the best quality. There are few things we do that are more important than eating, which is the primary way we interact with our environment. It is our technique for taking in the intelligence nature has organized for us in fruits and vegetables -- taking these substances external to us and incorporating them into ourselves. If we are not in the habit of giving thanks before meals, we might at least pause and consider: *This is going to become the new me. The person that I am going to be in the future is going to be built of this food I am about to eat. How can I expect to become a healthy person if I'm ingesting poor quality foods?* In that light, the chili-dog, fries and coke may be less appealing.

Food is best if warm and well-cooked. This doesn't mean it should be cooked to death, just appropriately cooked to begin digestion and simplify the job of the gut. Food should always be delicious and pleasing to all the senses. It should look good, taste good and smell good. The texture of it should be pleasing.

Ideally the food would be prepared by a happy, settled cook in a pleasant environment. If we eat out at restaurants a lot, finding a good-quality place with a contented and *sattvic* (*sattva* refers to purity and positivity) cook is important. That is why children often thrive best when they are fed food prepared by their mother. Even if Mom is not a great cook, her love and concern for those who are going to eat her food generates a powerful positive influence in the food.

As mentioned, mental problems -- stress, anger, upset of any kind -- will tend to have a deranging effect on agni. Also, problems in our eating patterns -- such as taking food too close to the previous meal or taking food at the wrong times of day will also have adverse effects on our digestion.

In fact, as we'll see in the next chapter, the times of day we engage in various activities and routines can have enormous effects on our health.

> To eat is human; to digest, divine.
> -- Mark Twain

## CHAPTER SEVENTEEN

# The Cycles of Nature

> The trouble with life in the fast lane is that you get to the other end in an awful hurry.
>
> -- John Jensen

Fred came to me with a complaint of chronic fatigue. Though he had been feeling fatigued for about a year and a half, he didn't quite meet the criteria for the chronic fatigue syndrome. He was still able to get up in the morning, go to work and do some exercise, but he would often fall ill, got a lot of sore throats and never felt he had the energy he used to have.

I asked when he went to bed.

"About midnight or so," he said. "I will fall asleep, often promptly, but sometimes I'll just lie there for a half hour or even an hour or more. It's the strangest thing, because I feel exhausted but I can't quite fall asleep."

I asked how he felt in the morning.

"Like death warmed over. The alarm goes off at about seven and I hit the snooze button until about quarter to eight, then I jump up, brew some coffee, shower and shave and hit the door just in time to make it to work. I do a good job but I drag, especially in the afternoon. When I get home in the evening I just don't have any energy to play with my kids. It makes me feel bad because they're sweet little characters, but they just get on my nerves in the evening, I feel so tired."

"Why don't you go to bed when you feel tired?" I asked.

"Well, I think I'm something of a night owl because I feel my best after I put the kids to sleep. I seem to get kind of a second wind. I'll feel okay for a while and won't even feel like going to bed because it's the best I've felt all day."

This is a common story. There are a number of errors in Fred's daily routine and we explored them in some detail. The understanding in Maharishi Ayur-Veda of *kala* or time is very helpful in understanding the origin of some of Fred's symptoms.

## Life Cycles

There are certain times when each of the doshas is predominant. Some of these periods are broad segments of our life. That is, from the time we're born until our third decade, kapha dosha is relatively predominant. (This is superimposed upon any imbalance; but anyone will tend to have more kapha in these first decades than later.) Pitta becomes more predominant in the middle decades of life. Then around the seventh and eighth decades of life and beyond, vata tends to predominate.

## Seasonal Cycles

Generally in temperate latitudes in North America, the vata season is November through February, the kapha season is March through June and the pitta season is July through October. In the vata season, the characteristics of vata are relatively predominant. That is, the weather tends to be cooling and drier, the wind tends to blow, the environment is more full of the characteristics of vata dosha. Kapha, on the other hand, being late winter and spring, tends to be cold (turning warmer as pitta approaches), but also wet. The snows are melting, the rain is falling, the ground is turning to mud -- these are manifestations of kapha dosha in the environment. Then pitta begins in July and lasts through the end of summer and into the early fall. Pitta, as you'll recall, is the only dosha that has the property of heat. These influences in the environment have influences upon us. That's why the aforementioned diets can be followed in those certain times of the year (vata pacifying diet during vata season, etc.) Consultation with a professional trained in Maharishi Ayur-Veda is helpful to prioritize the influences of season and imbalance in selecting a diet that is appropriate for you.

## Daily Cycles

In the course of one 24-hour cycle, there will be six four-hour periods when each dosha, in turn, is predominant. Kapha dosha predominates from 6 o'clock to 10 o'clock, pitta dosha from 10 o'clock to 2 o'clock and vata dosha from 2 o'clock to 6 o'clock. This is both a.m. and p.m. and it cycles twice through the day.

The ideal time to retire is during the kapha time of the evening, between six and 10. Practically speaking for us, in our culture, toward the end of the kapha time, at or before 10 o'clock at night. Kapha dosha is characterized by heaviness, dullness, slowness; the day is winding down and activity in nature is coming to a halt. Many of us will notice that nature sends us some impulse of fatigue during this time.

I have small children and I'll notice it if I put one or another of my kids to bed, I'll lie there with him or her, we'll sing a little song and talk for a moment and sooner or later, my child will begin to doze off. I will have a clear feeling that if I'd brushed my teeth I could roll over and in 20 seconds I would be out like a light right next to this child. But I look at my watch, which reads 14 minutes after eight, and I, like most of us, am culturally indoctrinated not to retire at 14 minutes after eight. I have checks to write and business to attend to, so I sometimes inappropriately override this natural impulse, get up off the bed and remain active.

If we don't go to bed before 10 o'clock, an interesting thing happens. We go from the kapha time, which is characterized by heaviness and dullness and inertia, into the pitta time which is characterized by heat, ambition, drive, dynamism and efficiency. Most people (particularly those with strong pitta dosha), will notice that they seem to get a "second wind" around 10 o'clock at night. Activities and chores that were unattractive at 8:30 become irresistible at 10:30. These people begin to feel as good as they've felt all day, and the prospect of now retiring to sleep, now that they've finally begun to feel good, is unappealing; and so they tend to stay up later. This second peak of energy is used by the body to cleanse and heal itself while asleep. It is unwise to deprive it of that chance.

193

Staying up late tends to aggravate vata dosha. Vata has to do with motion, and if we stay up late we're in motion, at least mentally, at a time of the 24-hour cycle when nature would have us be quiescent. The later we stay up, of course, the more fatigue accumulates, and eventually we can fall asleep. But over the long term, a pattern of staying up late tends to aggravate vata dosha. Then we can have this experience that Fred reported: he felt fatigued, yet it's as if his whole body was buzzing and the committee upstairs in his brain would not turn out the lights and stop talking. These are manifestations of vata imbalance.

> To rise at six, to bed at ten,
> Makes a man live for ten times ten.
> -- Inscribed in Victor Hugo's house on the Isle of Guernsey

The optimum time to awaken is at the end of the vata time, in the morning around 6 o'clock, around dawn. That time will not be comfortably available to us if we have gone to bed late. We will either awaken late or we will awaken tired. It's a cliché experience in our culture to hit the snooze alarm a number of times, awaken fatigued, drink coffee and then plunge into activity.

But the alternative is to sleep later. If we sleep in, past 6 o'clock, then we have gone once again into the kapha time. Kapha time of the morning is from 6 to 10. It also is characterized by some heaviness and dullness and inertia, which is why during this time it's best to perform counterbalancing activities that are enlivening to the physiology. If we continue to sleep, then the dullness of sleep is superimposed upon this inertia of kapha. One would think that after nine hours of sleep anyone would feel fantastic. But if our nine hours of sleep are from 12:30 a.m. until 9:30 a.m., almost invariably we'll awaken feeling lethargic. Just as staying up late aggravates vata, sleeping late or in the day between dawn and dusk aggravates kapha, making us feel dull and heavy like kapha.

Most of this late sleep is just an artifact of our culture. By virtue of our scientific prowess, we are able to manipulate our environment. With air conditioning, we can turn summer into winter.

With heaters, we can turn winter into summer. And, perhaps most insidious, with electricity we can turn night into day with lights, television sets, VCRs and radios. Having the capability to manipulate our environment and make it more comfortable is fine, but all too often it comes at a high price. We become out of touch with our own natural rhythms.

If you think of the tens of thousands of generations that have preceded us on this planet, they've been on a daytime program. The sun would go down and people would retire to sleep. There wasn't much else to do. There were no reruns on TV and our ancestors basically were living an agrarian life. Up until a couple of generations ago, even in the developed world, people still lived predominantly in the countryside. In the developing world, this is still the case. They would awaken in the early hours of the day in order to begin their activities, which were usually physical, often outdoors and almost universally beginning early in the morning.

Most of us are only a day or two away from recapturing this experience. If we go up to Uncle Arnold's cabin on the lake for a week of communing with nature, the first night everyone stays up until midnight and tells ghost stories, but that pattern is promptly extinguished. At night, there's nothing much to do up there, and if you forget the lamps there's no illumination, so soon after sunset everyone goes to sleep. In the pre-dawn then, having had an adequate quantity of sleep, we awaken feeling refreshed and enjoy our day's activity. The return to this natural rhythm can happen surprisingly quickly.

If we maintain the pattern of being late to bed and late to rise, it can become a vicious cycle that perpetuates itself. The human physiology is used to being asleep for roughly eight hours; perhaps a little longer -- nine or even 10 hours in persons with kapha dosha very strong -- and perhaps less than eight hours if pitta or particularly vata is strong. But, for purposes of illustration, let's say it's eight hours. And the remaining 16 hours is the amount of time the body is used to being awake.

If we awaken late, say at 9 or 10 o'clock in the morning, then 12 or 13 hours later, when it's time to retire to bed, the body is not ready to retire. It hasn't been awake quite long enough. If we try to retire to bed at that point, we're unable to fall asleep at the optimum time, and in the morning we're tempted to sleep in. If we do sleep in until 9 or 10, the whole cycle can perpetuate itself indefinitely. So we want to take some steps to break this cycle.

One approach is simply to continue to go to bed early and habituate the body to fall asleep at that time. Another approach, which is not good in the long term but can actually be helpful for a short period, is to set an alarm and get in the habit of getting up early and avoiding daytime sleep. I have also found that setting an alarm for about 9 o'clock at night is helpful: using the alarm as a signal to bring the day's activity to a close, brush teeth, perform our evening ablutions and retire to bed.

## Modern Confirmation

More and more these days, scientists are recognizing that disruptions in our sleep-wake cycles can be deleterious to our health. Many bodily functions follow a *circadian* rhythm, that is a daily rhythm. These include body temperature, sleeping and wakefulness, release of many hormones, alertness and memory.[1]

People who perform shift work often have difficulty sleeping as a result of trying to sleep at an hour conflicting with their circadian rhythm.[1] We can simulate the problems of these shift workers simply by having bad habits and going to bed too late. In shift workers, gastrointestinal disorders are more common[2] and the incidence of cardiovascular disease[3] is higher. Some studies also suggest that shift workers have an increased risk for miscarriage, pre-term birth and lower birth-weight babies.[2]

Millions of Americans are sleep deprived and get by on six hours of sleep or less, and about a third of Americans have trouble falling asleep or staying asleep. Between 60 and 90 percent of workplace accidents are attributed to human error, and lack of sleep is a major factor. The U.S. Department of Transportation reported that up to 200,000 traffic accidents a year may be related to sleep disorders.[4]

We disregard these circadian rhythms at our peril, for they are not just someone's idea of when it's good to go to bed but are actually entrenched in our physiology, in our DNA. Researchers have found that receptors in the forebrains of rats have circadian variations.  There are pacemakers in our brains and in the brains of animals that control these rhythms.[5]

There are significant circadium rhythms and variations in the metabolism of drugs and expressions of disease, something we didn't know when I was going through medical school.  We used to put people on constant intravenous infusions of anti-coagulant medications, for example, and would wonder why their clotting capability would be too thin at midnight and the blood would not be thinned enough at 8 o'clock in the morning.  Research[6] now has demonstrated that there are circadian rhythms in the metabolism of these anticoagulant drugs.  The same phenomena are found with regard to cancer medications[7] and the tolerance of anti-cancer agents,[8] as well as many other drugs and conditions.  Most angina occurs in the morning, and the first couple of hours after awakening are the peak hours for heart attacks, strokes, and high blood pressure.  The night belongs to asthma.  Rheumatoid arthritis pain peaks in the morning, osteoarthrosis pain peaks in the evening.  Stomach acidity peaks around 6 p.m.  Childhood acute lymphoblastic leukemia chemotherapy is three times more effective when administered in the evening.[9]

## Time: Master or Slave?

Our body-mind complex has the ability to influence the timing of biological phenomena.  This is most markedly shown by the ability of individuals to postpone their deaths.

One study looked at a sample of 1,919 deaths among Jews from 1966 to 1984, at or around the time of Passover.  Researchers found that the number of deaths was lower than expected the week before Passover and higher than expected the week after Passover.  The pattern of a dip prior to Passover and peak afterward did not appear in control groups, including African-Americans and Asians, or in Jewish infants.  This pattern of a dip and peak around Passover was most pronounced in the years when the holiday fell on a weekend, when it is most likely to be celebrated by the largest number of people.[10]

A similar study was found among the Chinese.  Mortality dips 35 percent in the week before the Harvest Moon Festival and peaks by about the same amount, 34.6 percent, in the week after.[11]

Again, this pattern does not appear in various non-Chinese control groups.

Persons in cultures all over the world who are destined to die are able to defer their deaths for some significant periods of time in order to remain alive long enough to experience a significant event.

It seems that death itself is subject to our point of view.

## Rhythm and Blues

Is there any evidence that having a regular routine is beneficial in other areas? In fact, there is.

In the classic Alameda Study[12] seven personal health practices and subsequent mortality was examined in 6,928 adults in Alameda County, California over 9-1/2 years. These seven health habits included: never smoking cigarettes, regular physical activity, moderate or no use of alcohol, seven to eight hours of sleep regularly, maintaining proper body weight, eating breakfast, and not eating between meals. The results of this study were striking. If a 45-year-old man practiced zero to three health habits, he had a life expectancy of approximately another 21.6 years, but, if he practiced six or seven of these health practices, he would have a life expectancy of another *33.1 years.* Thus we can add over a decade to our life expectancies simply by engaging in these health-promoting habits.

We all know the value of never having smoked. The value of regular physical exercise I'll discuss later in the chapter. Alcohol is clearly recognized as being toxic; maintaining proper weight addresses risk for a number of diseases. Eating habits have not been much studied in terms of their ability to prevent disease, and I'll discuss the Ayurvedic approach to them in a moment.

The value of seven to eight hours of sleep also has not been well explored, but there's plenty of data to provide theoretical underpinning for why sleep would be significant. Sleep deprivation has been associated with a decreased proliferation of lymphocytes and decreased ability of white cells to eat and kill bacteria.[13] In deep sleep 70 percent of our growth hormone is produced, and the production of cortisol, a stress hormone, is inhibited by deep sleep.[14] In volunteers who underwent a 77-hour wakefulness vigil,[15] researchers noted there was decreased ability of macrophages to eat bacteria. It is during the pitta time of the night that *agni,* the transformative aspect of pitta, is lively. This allows for the performance of the self repair we require after the day's activity. That is why sleep between 10 p.m. and 2 a.m. is so restorative, and is yet another reason we should retire and rise early.

It is recognized in Maharishi Ayur-Veda that there are also a number of seasonal influences that should be addressed. Modern medicine now recognizes a phenomenon called *seasonal affective disorder* (rhythm and blues), in which some people become depressed in the wintertime. Their depression lifts at other times of year. This problem has been treated with antidepressants and artificial full-spectrum lighting as well as with structured exercise programs. Advice from the Charaka Samhita thousands of years ago for such people to take a walk in the morning sun -- a prescription that provided for full-spectrum lighting as well as exercise -- made pharmaceuticals unnecessary.

There is a an ideal daily routine in Maharishi Ayur-Veda. The first element in this daily routine, as we've previously discussed, is to be early to bed. This allows us to begin our routine early in the morning, arising ideally around dawn -- usually at or before 6 o'clock. Then we should evacuate our bowels and bladder. This is the time to brush our teeth and to clean or scrape our tongue. Often ama will show up as a white coating on the tongue in the morning, an indicator that there are other steps we should be taking (diet, panchakarma, etc.) to reduce or eliminate this toxic influence.

The next step is an oil massage called *abhyanga* which I'll describe in some detail in a moment. The next, for men, would be to shave. This is followed by gargling with sesame oil. Subsequent to that, we would bathe or shower. Next is the time to practice TM.

After that we would dress, and *if we're hungry*, eat breakfast. From the Ayurvedic perspective, breakfast is an optional meal. Those who require it should have it (the Alameda study at least showed that it was a marker for regularity in one's life), but people who aren't hungry can skip it (we shouldn't be skipping it because we're time pressured). Then we would engage in our work or study.

At mid-day, in the pitta time of the day between 10 and two, we would take lunch, which ideally would be the largest meal of the day. It should be composed of food that is balanced according to our body type and the season of the year, taking into account any imbalance that may have been identified by diagnosis through the pulse. After lunch, we would briefly rest before returning to our work or study. At the end of work, in the late afternoon, we would once again practice TM.

In the evening, one would have an appropriate supper, with lighter foods than at lunch. Subsequent to supper we would take a walk for 10 or 15 minutes, and then have pleasant and relaxing activity which was not over-stimulating so that we would be able to retire before 10 o'clock at night.

A prelude to the practice of TM (or, if we have been instructed in it, the TM-Sidhi program) would be the practice of some *yoga* postures and another "Vedic exercise" called "salute to the sun." These are described in Appendix E.

The prospect of adding all these behaviors to our daily routine -- yoga postures, sun salutations, oil massage -- may be somewhat daunting. I can assure you that these can be quickly and comfortably integrated into anyone's daily routine.

## Abhyanga: Oil Massage

The Ayurvedic daily oil massage or abhyanga is purificatory in its function. Different oils can be used, including olive oil and coconut oil, but sesame oil is preferable. Ideally, the sesame oil would be *cured*. This is purifying to the sesame oil and is accomplished by heating it to the boiling point of water (not the boiling point of the oil!). In order to do this, you take a quantity of sesame oil and put it on the stove at low to medium heat. This is a fire hazard and you should never leave it unattended. One way to determine when it reaches the boiling point of water is with a cooking thermometer. If that's not available, another simple way is to put a drop of water in the oil. If you have a Pyrex or see-through pot, you'll see the water at the bottom, under the oil, and you'll actually be able to see it begin to boil. If that's not convenient, you can take a drop of water on your fingertip and just flick it into the oil every minute or so. When the water hits the oil it will begin to sink, but if the oil is at the boiling point of water, the drop of water will pop. That means the sesame oil is cured. You can turn off the heat, let it cool and pour it into a suitable container. Depending on how much oil you use each time, a quart of oil will cover probably 10 to 20 massages.

To do the oil massage, use a few tablespoons, up to a quarter-cup or so, of the cured oil and heat it to a warm temperature. We start at the top by massaging the head. Traditionally, the scalp, ears and soles of the feet are emphasized in this process. Place some oil on your hand or fingertips and massage your scalp vigorously. Alternatively, if you have long or thick hair and this is cosmetically unsuitable, you can place some of the oil directly onto the scalp (if you keep the oil in a container with some type of dispensing nozzle); in doing the massage, some of the oil may move up the hair shafts. If that's a problem for you, simply use a smaller amount of oil. The massage is done with the open, flat hand rather than with the fingertips. Massage your ears, your face, the front and back of your neck and the upper back of your back and spine as much as you can comfortably reach.

After a few minutes, you will apply some oil over the body. You may want to put enough oil on that you can perform the massage without having to retrieve more oil every time you want to massage a different extremity. You don't want to put on so much oil that it drips or runs onto the floor and makes a mess; estimating the right amount is quickly learned.

Next, massage your upper extremities. In performing the massage, we go in a circular motion around the joints and in a longitudinal back-and-forth motion over long bones. In that way you massage shoulder, arm, elbow, forearm, wrist, hand and fingers. Then gently you can massage your chest; over your heart it should be done very gently in an up-and-down motion. Massaging over the abdomen is done beginning in the right lower quadrant, going upward to the right upper quadrant, transversely across to the left upper quadrant and then downward to the left lower quadrant, back to the right lower quadrant in a circular motion, over and over again. The low back, as far as you can reach, is then massaged, as are the hips, buttocks, thighs, knees, legs, ankles and feet. Again, the soles of the feet would be emphasized.

Ideally, you should have the oil on for at least 20 minutes. That's done best by performing the massage for 20 minutes. If that much time is not available, spend as much time as you comfortably can doing the massage, but then avoid washing the oil off, perhaps while performing some other chores such as identifying the clothes you're going to be wearing or any number of other things that you may need to do before leaving the house in the morning that you can do as well covered with oil as not covered with oil. Then it would be time to bathe and/or shower, as previously noted.

It may not be necessary take a bar of soap and de-fat every square inch of your skin in order to get rid of this sesame oil. It's natural to have a modest mantle of lipid on the skin. By allowing the water to wash over the skin, perhaps shampooing excess oil out of the hair and using soap in strategic areas, some residue of the oil may remain on the skin; this actually is quite suitable and is not a problem.

The purpose of this oil massage, as I mentioned, is purificatory. The sesame oil gets onto the skin and it's the property of the sesame oil, since it is somewhat heating in its nature, to be able to penetrate the skin to whatever degree and lubricate the srotas, the subtle channels of circulation through which ojas and the body's intelligence flows and within which these doshas and toxins and ama tend to deposit. It is the property of the sesame oil to be able to emulsify and loosen these complexes of ama and doshas. They then are more available to be liberated by the particular massage that we're doing. This massage pushes these complexes through the channels in which they've been stuck so they can be mobilized and moved into larger and larger channels until eventually they can be eliminated through the urine, feces, perspiration and respiration. Some modest quantity may be so addressed at each oil massage, but by doing the abhyanga day in and day out, week after week, month after month, some very significant momentum of purification can be generated. Fortunately, most people report that this process is quite pleasant and nurturing to experience.

# Exercise

> A man falls into ill health as a result of not caring for exercise.
> -- Aristotle

In July 1996, the Surgeon General's report on physical exercise and health stated that 60% of American adults do not engage in recommended levels of activity, and 25% do no exercise at all.

The eternal cycle of nature is one of rest and activity. We've seen the value of meditation and rest, but to help stabilize the benefits of meditation, as well as to accomplish our goals in life, action is also required. The concept of setting time aside for exercise is a relatively new one in our culture. While there are some historical accounts of individuals such as Benjamin Franklin advising swimming and running back in the 18th century, most of our ancestors got more than enough exercise in their daily labors. It is only with the advent of modern society with its sedentary ways that we have seen the range of health problems that can occur if exercise is ignored.

A number of studies in recent decades have documented the health benefits of some degree of exercise.

## Exercise and Heart Disease

In Harvard alumni[16] who walked three to eight miles per week mortality decreased 15 percent compared to those individuals who were sedentary. Performing light sports for an hour or two a week decreased mortality by 24 percent, and exercising vigorously for an hour or two per week decreased mortality by 35 percent. This was mostly due to decreases in cardiovascular mortality. In 13,000 men and women mortality from all causes dropped[17] corresponding to the degree of exercise. In Canada, a health survey[18] also demonstrated that physical fitness decreased mortality. It's interesting that these studies showed that this trend held true only up to a point, indicating that too much exercise is not necessarily good for you.

## Exercise and Cancer

One study followed over 17,000 men for over 20 years and found that those who were active had 37 percent less colon cancer and 50 percent less lung cancer[19]. This was confirmed in another more recent study[20] that showed three hours of walking per week led to a 30 percent decrease in the incidence of colon cancer.

## Exercise Lite

A decade or so ago, the tenet of exercise was 'no pain, no gain.' Instructions to exercise and exercise vigorously were in every supermarket magazine. Many experts in this field now recognize that over-training is counterproductive and unnecessary. Twelve thousand men followed for ten years demonstrated[21] a 30 percent decrease in mortality with mild increases in exertion, as little as 150 kilocalories per day, which would correspond to such activities as walking, gardening, and bowling.

## The Vedic Approach to Exercise

Maharishi Ayur-Veda recognizes exercise as helpful: it pacifies kapha dosha, mobilizes ama, improves circulation, creates energy, helps to clear the body of accumulated toxic debris, enhances a sense of well being and fitness and, if done properly, need not produce stress in the body.

How much exercise we need varies from individual to individual. It also tends to vary with age. Exercise should feel comfortable while we're doing it, not just after we stop. For those less than 25 years old, as long as there's no discomfort there are no limits on exercise. For those between 25 and 40, exercise should be guided by the body build of the individual. Between the ages of 40 and 60, it's usually prudent to have some gentle reduction in the amount of exercise. After the age of 60, mild exercise is more appropriate.

Kapha generally requires more vigorous exercise. Kapha dosha leads to larger, more muscular body builds. By its nature kapha is heavy, slow and inert. Exercise tends to counter these properties and have a balancing effect. Pitta influence dictates moderate exercise, with a couple of caveats: avoid too-vigorous exercise, particularly in the middle of the day when exposed to the hot sun.

Also, competitive exercises (particularly if you're not quite as good as the person you're competing with), can often provoke pitta imbalanced people into exercising beyond a healthy range. A worst case scenario would be for an weekend athlete with a pitta imbalance to take up jogging at noon in the summer with a co-worker who is more fit and who wants to demonstrate that fitness. Vata dosha indicates mild exercise. Too strenuous and rigorous exercise will generate in the body too much influence of motion and movement which already exists in abundance in vata dosha.

You can see that the recommendations with regard to age also parallel the *kalas*, the times of life, that I discussed earlier. In the early part of life, when kapha dosha is more predominant, more rigorous exercise is suitable. In middle life, exercise can be more moderate, and after age 60, vata is more predominant, so one should do milder exercises such as comfortable walking, comfortable swimming, or easy cycling.

## Maharishi Yoga

The Maharishi Yoga program enlivens what are called *marma* points. Marma points are subtle junction points between consciousness and physiology. It is recognized in the ancient Ayurvedic texts that there are scattered throughout the body 107 such points that can be influenced the organizing quality of our attention. Of course, consciousness and intelligence are everywhere in our body, since the body is ultimately made of consciousness, but at these subtle points the interplay between consciousness and physiology is more accessible. Putting our body through the ranges of motion and movement, with our attention animated, has an enlivening effect upon these marmas. These marma points while located generally on the surface of the body, have particular connections to our musculoskeletal and nervous systems. They also have effects on particular organs throughout the physiology, so that a point on the surface of the body far removed from the actual organ may have an effect on our spleen or thyroid gland.

Of these 107 marmas, there are three especially important ones, called *mahamarmas*, located in the head, the heart, and the lower pelvis over the urinary bladder. These principal marmas are particularly related to rishi (the knower), devata (the process of knowing) and chandas (the known), respectively. Enlivening these marma points helps balance and integrate rishi, devata and chandas throughout the body-mind. When the marmas are injured or exposed to toxins, imbalances may block the connection between our consciousness and our physiology at these points, inhibiting the free flow of bliss and intelligence.

Virtually universally beneficial are yoga postures or *asanas* A preliminary set of these is described in Appendix E. The more complete understanding of the principles, and more in depth postures, of Maharishi Yoga can be found in the course offered by the Maharishi Ayur-Veda Universities and Schools listed in Appendix A. While neither the diagrams in the appendix nor this chapter's discourse can do justice to the knowledge offered in this course, perhaps I can give a preview here of some of the information.

There are certain principles we need to attend to in performing these postures. First, they should always be done comfortably and easily, without strain, without jerks and jolts. The yoga asanas mimic the dynamic of rest and activity that is fundamental to the cycles of nature. The stretching aspect of the posture is dynamic, the holding phase is resting, silent. While executing each posture, we allow the mind to be on any place in the body that invites our attention. We'll feel some stretch, naturally, in less flexible areas. This lack of flexibility is related to some decrease in the flow of biological intelligence in that area. Our attention supplies that intelligence.

These postures, then, are valuable not so much as calisthenic or stretching exercises but as techniques for neuro-muscular integration: mind-body integration. We start in a neutral position -- sitting, standing, supine, prone -- depending upon which posture we are about to execute. Then we begin to move in the direction of that posture. As we move, most of us will find that before we get the body into the "perfect" position (as diagramed in the Appendix), we encounter some threshold beyond which lies discomfort. Our universal rule is that we never go past that threshold. Now, it may well be that five or ten seconds into the posture, or during the holding or resting phase, that threshold may move beyond where it was. In that case, we can comfortably move with it and come closer to approximating the posture as diagrammed. But, we should never get target-fixated on getting our body into that particular posture.

There are many traditions in the West and in India that re-gard these postures as having value only when perfectly executed. They believe that until we get the body into this particular position there is no benefit; then, once we get the body matching the template of this position, everything lines up, the energy flows and good things happen. The tradition of Maharishi Ayur-Veda does not re-gard postures that way. They should be subtle and easy. Just mov-ing in the direction of the posture is stimulating to our various marma points. The marma points, when stimulated, tend to elicit our attention; our coherent attention being brought to these marma points has organizing power, and it's that organizing power which enlivens our healing response and affects organs throughout our body.

You can see, then, that in this process I've outlined it doesn't matter so much how far you get in a posture. Each time you do the posture, it's brand new. All we need to do is pay attention to the body as we're performing that particular posture. If we are com-fortably able to go further than we could yesterday, that's wonderful. If we find that we're not quite able to go as far as we could yesterday or last week, that's fine too.

You can see also that it's not wise to divide the mind during exercise because our attention should be comfortably on our body, sensitive to the signals the body is sending. Putting on headphones, listening to music, watching TV -- all these things divide the mind and weaken the quality of our attention on the body. When we dis-tract ourselves this way, we often ignore signals from the body that warn us of stress and imbalance due to overexertion.

> Regimen is superior to medicine.
>
> -- Voltaire

## CHAPTER EIGHTEEN

# The Discovery of the Veda Within: Our Birthright

> The verses of the Ved exist in the collapse of fullness in the
> transcendental field, self-referral consciousness, the Self.
> In which reside all the devas, the impulses of creative intelligence,
> the laws of nature responsible for the whole manifest universe.
> He whose awareness is not open to this field, what can the verses
> accomplish for him?
> Those who know this level of reality are established in evenness,
> wholeness of life.
>
> -- Rik Ved (I.164.39)

*Veda* means pure knowledge, as old as time. But Veda also refers to books. The Vedic literature describes how the universe works. As a philosophy, as a body of writing, these books are often incomprehensible. Maharishi Mahesh Yogi has brought to light the significance of the structure and organization, as well as the *sound* value of these works. The laws of nature, virtual and potential, reside in the inner silence experienced by the seers. This field subtly fluctuates, and the fluctuations are appreciated as sounds. These sounds are the Veda, and their more complex harmonics are the Vedic literature, the commentaries on Veda. The value of the Vedic literature, then, lies not so much on the level of meaning, but on the vibrational quality of the sound, the series of syllables and gaps between the sounds.

There are dozens of components of Veda and Vedic literature, each with numerous divisions and subdivisions, and each presenting studies in various aspects of creation. The entire universe then, including ourselves, is a material expression of the vibrations within the field of Veda. Indeed, in the Rik Ved, the first and most fundamental of the Vedic texts, it states explicitly that the *verses* of the Veda exist in the Self. Logically we can see that the human body also is a form of Veda.

This may seem extremely alien. But in fact, virtually all religious and philosophical traditions have indicated this reality. The gospel tells us that in the beginning was the Word, which then becomes everything else. From India come many expressions such as, "As is the individual so is the universe." In the Koran we read, "On earth are signs of God, they are within you; do you not see them?" This understanding became the starting point for some remarkable research.

## The Discovery of Veda and Vedic Literature in Human Physiology

Tony Nader M.D.,Ph.D., a physician and neuroscientist, explored (with Maharishi's guidance) the organization of the Vedic literature and found parallels between the structure of those books and human anatomy. He also discovered* exact recapitulation of the topics and functions of the Vedic literature and the activities of human physiology.

For example, Yoga has four chapters, each with a number of sutras (51, 55, 55, and 34). The number and the topics of the sutras in each of those chapters correspond to the anatomy and function of those parts of the respective lobes of the brain. I had an opportunity to discuss these findings with Dr. Nader; I didn't understand for instance how we could have an odd number (51, 55, and 55) of structures in a bilaterally symmetric organ such as the brain. He was able to point out to me the "odd" structures which travel between the hemispheres of the brain, and the corresponding verses. The conformation of Vedic literature to human physiology recurs incessantly and is beyond coincidence. This is because, continuing with the ex-

---

- * This discovery is explained in a new book, *Human Physiology: Expression of Veda and the Vedic Literature:* by Tony Nader M.D., Ph.D. Vlodrop, The Netherlands: Maharishi Vedic University. 1995.

ample from the four chapters of Yoga, the sounds of the yoga sutras express themselves as the four lobes of the brain; the reality of these lobes has its basis in the sounds of the yoga sutras.

A partial synopsis of this discovery is listed in Appendix G.

This disclosure graphically demonstrates that each of us contains within ourselves all the laws of nature. The Veda, the unified field, is within us; if we enliven this total potential, we will be able to think and act in accord with natural law, and never violate natural law (don't eat the wrong food, don't have wrong routine, etc.). This means we don't make mistakes, don't suffer and don't generate problems for ourselves or for others. Practical approaches to disease can be located in this body of Vedic literature.

After this discovery, it was appreciated that the term Maharishi Ayur-Veda did not encompass all the possible applications of this tradition to health. Again recognizing the unique contribution of Maharishi to our understanding of the significance and the roles of the Vedic literature in health, a broader characterization has now arisen: the Maharishi Vedic Approach to Health.

# A Comprehensive Approach to Health

It is beyond the scope of this book to consider all the interventions of the Maharishi Vedic Approach to Health in detail. But it can be helpful to think of the approaches of Maharishi Ayur-Veda as falling into four broad areas.

- First is the approach through the **mind**.
- Second is the approach through the **body**.
- Third is the approach through **behavior**.
- Fourth is the approach through the **environment**.

The approach through the mind is through consciousness, and I discussed this in some detail in the chapter on Transcendental Meditation. There are number of advanced techniques of TM as well as the TM-Sidhi program which I'll be talking about in the next chapter. Behavioral rasayanas, emerging as they do from the level of thought and feeling, fall into both this category and that of behavior.

The approach through the body is basically a medical approach. It involves attending to what we're putting into our body and we're eliminating from it. We put into it foods, herbs and sensory input, and we eliminate waste products, doshas and toxic debris.

The third approach, through behavior, involves the more expressed aspects of the behavioral rasayanas, as well as what is called in contemporary medicine *chronotherapy* or time-related treatments. This has to do with daily routine (*dinacharya*) as well as seasonal routines (*ritucharya*).

Last is the approach through the environment which we'll consider in the next chapter.

## The Body as Process

We spontaneously use the approach through our body, for good or ill, every day. We ingest and metabolize our sensory experiences in just as real a way as we metabolize any other experience. The body is more a process than a structure. It is through the processes of sensory perception and ingestion -- eating, digesting, breathing, metabolizing, eliminating through the urine and feces and perspiration and respiration the waste products that we elaborate, our psychological and physiological responses to persons and situations -- that we determine what our body becomes day by day, month by month, year by year.

## Pulse Diagnosis

The primary physical diagnostic tool used in Maharishi Ayur-Veda is diagnosis through the pulse (or *nadi vigyan*). Western medicine also uses some diagnosis through the pulse. We were all taught in medical school how to take the pulse, how to count it, and aspects of the pulse's strength and regularity (or lack thereof) that can have diagnostic value. But these are nothing to compare with the refined and subtle information that can be gained from the pulse through Ayurvedic techniques. I have seen master pulse diagnosticians (such as Dr. Triguna, past president of the All-India Ayur-Veda Congress) make remarkable diagnoses using only the pulse. An

Ayurvedic practitioner can determine from a person's pulse imbalances among the doshas, and the strength and functioning of the tissues (or *dhatus*).

Information about a person's doshic imbalance is important in determining proper diet. Food that is suitable for you may be unsuitable for your friend. That is why dietary recommendations are specific to individuals.

## Herbs

There are a number of substances one can ingest to promote health. Ayurvedic teas pacify specific doshas, and combinations of spices (called *churnas*) supply all six tastes in an appropriate proportion to pacify a given dosha.

There is a wealth of knowledge about the use of medicinal herbs in Maharishi Ayur-Veda. Herbs, even more subtly than foods, are packets of both intelligence and wisdom, concocted such that the body can most favorably utilize the health giving information present. Herbs have been used and prepared in this tradition literally for millennia, and these herbal preparations are extremely complex. In Western medicine there are a number of pharmaceuticals that are single molecules, and some of them are single atoms (such as lithium). Many of these drugs, while used frequently, are of unknown mechanism; that is, we really don't know how they work. These herbal preparations are much more complex than pharmaceuticals. They often contain dozens of plants, and each of these plants may have dozens, even hundreds, of different molecular components, any one of which may have some specific effect. The combination of all of these substances, plus all their possible interactions, makes the potential activities of these herbal preparations utterly labyrinthine and unfathomable on the level of the intellect. It is only by the knowledge of these clear-thinking seers who have directly cognized the effects of these plants and handed this information down through generations that we are able to use them appropriately.

Those responsible need to understand the appropriate handling of these plants. If that expertise is lacking, one could have a jar of an herbal preparation which lists on the label the very same plants as another jar, yet one product might be extremely beneficial and the other relatively inert. This could be due to a number of factors which might seem opaque to the uninitiated. Was this plant harvested on a north- versus a south-facing slope? What time of the year was it harvested? Was the leaf used, or the stem, or the root? Was it heated enough or too much? Was it processed in the appropriate way? Was it added in the appropriate order along with all the other components of all the other plants that are included in this preparation? Without access to a tradition with such knowledge, the actions of these herbal preparations may not be helpful clinically nor measurable scientifically.

Herbs are different than drugs. Pharmaceuticals make war on disease; herbs, if prepared properly, act to promote health. As in any war, some noncombatants get in the way and are injured or killed by the side effects of drugs. But these herbs are virtually free of side effects. Drugs tell the body what to do, even if they tell it the wrong thing; they are a single molecule, playing one note stridently, insisting that the body dance to that sound. The herbs gently offer an entire symphony of possibilities to the body; and if some selections aren't needed, they aren't used. Drugs operate on the principle of the *active ingredient*. It is understood in Maharishi Ayur-Veda that many of the components of an herb may not be specifically "active," but do act to buffer and integrate the activities of other parts of the herb. If you attempt to extract the active ingredient, you may succeed in drawing some of the intelligence from a plant, but at the price of leaving the wisdom behind.

## Maharishi Amrit Kalash

There is a class of herbal preparations called rasayanas that, like the behavioral rasayanas previously discussed, enhance the flow of ojas. These herbal rasayanas are not tailored for a particular season of the year or doshic imbalance. These rasayanas are more globally health enhancing, and perhaps since they are more widely used, they've been studied more.

A particular combination of two herbal complexes is called *Maharishi Amrit Kalash*. This herbal combination is a potent antioxidant. You may be familiar with anti-oxidant vitamins: if you are having a heart attack you're advised to take Vitamin E because it salvages myocardial tissue by scavenging *free radicals*. Free radicals are extremely reactive chemicals, metabolic sharks that are born of the biochemical rough-and-tumble of our bodies. These free radicals inflict damage on our DNA, our cells, our lives.* The Maharishi Amrit Kalash (MAK) is a powerful free radical scavenger. In fact, one component of it is a few hundred times more potent and the other component is about a thousand times more potent[1] than either Vitamin C or Vitamin E, two big players in the field of vitamin anti-oxidant free-radical scavengers.

Also, the Maharishi Amrit Kalash (MAK) has a number of other effects, against cancers. It inhibits the induction of breast cancers[2] and causes the regression of established lung cancers[3], breast cancers[4] and papillomas[5] in animals. *In vitro*, which means in the test tube, it will take neuroblastoma cells (a type of cancer) and convert them into normal-appearing, normal-functioning cells[6]. It also inhibits adrenaline-induced platelet aggregation,[7] which has been associated with heart attack and stroke. It also binds to endorphin binding sites[8] in the brain, enhances lymphocyte functioning,[9] and has a wide range of other beneficial effects.

Now the interesting thing about this is that MAK is not a cancer herb, it's not a rat herb, it's not a platelet herb. This is not what the formulation is designed to address. The very range of beneficial effects of MAK confirms that the model we have for understanding the functioning of these herbs** is probably correct. The model tells us that these herbs are operating at a fundamental common denominator of life which, when enlivened, tends to give rise to a number of beneficial effects in different tissues throughout our bodies, even in different species.

## The Senses

In attending to our body, we also must attend to our sensory input. All our senses are supplying our body-mind with raw material that we are experiencing and processing and turning into ourselves.

---

* For an extensive and very readable review of the whole area of free-radical scavenging, antioxidants and the role of these herbal preparations, read an excellent book written by Dr. Hari Sharma of Ohio State University entitled Freedom From Disease.

** Maharishi Amrit Kalash is commercially available. See Appendix A section III.

There are a number of therapeutic modalities that address each of our senses. The sense of touch, for instance, is addressed by the sesame oil massage as well as the yoga postures and sun salutations. We've discussed taste with regard to the foods and teas and churnas. There are specific aromas that can be tailored to doshas and subdoshas.

## Sound

But subtlest among these senses is that of hearing. The relationship of sound to thought is utilized in TM. Also, the sound of the Veda itself can be used to reestablish order in human bodies that have become imbalanced. These sounds can be used in ways that address the sequential unfoldment of Veda from this state of pure potentiality, virtual and unexpressed, in the unified field as previously discussed. Errors, born of pragya aparadha (the "mistake of the intellect"), which slip into this process of the orderly elaboration of Veda into manifest creation can be corrected by these sounds which reset this sequential order appropriately. This reestablishes the orderliness of the entire physiology.

While perhaps abstruse to us now, these approaches are the therapies of the future. Healing through sound is subtle. You may find this approach to be abstract. You are right. That which is closer to the source of Natural Law will inherently be more abstract, less differentiated. It is for this reason that Vedic sounds, properly utilized, can have such a powerful effect on the physiology. It takes expertise and very clear awareness to be able to discern the proper use of these sounds. The programs using these sounds are parts of the Maharishi Vedic Approach to Health which are just coming into use.

## Music

A more expressed value of sound is found in Gandharva Veda which is the traditional system of music from this Vedic civilization. It is a precise and sophisticated science of Vedic melodies. Music is recognized even in the West as having beneficial effects on health, and there are studies which have examined different types of music and noted their effects on diverse subjects, from plants to surgeons in the operating room. Even though our Western investigations have not been systematic, at least we recognize that there is a worthwhile effect here. Fortunately, we don't have to reinvent the wheel, since this knowledge of Gandharva Veda and sound is already available through this Vedic tradition, currently being enlivened and made applicable by a contemporary sage.

Dr. Nader's discovery has identified the role of Gandharva Veda in all the rhythms and cycles of the physiology. The sequences of these notes have integrating qualities which keep the mind and body in tune with the rhythms of Nature.

## Panchakarma: Cleansing the Channels of the Body

> In treating a patient, let your first thought be to strengthen his natural vitality.
>
> -- Rhazes (850-923)

The last point that I want to consider among these approaches through the body is that of *panchakarma*. There is no good analog to panchakarma in Western medicine. Methods of eliminating toxic build-up in the physiology (outside of acute intoxications and poisonings) are not much addressed in Western medicine.

Panchakarma comes from two Sanskrit terms: *pancha*, which means five, and *karma*, which means action or therapy. Panchakarma, then, is the five main purificatory and rejuvenative treatments of Ayurveda. Panchakarma includes:

- *Snehana* or oleation, which means lubricative types of treatments.
- *Virechana*, which refers to purgative and cathartic types of treatments.
- *Swedana*, which refers to fomentation or heat treatments.
- *Basti*, which gets translated as being enemas, herbal decoctions administered rectally (some are small, more like herbalized suppositories).
- *Nasya*, which refers to treatments administered through the nose and/or respiratory tract.

217

The purpose of these treatments is to purify and rejuvenate. I described earlier the build-ups of ama, doshas and toxins that clog our body's channels. In performing the panchakarma we lubricate the channels and so help loosen and emulsify these toxic build-ups. We do particular types of massage that are forms of (external) oleation. We use heat to dilate the pores and channels to help further loosen these toxins and allow them to come out through the skin. The purgative therapies help flush out materials that have been loosened and mobilized and shunted into the gut. Nasya (nasal treatment) facilitates elimination through the respiratory tract and sinuses, and basti (enema) is used to pacify and eliminate vata dosha, that has its seat in the colon.

There are three main phases to these panchakarma treatments. One is usually done at home for about a week or two before your treatments at the clinic begin. It involves a simple diet and some substances you take at home that loosen and mobilize these toxic materials so that the panchakarma will be more effective. The second phase involves the panchakarma treatments themselves. These are performed typically for over two hours each day, a number of days in a row. On any given day, one would have a number of these treatments as prescribed. Some of them are not administered on the same day but might be administered some other day. In the best of all possible worlds, healthy people would have around eight days of panchakarma three times a year, just for routine health maintenance. Shorter or longer programs may be prescribed. After the panchakarma treatments are finished, the third phase involves an easy transition from the panchakarma back into your (perhaps improved) routine of diet and activity.

There are a number of things we do at home to avoid forming toxic wastes such as ama. By using the interventions I discussed earlier, by doing abhyanga (oil massage) and eating appropriately and strengthening our digestion, we make sure that we're not generating any more imbalances in our doshas.

All these routine interventions are like a man raking leaves and sprinkling his lawn. This helps maintain the good appearance of his home. But it's important every so often to have a rainstorm that saturates the earth and washes away all the unwanted debris. That rain is analogous to the panchakarma, which, as Maharishi says, "helps to get the doshas out by the truckload."[10]

Panchakarma is a rich field for researchers, who have already found a number of beneficial effects: anxiety and other psychopathology decreases,[11] indicators of free radical activity fall,[12] beneficial neuropeptide levels rise,[12] and cholesterol decreases.[13]

Even though the term purificatory may not sound appealing, panchakarma actually is an enjoyable experience; one can imagine oneself as being a member of some royal family back in the time of the Upanishads in ancient India having these nurturing, restorative and health-promoting treatments. It's a charming contrast to the unpleasant treatments we usually experience in the medical model, which is destructive and adversarial with regard to disease.


This is not an eclectic field. That is, the Maharishi Vedic Approach to Health does not borrow from other traditions. Some people find this difficult to understand. But it's quite simple: changing it weakens it. Maharishi has stressed the necessity of keeping this tradition of knowledge pure. This is not ethnocentric chauvinism. (Nor is it to say that other approaches have no value, that would be silly. As I've discussed, anything that serves to help mobilize the coherence generating effect of our attention could be expected to have at least some benefit.) But a program that has complete support of Natural Law cannot be enhanced by mixing it with other approaches. It will always be the policy of the organizations that propagate these programs that they remain unadulterated, and thus, most effective. This approach can serve as the basis for integration of life, individually and internationally.

> The doctor of the future will give no medicine, but will interest their patient in the care of the human frame, in diet, and in the cause and prevention of disease.
>
> -- Thomas A. Edison

## CHAPTER NINETEEN

# Amazing Grace:
# A Proven Technology
# for Changing Society

> The health of the people is really the foundation upon which all their hopes and their powers as a state depend.
>
> -- Benjamin Disraeli, 1877

We have a symbiotic and reciprocal relationship with our environment. As the poet said, "Thou canst not stir a flower without troubling a star." Most important are our own internal dynamics -- the sources of the influences we subsequently experience -- generating actions that affect our environment. But it's appropriate also to look outside ourselves and optimize our environment.

For instance, there is a branch of Maharishi's Vedic Science called *Sthapatya-Veda*, Vedic architecture, elaborating principles known since antiquity, recognized to be valuable today. These principles tell us that housing should not be dense. Home designs should allow for fresh air in the building, and the building should be constructed of non-toxic materials (to avoid the "sick-building syndrome" that is currently a problem in American cities). Construction needs to be energy efficient, with minimal impact on the environment. Green space must be generous, and the siting, design and orientation of the house support the function of its various rooms. That is, dining rooms stimulate appetite, bedrooms facilitate sleep, and so forth.

Unknown to modern architecture is the importance of such points as the direction of the entrances to houses and offices.

## The Super-Radiance Effect

Especially provocative and encouraging among the environmental effects of principles I've been discussing in this book is what has been called the *super-radiance effect* or the *Maharishi effect,* named after Maharishi Mahesh Yogi, who was the first person to predict its existence. This is the effect of group practice of TM and an advanced technique based on TM, the TM-Sidhi Program. Thirty years ago, Maharishi wrote:

> When people behave rightly, a corresponding atmosphere is naturally produced, and when such an influence is dominant, the individual's tendencies are affected by it. If in such an atmosphere of grace and glory, an individual is tempted to follow a wrong path, he is protected by the unseen influence of righteousness which surrounds him. [1]

The Vedic literature has long noted that the influence of meditation spreads coherence in the environment. When we go into a home where there has recently been a fight, we notice tension in the atmosphere, even though no harsh words are currently being spoken. In contrast, a home where harmony predominates is pleasant to enter. There may actually be substances similar to pheromones, products that are actually secreted by the body, lingering in the atmosphere, but our perception is also a manifestation of the subtle effect of consciousness.

Social scientists have always envisioned social interactions as linear and Newtonian. That is, unless someone talks to someone, shoots someone, gives someone a job or some money (or influences someone else who performs these actions), there is no interaction among these people. This model sees people interacting the way billiard balls interact on a pool table. One ball hits another and hits another, and, in this way, the interaction is propagated; otherwise, a miss is as good as a mile. But our understanding now is that consciousness is not like a pool table. Rather, consciousness is more like a bathtub.

Try to visualize a bathtub that is calm and has floating in it a dozen or so corks. If we push down on one cork, then let it go, it begins to bob up and down. As it bobs up and down, even though it's not touching any of the other corks, it propagates some effect through the *field* of the water that causes all the other corks to respond by bobbing up and down. This is analogous to the field effect of consciousness. Influences generated in the consciousness of individuals or groups can have effects on the consciousness of people who are not involved in the specific intervention being done. So, people meditating can have effects on persons not meditating, and can generate influences of coherence in society at large.

One could derive from the Vedic literature the hypothesis that a certain number of people meditating in a community will change the trends in that community, increasing positive influences and decreasing negative ones.

This hypothesis was first put to the test back in the 1970s when a number of cities in the United States were found to have one percent or more of their population practicing Transcendental Meditation. These were compared with comparable cities that did not have one percent of the population practicing TM. It was found that those cities that reached the one percent level had trends toward decreased crime rates,[2] increased employment, enhanced quality of life.[3]

The behavior of certain coherently behaving systems in physics (such as lasers) led to the further prediction that this super-radiance effect would be even more profound when generated by those persons practicing an advanced technique of TM called the TM-Sidhi Program. The prediction was that one percent of the population practicing TM would generate this effect of coherence significantly enough in the environment to induce changes in the behaviors of persons not practicing the technique. Further, the same effect would be generated when only the *square root* of one percent of a given population was practicing the TM-Sidhi Program.

> In the vicinity of Yoga, all enmity ceases.
> -- Maharishi Patanjali, Yoga Sutras

This introduced the practical possibility of actually mobilizing teams of individuals practicing the TM-Sidhi Program and sending them to trouble spots in the world. This was accomplished on a number of occasions, and its effects were documented prospectively. That is, certain trends were evaluated, particularly in places that were hotspots during the 70s and 80s, such as South Africa, Nicaragua, Iran, Lebanon, and Israel. Teams of TM-Sidhi Program practitioners were inserted into these areas at the time of social disturbance. It was found that these teams were able to decrease disorder in society and increase coherence and positivity.[4,5] It was further noted that when the teams were removed from these areas problems tended to resume. This finding was replicated multiple times to an extremely high degree of statistical significance. Further, groups were established in certain cities in the United States and demonstrated decreases in crime rate and other indices of social disorder and distress, and increases in indices of improvement in quality of life.[6] In fact, 41 such studies involving this super-radiance effect had been performed and this effect was found to be significant in all of them.[7]

## Mister Meditator Goes to Washington

With this in mind the organization that teaches the TM and TM-Sidhi Programs approached the mayors of American cities with the proposal to decrease crime in those cities in this most cost-effective means of inserting teams of persons practicing the TM and TM-Sidhi Programs. The mayors were impressed by these findings; a demonstration of this effect was organized and performed in Washington, DC, in the summer of 1993. This study design was rigorous. The hypothesis, again, was that the insertion of a group of persons practicing the TM-Sidhi Program into the District of Columbia would lead to reduction in violent crime and social stress and improvement in the effectiveness of government. It was predicted, based on the population of Washington, DC, that bringing in 4,000 experts would lead to a decrease in violent crime of 20 percent in the District of Columbia in the summer of 1993.

> Because of the association of their name with crime, the Washington Bullets basketball team will change their name: next season they'll just be called the Bullets.
>
> -- Jay Leno

The study was executed in concert with the District of Columbia Metropolitan Police Department, which supplied the crime result statistics and was overseen by an independent project review board of scientists from leading institutions around the country. Despite the success of previous interventions in this matter, this demonstration was met with some skepticism. A Deputy Chief of the Washington, DC Police was quoted as saying, "The only thing that will reduce crime by 20 percent in the District this coming summer would be 20 inches of snow."

Now, demonstrating a decrease in crime rate might seem simple but in fact, it's not. Simply taking the rate of crime from one month to the next or one year to the next is not reliable. A number of factors influence crime rates and all of them have to be taken into account. It's a complex procedure that requires the input of many social scientists and statisticians to generate a model that will allow one to predict crime rates (and so demonstrate a change from those predicted rates).

Let me give an example. If a charlatan wanted to claim a reduction in crime rate all he would have to do is walk into your town in July, say that you have a terrible crime problem and promise that in six months he could reduce crime significantly. Six months later, in January, crime would indeed be much lower: but not due to anything he had done! Crime would be lower because crime is virtually always lower in January than in July. There are seasonal influences, influences of temperature, precipitation, weekend effects, number of hours of daylight; some even hypothesize that geomagnetic fields have effects on crime.

All these factors were evaluated and were controlled for in this Washington DC study. That is, a model was generated which could account for all fluctuations in crime rates over the past year and a half or so, and once that model was demonstrated to account for those crime rates it was then viewed prospectively, looking forward, to see whether it would continue to account for changes in crime, and, indeed, this model did work. As it turned out, the three primary considerations are: temperature, precipitation and weekend effects. That is, the hotter the weather the more crime there is. When it rains, there is less crime. Now, it doesn't matter if there are two inches of rain or eight inches of rain (crime does not drop four times as much with eight inches), it just matters whether it rains enough or not, and this has to be accounted for mathematically in modeling the amount of crime that is going to take place. Weekend effects are clear: crime rates tend to increase over the weekend compared to the weekdays.

In predicting a reduction in crime one can't say that the number of violent crimes will be exactly a particular number because that is going to vary depending upon these three factors: temperature, precipitation and weekend effects. Rather, what one does is generate a model (one that has demonstrated reliability), and show that by accounting for the variables, crime will be at a certain rate. You may have a particularly hot summer with little precipitation, which would be a high-crime summer, or you may have an especially cool summer with high precipitation, which would be a low-crime summer; but whatever the crime rates were going to be, based upon the statistical predictions, there would be a reduction in crime by 20 percent due to this intervention. That was the nature of the prediction made by these researchers.

This approach was reviewed by an independent review panel composed of scientists from the University of Maryland, University of Texas, Temple University, University of Denver School of Law, University of the District of Columbia, American University and Howard University. Before the project was undertaken all these researchers signed off on it and recognized that if the intervention was going to have an effect this was the best way to measure it and account for it.

Violent crimes were what are called HRA (Homicides, Rapes and Assaults). These were kept track of by the District of Columbia Metropolitan Police Department and the statistics were analyzed by the Institute of Science, Technology and Public Policy's Research and Evaluation Division.

Emmanuel Ross of the Planning and Research Division at the District of Columbia Police Department said, "The data on violent crime used in the experiment was provided by the Police Department. The experiment appears to have been competently undertaken and to be a good-faith effort on the part of the Institute of Science Technology and Public Policy and the Independent Project Review Board of Scientists formed to oversee the project."

## Results

The results were stark and unequivocal: crime dropped as predicted.[8]. The project took place over two months. In the first month of the project, crime rates dropped modestly. There were only about 1,000 TM-Sidhi practitioners in the group at that time. In the fifth and sixth weeks, the numbers increased to 2,500, and by the end of the demonstration project, the last two weeks of July 1993, there were almost 4,000 people participating in the demonstration. By the end of the demonstration project, when the group was largest, actual crime decreased markedly below the predicted level. This decrease was initially thought to be approximately 18 percent and was highly statistically significant. By 1995 clearer data derived from FBI statistics put the reduction at 20 percent.

A methodology that can decrease crime by 20 percent in just a few weeks is amazing. If there were a drug we could put in the water supply to accomplish this, it would be the greatest breakthrough in the history of pharmaceuticals. When the demonstration project was ended due to lack of funding at the end of July 1993, crime rates promptly came back up to the predicted level.

Dr. John Davies is the Research Coordinator for the Center of International Development and Conflict Management at the University of Maryland. He was a member of the Project Review Board who evaluated the project. He stated, "The project design was rigorous, the analysis was conducted in a highly competent manner and the results are impressive."

A Professor of Government from the University of Texas at Austin, Dr. David Edwards, was also a member of the Project Review Board. According to him, "The claim can be made plausibly that the promised practical societal impact of this research significantly exceeds that of any other ongoing social-psychological research program. For this reason alone the research along with the theory that informs it deserves the most serious evaluative consideration by the social science community." Dr. Edwards is not a practitioner of Transcendental Meditation.

Dr. Beverly Rubik, Biophysicist and Director of the Center for Frontier Sciences at Temple University, who was also a member of the Project Review Board, said, "The data show an impressive, statistically significant correlation: a decrease in violent crime for the time period over which the group meditated. An impressive number of variables were considered in analyzing the data and I'm satisfied that the research team made a serious effort to examine the data in the light of numerous other possible influences."

Another member of the Project Review Board, Ann Hughes Ph.D., Professor of Sociology and Government at the University of the District of Columbia, who also does not practice TM, asks a pointed question: "To a skeptic I would say, 'What is your solution?' I haven't seen one yet."

## A Light Kept under a Bushel

The man who reads nothing at all is better educated than the man who reads nothing but newspapers.

-- Thomas Jefferson

While remaining committed to the reduction of crime and all human suffering, Maharishi Mahesh Yogi has indicated that the need for such demonstration projects has passed. Forty-two consecutive studies have demonstrated the value of this approach, yet those in a position to implement these techniques on a broader scale have not moved forward. Maharishi had been assured, back in the

228

1960s, that if he subjected his programs to rigorous scientific scrutiny they would be recognized and acted upon by a society that prides itself on being able to separate the wheat from the chaff -- to evaluate something promptly and, if it is worthwhile, adopt it.

The efficacy of this approach has been demonstrated as dramatically and as rigorously as our modern science can demonstrate it. Further, the model that was used predicted that, had the group not disbanded, crime rates would have been reduced by 42 percent in a couple more months. A larger group and/or the same group working for an even more extended period would have brought about even greater decreases in crime. We have a technology that is utterly benign, that has been rigorously tested, that has demonstrated its ability to alleviate human suffering, yet it is not being fully used.

The degree of sophistication of the analysis may have put off some people. Perhaps looking at the raw numbers was confusing. I have described the methodology of what is called *time-series analysis*, which is really the only way to analyze such data. As I mentioned, you can't just take the number of robberies in January of 1993 and compare it to the number of robberies in July; nor can you take July 1992 and compare it to 1993, without accounting for these confounding factors of time, temperature, precipitation and weekend effects.

The reporting about this has been lethargic. Most of the articles I saw approached the story tongue-in-cheek. Many seemed to presume that the hypothesis that consciousness is a field that can be influenced by mental activities and can then propagate effects to others, is absurd; and that any experiment that could demonstrate its efficacy is *a priori* a flawed experiment. This is a completely unscientific and prejudiced attitude.

Perhaps the best insight into this prejudice comes from Goethe who said, "One should never bother to try to prove things much, because our proofs are only variations of our opinions, and the contrary-minded listen to neither the one nor the other."

But journalists have a job to do and I would ask only that they do it well. Either this experiment is a fraud and those persons who have perpetrated it deserve to be held up to the strongest of public and scientific censure; or, it is not. If it is fraudulent, it would be playing upon the fears and hopes of people in a most callous and unforgivable way, and those responsible would deserve to be exposed. But, if the technology does what it has been proved to do, then it is one of the greatest discoveries of our time and deserves the widest possible attention.

We have elected representatives whose job it is to hold the reins of control in society, to take the taxes which the population generates and use them in appropriate fashion. Frighteningly, concern was expressed by some municipalities that if this approach worked, they could be faced with the loss of federal crime-fighting funds. We have crime bills that have billions of dollars to spend on crime prevention, and yet the best they can come up with is midnight basketball! I'm glad to have brighter streetlights but this is a pathetic effort in the prevention of crime. It certainly does not compare to the reduction of crime by 20 percent simply by having people generate coherence in the depths of their own awareness.

By not acting, we are still acting. We are acting to defer implementation of an effective policy. Every day we don't do something about this, more persons are maimed and killed in drive-by shootings, more robberies are perpetrated, more assaults occur, more human suffering is generated. To fail to act because nothing can be done is frustrating, but to fail to act when something can be done is either negligence or ignorance.

## CHAPTER TWENTY

# Platform for a New Tomorrow

> Your public servants serve you right.
> -- Adlai Stevenson

Our attention thus far in this book has been largely on our own internal dynamics, and for good reason -- those are most important. For all the reasons I've discussed in this book, what is going on in our hearts and minds is in large measure going to dictate the quality of our life experience. By operating on this subtle aspect of life, we generate pervasive positive influences throughout our environment.

This is in contrast to most of what we see about us in fields of human interaction. Now certainly you can appreciate that the means of bringing about change in the larger world are usually hamhanded. Perhaps the grossest aspect of life in the United States is political life. Indeed, a poll published in Time Magazine found that most people believe that crime and politicians are the two greatest problems facing the nation. Politics as a field is a quagmire. Party politics seems to be contributing to problems more than helping them. Partisan opposition generates paralysis in government. Partisan agendas take precedence over the needs of the people and of the nation as a whole. Winning power is more important than using it for anything constructive. In the meantime, we continue to experience the brunt of all of the problems.

But is this really the fault of the politicians?

The political life of a nation mirrors the level of awareness of that nation. More simply put, we get the government that we deserve. That is true particularly in the United States where we continually have the opportunity to change the government. We, the electorate, are possessed with the power to turn out any or all of our elected representatives and replace them with those of our choice. Similarly, we are the members of the political parties; their platforms are our platforms. Sometimes it happens that there is some discrepancy between the beliefs and attitudes of the population and the political parties or the governments that represents them. In extreme cases, this leads to revolution. Discrepancies extant in the United States are not nearly so devastating, I believe, but there clearly is need for change.

## The Natural Law Party

There is a new political party in the United States based on the idea of prevention-oriented government providing proven solutions for problems through scientifically proven methods. Also, it brings a message of conflict-free politics. While disagreements naturally tend to take place among independently minded persons, the type of conflict and divisiveness we see now in our political arena is disturbing to the progress of the nation as a whole.

The Natural Law Party was founded in 1992 to bring the light of science into politics; to introduce common sense and cost-effective, tested solutions to our nation's problems. (While some members of this party practice TM, most do not, yet.) The Natural Law Party advocates fundamental reform in virtually every aspect of national life, including education, the economy, health, crime and rehabilitation, energy and the environment, agriculture, defense, government waste and the strength of the family. There is no reason why our nation should not be experiencing the peace, prosperity and happiness that are the natural consequences of properly using the bounty nature has provided for us.

The Natural Law Party is the only political party that provides these powerful techniques to eliminate stress, tension and disorder in both the individual and society. The other parties have not yet demonstrated their competence to create a government that can effectively prevent problems and produce a society free of violence and suffering.

Let's consider some aspects of the platform of this political party.

## 1. Health Care.

As I've mentioned before, America now spends over a trillion dollars per year on health and this health bill continues to escalate. To extend meaningful health benefits to all Americans without ruining the economy, we must decrease health care outlays per person. Since curing disease is becoming constantly more expensive, the only effective way to decrease expenditures is to prevent disease. Most disease in the United States is preventable. Let's look at the percentage and number of deaths in the United States and their causes.

According to the Journal of the American Medical Association, tobacco caused 400,000 deaths in 1990. This is 19 percent of total deaths in the United States. About two million people die each year in the United States and 400,000 of those deaths can be attributed to tobacco. If you recall, over 50,000 Americans died in the entire Vietnam War; yet, almost *eight times that many die every year in the United States due to tobacco* use, which obviously is completely preventable, as I've previously discussed.

Three hundred thousand deaths, or 14 percent, are due to problems with diet or exercise. One hundred thousand deaths are due to alcohol; that's five percent of total deaths. Ninety thousand deaths are due to microbial agents, infections. Sixty thousand are due to toxic agents. Thirty-five thousand are due to firearms. Thirty thousand are due to sexual behavior. Twenty-five thousand are due to motor vehicles. And, twenty thousand are due to the illicit use of drugs. The vast majority of these are preventable.

Most people believe that prevention is important even though it's not what we're trained to address in medical school.[1,2] Ninety three percent of patients believe that promotion of preventive care is very important, but only 46 percent rate their physician as excellent in that area. And only 10 percent of physicians rate their training in prevention as excellent.[3] This demonstrates the need for a new approach in medical education. Maharishi Medical Colleges and Maharishi Institutes for Medical Education are being established in the USA and around the world to address this need.

233

In 1990, the nation's health goals were set forth by the US Public Health Service.[4] Many of these targets seem unlikely to be met by our current approaches. This is especially true in the areas of nutrition, tobacco, drug abuse, mental health and mental disorders, violent and abusive behaviors, as well as cardiovascular disease, cancer and other illnesses. The Natural Law Party offers programs that we can more readily fulfill these objectives.

The Natural Law Party promotes prevention-oriented health education and prevention-oriented natural medicines that have the demonstrated capacity to create healthier citizens and cut health-care costs by more than half.[5] Through proper prevention, the Natural Law Party could promote a disease-free society, and prevent untold pain and suffering while saving the nation five hundred billion dollars a year in health-care costs. These savings would realistically allow the government or private sector to extend high-quality health care to the tens of millions of Americans who do not currently qualify for government-sponsored health care and have not been able to afford the high cost of private health insurance. The Natural Law Party is unique in offering health care for all while providing a net cost savings for the nation.

## 2. Crime.

Most violent crimes are committed by hardcore repeat offenders. There are four reasons to incarcerate these people: 1) to punish them 2) to deter others 3) to remove them from society, and 4) to rehabilitate them. Unless they serve a life sentence, they'll be back on the street sometime. Unfortunately, prison life does not tend to rehabilitate, it rather reinforces the tendency toward a life of crime. Despite a couple of decades of get-tough policies with longer mandatory sentences, crime in America is still a nightmare.

The Natural Law Party recognizes that criminal tendencies arise from accumulated stress and the inability to fulfill one's desires in a lawful way. By eliminating stress in the collective consciousness of society by promoting education that develops the creativity and intelligence of every person and by providing effective rehabilitation of prison inmates, the Natural Law Party is unique in its ability to eliminate the root causes of crime. For example, 22 demonstration projects in this country and many more abroad have shown that pro-

grams supported by the Natural Law Party, including Transcendental Meditation, decrease stress and hostility among even maximum-
security prisoners and reduce the rate at which released prisoners
return to prison (recidivism) by 30 to 40 percent,[6,7] whereas prison
education, vocational training and psychotherapy did not. Also, as
discussed in the previous chapter, 42 studies have shown that groups
practicing the TM-Sidhi Program together reduce social stress, violence and crime.

## 3. Capital Punishment.

In the current epidemic of crime and lawlessness in America,
capital punishment has gained a broad base of popular support as a
strong incentive against the most severe crimes and as a cost-
effective alternative to the high cost of incarceration for those with
long prison terms resulting from severe crimes. However, history
and recent research have convincingly shown that capital punishment neither deters crime nor saves the taxpayer money. We believe
a shift in public sentiment concerning capital punishment would
naturally occur once the Party introduced the following proven solutions to the problems of violent crime.

- 1. Effective crime prevention based on programs that reduce
  stress in the society and bring the life of the nation into accord
  with both natural law and national law.
- 2. Effective rehabilitation programs in the nation's prisons that
  have shown to dramatically reduce recidivism; and,
- 3. Modern and effective means of assessing the level of rehabilitation of the nation's prison population in order to determine the
  readiness of inmates to return to society and contribute produc-
  tively to the life of the nation.

## 4. The Economy and Jobs.

Lowering taxes is the single most powerful fiscal action a
government can take to stimulate the economy and provide the basis
for long-term economic growth and prosperity. The Natural Law
Party alone has the ability to cut taxes significantly on a realistic
and responsible basis. Most other parties have promised lower taxes
but have been unable to live up to those promises because of their

inability to address effectively the extent and complexity of problems faced by the government in the areas of crime, spiraling health costs, etc.

Sumitomo Heavy Industries in Japan found that TM improved health[8,9] and performance among its workers. Some U.S. employers have also been as innovative, finding increased productivity, decreased labor costs, decreased absenteeism,[10] increased job satisfaction, improved work and personal relationships and decreased desire to change jobs.[11]

The Natural Law Party, through these and other cost-effective solutions to the nation's health care crisis, crime, rehabilitation and other problem areas, would save the nation hundreds of billions of dollars annually. These savings would allow the government to eliminate the budget deficit while lowering taxes significantly for both individuals and industry. Lowering taxes and lifting the burden of health care costs from our nation's businesses and industries would provide the basis for long-term economic growth, create new jobs and eliminate unemployment now and in the future. The economy would also flourish on the basis of the increased creativity and intelligence provided by the Natural Law Party's effective programs in education.

## 5. Education.

Education should prepare our youth to compete successfully in the 21st century and to develop their full potential. Thus, education should be for higher consciousness. The Natural Law Party promotes education that has been shown to enhance academic performance,[12] and to develop intelligence,[13] creativity, moral reasoning and higher states of consciousness for all students[14,15,16]. Consciousness is the most basic element in education, but existing educational programs contain no knowledge of consciousness and no scientifically-proven technologies for the development of consciousness. The Natural Law Party would supplement traditional academic knowledge with knowledge of the knower, or consciousness, along with scientifically validated programs to develop the full potential of consciousness. Education should provide the ability to think and act spontaneously in accord with natural law along with the intellectual understanding provided by existing education. Education should include development of consciousness and those procedures that allow the student to access natural law, to take natural advantage of the laws of nature, and to fulfill his or her desires in the most effective and life-supporting manner.

The Natural Law Party promotes education that expands human comprehension to include the most fundamental and universal level of natural law: the unified field of all the laws of nature, unfolding life at every level of the manifest universe, thereby creating universal individuals -- global citizens who know how to fulfill their own interests while simultaneously promoting the interest of their families and of society as a whole. Only education that promotes ideal citizenship can stem the tide of crime and lawlessness that afflicts the nation. Only education which develops the student's ability to use natural law in daily life will make education relevant to the student and stop the growing attrition from our nation's schools and colleges. One such university is already established in the United States: Maharishi University of Management in Fairfield, Iowa, which provides a model institution that has incorporated the educational programs promoted by the Natural Law Party, resulting in demonstrably improved educational outcomes[17,18] and a higher quality of life among its students, faculty and alumni.

> It is an axiom in political science that unless a people are educated and enlightened it is idle to expect the continuance of civil liberty or the capacity for self-government.
> -- Texas Declaration of Independence

## 6. The Drug Problem.

Drug abuse is destroying lives and destabilizing societies. The practice of the United States has largely been one of trying to interdict drugs as they enter the country and arresting and incarcerating those who supply them. But almost everyone agrees that the damage can be stopped only by reducing the demand for drugs and alcohol. No one, up to now, has had an effective program to prevent and reverse addiction. The drug problem has its origin in accumulated stress in individual life and in the collective consciousness of society. The accumulation of stress, particularly in the nation's urban environments, is born of continued violations of natural law by the citizens of the nation. This violation of natural law is, in turn, due to families' ignorance of natural law and an educational system that does not train the individual to think and act spontaneously in accord with natural law.

The most effective defense against drugs is proper education, in the home and in the schools. We need education that brings life into harmony with natural law, develops intelligence and creativity, builds self-confidence and reduces stress, thereby eliminating the tendency toward drug dependence. Education must be satisfying and relevant to the student's own life if it is to prevent drop-outs who become the principal targets of drug-related crimes. When education succeeds in promoting enjoyment in life, the experience of taking drugs becomes less appealing by contrast. In that context, drug abuse cannot be established because people have no desire for drugs.

For those currently suffering from drug dependency, the Natural Law Party promotes programs that dramatically reduce drug dependence by eliminating stress and restoring balance to the individual physiology and psychology.

The total cost for addiction in the United States is higher than for any other health problem, including cardiovascular disease and cancer. Alcohol and other drugs are involved in 52 percent of all traffic fatalities and 54 percent of violent crimes in the United States. The number of people with substance abuse problems added to the number of people whose lives are affected by drug addicts totals almost 70 percent of the American population.[19] The Office of National Drug Control Policy estimates the annual social costs of illicit drug use (including health care, criminal justice, lost productivity, etc.) to be $67 billion.

A meta-analysis of 198 studies published for the first time in the book Self Recovery[20] reveals that TM produced a significantly higher recovery rate from addiction than conventional recovery programs. Over an 18- to 24-month period, abstinence ranged from 51 percent to 89 percent for subjects practicing TM, compared to 20 to 30 percent for subjects using other treatment programs.

Particularly encouraging were the results with severe, transient skid-row alcoholics, who were the subjects of one of the studies published in Self Recovery. Of course, as one would imagine, this group is particularly difficult to treat and to study because they are not only the most prone to relapse but are difficult to track after their release from a treatment program. Researchers found that adding TM to their routine professional counseling and attendance at meetings of Alcoholics Anonymous more than doubled the sobriety rate for these severe alcoholics. This finding was all the more powerful because follow up was extraordinarily thorough. Researchers were able to maintain contact with 69 out of 70 subjects over a two-year period.

Dr. Skip Alexander, the editor of this book, explains why one is able to get such surprising results with skid-row alcoholics. He explains that he saw similar results as a graduate student when he studied the impact of Transcendental Meditation upon prisoners. "When someone has truly given up," Dr. Alexander said, "and then is given a first-hand experience of well being deep within, they're prepared to go all the way. The experience replaces their despair with hope and continues to support them on their journey to full recovery."[19] For all of us who feel despair at the magnitude of drug abuse and crime, this can only be encouraging.

## 7. Restoration of the Inner-Cities.

The Natural Law Party strongly promotes programs to improve the quality of life in our nation's inner-cities. Job training, technical training and management training are essential as programs that allow our citizens to use more and more of their creative potential. Reducing deep-seated stress and tension in our inner-city environments is essential if such programs are to have any chance of success.

The Natural Law Party supports programs that have already been used in inner-city environments throughout the country and have been shown to reduce stress and tension in the collective consciousness of society. These programs, which have been implemented in community centers and prevention-oriented health, education and stress management centers in the inner-city environments, have been shown to reduce not only physiological symptoms

of stress such as high blood pressure but also the symptoms of societal stress such as crime, violence, accidents, and hospital admissions,
while promoting positive trends throughout society.    It is only
through the addition of such programs to dissolve stress and create
coherence in the collective consciousness of society that we can prevent the build up of stress and frustration that leads to outbreaks of
violence such as we saw here in Los Angeles in 1992.

## 8. Strengthening Families.

When stress and frustration increase in society, the integrity
of family life, so important to the youth of our nation, is severely un-
dermined by domestic violence and divorce.   The only solution is to
reduce and eventually eliminate accumulated stress in the whole
population so that individuals are spontaneously able to make the
most life-supporting decisions in their personal lives -- decisions that
are most nourishing to the tender lives of their children.   While the
Natural Law Party recognizes that diversity is natural in society, the
Party's programs would create a harmonizing influence on individual
and collective consciousness so that diverse cultures and individual
values could coexist without creating conflict among family members
and in society as a whole.

The Natural Law Party also upholds the role of the senior
members of our society as a source of wisdom and guidance for the
family and the community.  With the growth of consciousness, this
significant role for the older generation would spontaneously unfold,
and it would become a delight for different generations of a family to
live together, enriching each other's lives and helping to overcome
the problems of isolation, loneliness and childcare prevalent today.

## 9. International Instability and Defense Spending.

The Natural Law Party appreciates the need to maintain the
alertness of our nation's armed forces even as the nation naturally
shifts from the military economy of the Cold War era to a new peace-
time economy.   The Natural Law Party cautions against a too-rapid
deescalation of military preparedness until a stable state of world
peace is achieved.   At the same time, the Natural Law Party is
unique in offering a peace-promoting technology that would serve to

neutralize international tensions and promote stability and harmony within the family of nations. As a result of this peace-promoting technology, which is based on groups of experts collectively practicing TM and the TM-Sidhi Program, the Natural Law Party can ensure a peaceful world and thereby guarantee a steadily growing peace dividend to sustain life-supporting programs at home. Political parties that promote decreased defense spending without the technology to ensure world peace are not acting responsibly. Only through the addition of technology to generate an actual physical influence of peace among the family of nations can a political party responsibly cut defense spending and divert the precious resources of the nation toward more humane programs at home and abroad.

The Natural Law Party believes that U.S. foreign policy should shift immediately from one based principally on military aid to one based on the exportation of knowledge. American expertise in the areas of business administration and agriculture, supplemented when necessary with economic support, should replace military aid as the principal role of America in foreign affairs. This type of assistance would allow developing countries to become self-sufficient financially, eliminate poverty and create a more prosperous world. The U.S. and every other nation would be the beneficiaries of such a foreign policy by creating more affluent markets for our exports.

In addition, the Natural Law Party supports the immediate creation of a prevention wing within the military: a group whose primary purpose would be to prevent the outbreak of war while preserving and strengthening international peace. By training even one percent of military personnel in the Natural Law Party's proven programs for reducing stress in individual and national life, every nation could create a true peace-keeping force that could maintain a powerful, integrated, coherent national consciousness and thereby keep enmities from arising. By applying the Natural Law Party's technology for ensuring world peace, all nations could enjoy strength and harmony in international relations.

## 10. The Rights of Women and Minorities.

The rights of women and minorities are guaranteed by the Constitution, and the Natural Law Party would support any legislation deemed necessary to uphold those Constitutional rights. At the same time, the Natural Law Party recognizes the difficulties in legislating equality and regards such legislation as a stop-gap measure.

Ultimately, the Natural Law Party believes prejudice can be dissolved at its base by eliminating stress in society, expanding comprehension through proper education and enlivening the harmonizing and unifying characteristics of natural law in the collective consciousness of society. Natural law is the element in the universe that constantly nourishes the lives of every individual and every species.

Until now, democracy has stood ready to compromise the interests of the minority for the sake of the majority. This is because it has been based on principles that are not sufficiently comprehensive to be simultaneously nourishing to everyone. By compromising the interests of the minority, democracy inevitably leaves some segments of the population unfulfilled. As a result, stress and frustration grow in the collective consciousness of the nation and inevitably erupt as crime, sickness and other problems. By basing its administration on natural law, the Natural Law Party would offer a form of administration so universally nourishing that all citizens, including currently disadvantaged groups, would be simultaneously fulfilled.

## 11. Abortion.

The Natural Law Party's prevention-oriented approach to government includes prevention of abortion on a realistic basis.

The Natural Law Party promotes education that expands comprehension, develops intelligence and creativity, dissolves stress and promotes far-sighted action, free from problems. Through such education, we could reduce the number of abortions more than through any legislation that would restrict or prohibit abortions.

History shows that it is difficult to legislate morality. New legislation to restrict abortions would be effective only in reducing the number of legal abortions; the decisions and behaviors that lead to unsafe illegal abortions would persist. The role of government should be to provide the type of leadership and education that brings life spontaneously into accord with natural law, prevents mistakes and brings the support of natural law to the individual and the nation.

This policy of prevention would unite two heretofore irreconcilable factions. Those who are pro-life have found fulfillment in this position because they wish to effect real decreases in the number of abortions occurring in this country; this can be achieved through education and prevention, not effectively through legislation. Those who are pro-choice would also be satisfied because they want to keep this difficult moral and emotional decision in the hands of those whose lives are affected most, a principle the Natural Law Party also upholds.

The Natural Law Party believes government's role should not be to regulate details of citizens' lives through ever-increasing legislation but rather to provide the education, leadership and programs that allow all citizens more effectively to govern their own lives in greater harmony with natural law.

> Those who are too smart to engage in politics are punished by being governed by those who are dumber.
>
> -- Plato

More information about the Natural Law Party can be obtained by contacting its National Headquarters at (515) 472-2040 or (800) 465-7971; the address is 51 N. Washington St., Fairfield, Iowa 52556.

It has been interesting for me, personally, to witness the hoops through which the Natural Law Party has had to jump over the last few years. I was completely unaware that there is a strong disincentive in this country for third parties to succeed. The laws with regard to ballot access are tilted quite unconscionably toward the two established parties.

This should not be surprising, since the laws are written by legislators who by and large are members of either the Republican or Democratic Party and it is not in their best interest to invite further competition or new ideas. Despite this, the Natural Law Party is the fastest growing political party in the country, and is the third largest party in many states, including my home state of California.

It has been suggested that participation in a third party (or in politics in general) is a waste of time since you can almost guarantee that either a Republican or a Democrat is going to be elected to any significant office and that a vote for someone other than a Republican or a Democrat is just a wasted vote. I submit that in fact the opposite is true.

If we cast a vote out of expedience -- if we cast a vote for someone we do not believe is the best candidate but who is more likely to win or who is not as far from our point of view as the other major candidate -- we're not really voting our conscience. If we do not vote our conscience, if we, the electorate, do not vote for what is right and what are real solutions to the problems of our nation, how can we expect those we elect to vote their consciences, to do what is right for the nation? They are our representatives. The influences we generate in casting our vote will be recapitulated in the awareness of those for whom we vote. So we should vote for those candidates -- Republicans, Libertarians, whatever -- who will be simple and honest and oriented toward solutions rather than just oriented toward politics as usual; but more importantly we should be simple, truthful, and vote for the candidate we believe in.

## CHAPTER TWENTY-ONE

# Heal Your Self,

# Heal Your World

> Anyone willing to be corrected is on the pathway to life.
> Anyone refusing has lost his chance.
>
> -- Proverbs 10:17

The scope of this book has ranged from the molecules of neurotransmitters to the behaviors that lead to enlightenment; from the minute scale of subatomic particles to the laws of nature which govern the universe; from the small individual decisions we make regarding our state of mind to the societal changes group meditative practice can bring about. There is really nothing outside of our range of potential influence.

So what are we to do now? I will synopsize some steps you can take to promote health in yourself, your family, your community and the world.

1. Attend an introductory lecture on **Transcendental Meditation**, then begin the practice of TM and practice it regularly. The times and locations of these free lectures can be ascertained by calling one of the Maharishi Ayur-Veda or Maharishi Vedic Universities or Schools nationwide. A list of them is in Appendix A. You can also get information from them on all of the other programs and approaches discussed in this book (such as consultations with physicians or other experts, herbal preparations, and so forth).

2.     Review and attend to these pillars of Maharishi Ayur-Veda and integrate them into your life: **mind, food and digestion/ingestion**, and **routine**.

3.     You may find it difficult to implement these interventions on your own. **Consult a doctor** who has been trained in Maharishi Ayur-Veda. Such a doctor can be found by calling 1 800-THE-VEDA (843-8332) and/or by calling one of the Maharishi Ayur-Veda Schools listed in Appendix A.

4.     By calling the same 800 number, you can get information about the **courses** offered by the Maharishi Ayur-Veda Universities and Schools and Maharishi Vedic Universities and Schools. There are courses on the Discovery of Veda and Vedic Literature in Human Physiology, self-pulse diagnosis, diet, prevention, yoga asanas and a number of others (see Appendix A).

5.     Read through the chapters on **behavioral rasayanas** in this book. There is a list of the behavioral rasayanas on page 119. Make a copy and tape it to your refrigerator or bathroom mirror. It's not important to dwell on them, but if you simply read through them each morning they'll be livelier in your awareness.

6.     **Panchakarma (Maharishi Rejuvenation)**. While many of the programs of Maharishi Ayur-Veda are essentially daily recommendations you can follow on your own at home on a daily basis, you cannot administer panchakarma to yourself. These purificatory and rejuvenative treatments are offered at many of the Maharishi Ayur-Veda Medical Centers which are usually co-located with the Maharishi Ayur-Veda Schools. Information about these also is available in Appendix A.

7.     There are a number of **books** that one can read on these topics. They are listed in Appendix B.

It is beneath the dignity of humankind to live lives fettered by misery and ignorance. The means to rise above such a life are available to us and it is part of the wonder of nature that the things we do to strengthen and enlighten ourselves also have these heavenly effects on the world around us.

There is a new world waiting for each of us. We need only create it.

# Appendices

# Appendix A

## Resources

## Section I: Course Offerings of the Maharishi Universities and Schools

The text of this book introduces many of the topics covered in these courses. The scope of this book, though, is necessarily limited. The courses are much greater in depth and breadth; the participant will find knowledge much richer than I have been able to provide in these pages. This list is not all-inclusive; more and different programs will probably be added to the curricula of the schools as time goes on.

### Transcendental Meditation Program

This seven step program is the cornerstone of Maharishi's Vedic Approach to Health. Each step is about 90 minutes to two hours long.

Step 1: Free introductory lecture

Step 2: Preparatory lecture

Step 3: Private interview with your TM instructor (may be brief)

Step 4: Personal individual instruction in TM

Steps 5, 6, & 7: Verification and validation of experience ("three nights checking"). Always done on three consecutive days or evenings.

At the end of this course one is expert and self-sufficient in the practice of TM, on your own, 20 minutes twice a day. It is recommended though that one has one's TM "checked" weekly for the first month and monthly for the first year, and take advantage of the free life-long follow-up program.

"Meditation is making research into yourself and into the subtler fields of activity. Day after day we culture our minds with the deep silence of our own Being. This is not the inert silence of a stone, but creative silence. We decrease activity until silence becomes creative, and we sit in creative silence and close the gates of perception for insight into the content of life. In meditation, we research the field without time and space and activity and yet produce a useful effect while conducting the research. In the non activity of meditation, we dwell in the glorious field of life, and we are supported by the love of God."[1] -- Maharishi Mahesh Yogi

## 33 Lesson Videotape Course on the Science of Creative Intelligence

This is the original complete description of the source, elaboration, and expression of the field of creative intelligence in multiple aspects of life. First taped in 1972, it is clear that all of the nuggets of knowledge about pure consciousness amplified upon in subsequent years were present in this course.

## 16 Lesson Course on Self-Pulse Reading

This course provides the student with the theory and practical technique necessary to detect and evaluate one's own pulse. In the process of learning Self-Pulse, one not only detects states of physiological balance and imbalance, but also, through the flow of attention, one has a balancing influence on any area of imbalance, thereby spontaneously enhancing physiological integration. The student gains the ability to distinguish the superficial, middle and deep levels of the pulse. The course unfolds the structure of human physiology from the perspective of Maharishi's Vedic Science. This perspective is integrated with Western knowledge of the bodily systems. Students learn to detect and correct not only obvious physiological imbalances, but also imbalances that are developing before any overt symptoms appear. This 16 lesson course provides a gradual, systematic and effortless mode of learning Self-Pulse reading.

The format allows ample time to learn, practice and master the principles and evaluation of the pulse.

## 16 Lesson Course on Prevention

"Avert the danger which has not yet come." This course offers each student a holistic approach to perfect health through prevention oriented Maharishi Ayur-Veda. It provides insight into the fundamental structure of health and the relationships among all aspects of nature: individual, social, and cosmic. One is introduced to the different aspects of the Vedic literature -- the blueprint of creation in its total perfection. We learn to enhance purity and balance in Vata, Pitta, and Kapha through recommendations regarding diet, behavior and the cycles of nature. By aligning the physiology with the physiology of nature we create a state of perfect balance. This provides an understanding about how this balance is created and maintained through the various approaches of Maharishi Ayur-Veda by enlivening the symmetrical unbroken flow of life in bliss. This permits life to be lived in a state of perfect balance, "averting any danger," and creating a life of health, happiness, and enlightenment, as well as promoting the creation of heaven on earth.

## 16 Lesson Course on Maharishi Yoga

This course teaches the Asanas (postures) of the body through which the individual experiences the state of Yoga (union) in mind and body. Yoga Asanas are described in the Vedic literature as reestablishing the individual physiology on the level of the cosmic physiology. The ultimate purpose of making the body as flexible as the cosmic physiology is to support the state of complete self-sufficiency, immortality, and invincibility. These qualities of pure consciousness as Maharishi Patanjali defined in his Yoga Sutras, can be infused into the physiology. The Yoga Asanas are complementary and preparatory to Transcendental Meditation and the TM-Sidhi Program. During the course, the holistic understanding of the Yoga philosophy in terms of mind-body integration as taught by Maharishi will be understood. Through the 16 lessons students will learn different asanas. Each asana will be examined on the level of personal experience and intellectual understanding. The influence of each asana on the physiology is examined from the perspective of modern science and scientific research and from the perspective of Maharishi Vedic Science to create perfect health for the individual and society.

## 16 Lesson Course on Diet, Digestion & Nutrition

This course studies the fundamental constituents of human physiology and of the food we eat, and of their common origin in the field of pure intelligence. The nature and quality of different foods and their effects on physiological functioning are examined in detail from the perspective of Maharishi Ayur-Veda. The influences of nature's cycles and one's own constitution on digestion and metabolism are discussed. One learns practical dietary recommendations such as the how, when, and where of eating for optimal digestion, including the influences of mind, senses, and behavior on digestion, in order to promote balance in the body. The student is introduced to the nature of the final and finest product of metabolism, Ojas, and ways to enhance its appearance. The production of Ojas is considered to determine the overall strength and immunity of the body. The ability of the body to remain free of the accumulated impurities that result from incomplete digestion and metabolism is examined. The course concludes with an analysis of the relationship of diet and digestion to consciousness, intellect, emotions, mind, senses, motor organs, and behavior.

## The Discovery of Veda and Vedic Literature in Human Physiology

This course will explore in depth the findings of Dr. Tony Nader (see the end of chapter 18). It is not necessary to have previous knowledge of anatomy, physiology or Vedic Literature, as all the required information will be covered in the course.

Many other courses may become available soon, depending on location, including: Higher States of Consciousness, The Art of Metabolizing Experience, Maharishi Jyotish, Maharishi Vedic Observatory, Maharishi Sthapatya Veda, One Verse of Rk Veda Offers Total Knowledge, Sanskrit Language, Reversal of Aging, Crime Prevention and Rehabilitation, Maharishi's Supreme Political Science -- Automation in Administration, How to Gain Support of Nature, Invincible Defense to Prevent the Birth of an Enemy, Courses for Doctors, and more.

# Section II: Maharishi Schools, Maharishi Ayur-Veda clinics and TM Centers Nationwide

The author's clinic is in Pacific Palisades (Los Angeles), CA:

**17308 Sunset Blvd      Phone: (310)454-5531      fax: (310)454-7841**
**Pacific Palisades, CA 90272**

The Maharishi Vedic School is next door at 17310 Sunset Blvd.

   Phone: 459-3522      fax: 459-8146

| City and State | Phone | Fax | Address | Zip |
|---|---|---|---|---|
| Fayetteville, AR | (501)443-4013 | 582-9029 | 21 S. College Ave | 72701 |
| Phoenix, AZ | (602)254-2552 | 254-8614 | 1110 N. 16th St. | 85006 |
| Cobb Mt., CA | (707)928-5213 | 928-4329 | 15205 Hwy 175 | 95426 |
| Tustin, CA | (714)832-0328 | 832-0320 | 18682 E. 17th St. | 92705 |
| Mtn View, CA | (415)967-7242 | 967-4373 | 2525 Charleston | 94043 |
| Fair Oaks, CA | (916)961-0320 | 961-8140 | 10112 Fair Oaks#4 | 95628 |
| San Diego, CA | (619)296-6565 | 296-6182 | 3878 Old Town#200 | 92110 |
| San Jose, CA | (408)247-8963 | 247-8974 | 3920 Williams Rd | 95117 |
| Aurora, CO | (303)360-7014 | 344-9479 | 13650 E. Colfax | 80011 |
| New Haven, CT | (203)562-7000 | 562-0432 | 205 Whitney Ave. | 06511 |
| **Washington, D.C.** | **(202)244-2700** | **244-7695** | **4910 Mass. Av NW #315** | **20037** |
| Avon Park, FL | (813)453-6819 | 453-5551 | 1609 Lake Lotela | 33825 |
| Gainesville, FL | (904)338-1249 | 378-3967 | 1125 SW 2nd Av | 32601 |
| Tampa, FL | (813)831-7181/7979 | 831-1625 | 4525 S Manhattan | 33611 |
| Atlanta, GA | (404)351-9897/250-9560 | 352-1886 | 1750 Commerce Dr NW | 30318 |
| Honolulu, HI | (808)988-2266 | 988-5129 | 2407 Parker Pl | 96822 |
| **Fairfield, IA (The Raj)** | **(800)248-9050 or (515)472-9580** | | **Box 503 RR 4** | **52556** |
| Boise, ID | (208)336-5144 | 336-5388 | 928 Main St. | 83702 |
| Chicago, IL | (312)431-1212 | 431-0404 | 636 S Michigan Av | 60605 |
| Indianapolis, IN | (317)923-2873 | 923-0536 | 3434 N Washington | 46205 |
| Overland Park,KS | (913)341-1444/1888 | 341-2545 | 9303 W 75th St. #210 | 66204 |
| Baton Rouge, LA | (504)355-6638 | 355-6618 | 7370 Airline Hwy | 70805 |

| City and State | Phone | Fax | Address | Zip |
|---|---|---|---|---|
| **Lancaster, MA** | **(508)365-4549** | **368-7557** | **679 George Hill** | **01523** |
| Cambridge, MA | (617)876-4581 | 497-5597 | 33 Garden St. | 02138 |
| Bethesda, MD | (301)652-7002 | 652-1080 | 4818 Montgomery Ln | 20814 |
| Portland, ME | (207)774-1108 | 874-2455 | 575 Forest Ave. | 04103 |
| Rochester Hills,MI | (810)299-4814 | 853-5165 | 43 Timberview | 48307 |
| St. Paul, MN | (612)641-0925 | | 266 Summit Ave. | 55102 |
| St. Louis, MO | (314)367-1112 | 367-9351 | 275 Union Bl #1602 | 63108 |
| Waverly, MO | (816)493-2285 | 493-2287 | RR1, Box 90 | 64096 |
| Ashville, NC | (704)254-5301/4350 | 254-4352 | 301 E Chestnut Rd | 28801 |
| Raleigh, NC | (919)783-5544 | 783-0474 | 3916 E Knickerbocker Pkwy | 27612 |
| Omaha, NE | (402)345-6656 | 345-3221 | 306 S 16th St | 68102 |
| Antrim, NH | (603)588-2063/2012 | 588-2055 | 78 Old N Branch Rd | 03440 |
| Goffstown, NH | (603)644-0890 | 644-3790 | 214 St. Anselm Dr | 03045 |
| Asbury Park, NJ | (908)774-4000/9446 | 774-6969 | 1401 Ocean #718 | 07712 |
| Montclair, NJ | (201)746-2120 | 746-1003 | 109 Valley Rd | 07042 |
| Livingston Manor,NY | (914)439-3880 | 439-5014 | PO Box 370 | 12758 |
| New York, NY | (212)645-0202 | 645-0205 | 12 W 21st St | 10010 |
| Rocky River, OH | (216)333-6700 | 333-4180 | 19474 Center Ridge Rd | 44116 |
| Oklahoma City | (405)840-0108 | same | 2125 SW 65th St. | 73159 |
| Tulsa, OK | (918)747-0171 | 743-5849 | 4956 Peoria Ave. | 74105 |
| Philadelphia, PA | (215)732-8464 | 732-0258 | 234 S 22nd St. | 19103 |
| Providence, RI | (401)751-1518 | 751-7448 | 141 Waterman St. | 02906 |
| Sioux Falls, SD | (605)330-1940 | same | 4201 S Minnesota | 57105 |
| Arlington, TX | (817)649-8686 | 640-7874 | 601 Ave H East | 76011 |
| Dallas, TX | (214)821-8686 | 821-8703 | 5600 N Central Expwy | 75206 |
| Houston, TX | (713)659-7002 | 659-2846 | 801 Calhoun St. | 77002 |
| Fairfax, VA | (703)273-6631 | 273-4410 | 10801 Main St. | 22030 |
| Burlington, VT | (802)658-9119 | 658-7751 | 88 N. Prospect St. | 05401 |
| Bellevue, WA | (206)646-9429 | 646-0818 | 12320 NE 8th St. | 98005 |
| Seattle, WA | (206)281-7758 | 217-9021 | 321 1st Ave. West | 98119 |
| Madison, WI | (608)255-4447 | 255-4489 | 23 Pinckney St. | 53703 |

Those in **bold** face are currently offering panchakarma treatments.

# Section III: Other resources

Maharishi Amrit Kalash and other products are commercially available through Maharishi Ayur-Veda Products International; Phone: 1 800 ALL-VEDA (1 800 255-8332).

More information about the Natural Law Party can be obtained by contacting its National Headquarters at (515) 472-2040 or (800) 465-7971; the address is 51 N. Washington St., Fairfield, Iowa 52556.

To find a doctor trained in Maharishi Ayur-Veda, call 1 (800) THE-VEDA (843-8332).

In Canada, call 1 (800) 461-9685

For information on training programs for professionals in Maharishi Ayur-Veda, call your local center as per Appendix A; or, call or write:

College of Maharishi Ayur-Veda at
Maharishi University of Management
Office of Admissions
1000 N. 4th St., DB 1155
Fairfield IA 52557-1155

1 (515) 472-1166.

# Appendix B

# Suggested reading in the Maharishi Vedic

# Approach to Health

Books by Maharishi Mahesh Yogi (Founder of the Transcendental Meditation program, and primarily responsible for the current restoration of the complete knowledge of Ayur-Veda known as Maharishi Ayur-Veda)

- *The Science of Being and Art of Living.* Copyright 1963. Livingston Manor , New York: Maharishi International University (MIU) Press. Ninth printing, 1976. Hardback.
- *On the Bhagavad-Gita: A New Translation and Commentary Chapters 1-6.* Copyright 1967 New York, NY.. Penguin Books, Ninth printing, 1979. Softcover.
- *Life Supported by Natural Law.* Fairfield IA. Maharishi International University (MIU) Press. 1986.

Books by others:

- *Human Physiology: Expression of Veda and the Vedic Literature* by Tony Nader M.D., Ph.D. Vlodrop, The Netherlands: Maharishi Vedic University. 1995.
- *Self Recovery: Treating Addictions Using Transcendental Meditation and Maharishi Ayur-Veda* Alexander CN, O'Connell DF, editors. Harrington Park Press: New York. 1994.
- *The Physiology of Consciousness* by Robert Keith Wallace Ph.D. Fairfield, IA: Institute of Science, Technology and Public Policy; and, Maharishi International University Press; 1993.
- *Freedom From Disease* by Hari Sharma, M.D. Toronto: Veda Publishing. 1993.

- *A Woman's Best Medicine* by Nancy Lonsdorf M.D., Veronica Butler M.D., and Melanie Brown Ph.D. New York: Jeremy P. Tarcher/Putnam; 1993.
- *Higher Stages of Human Development: Perspectives on Adult Growth* Alexander CN, editor. New York; Oxford University Press 1990.
- *Maharishi Mahesh Yogi's Transcendental Meditation* by Robert Roth. New York: Donald Fine, Inc. 1987.
- *The Neurophysiology of Enlightenment* by Robert Keith Wallace Ph.D. Fairfield IA: MIU Press; 1986.
- *The TM Book-How to Enjoy the Rest of Your Life* by Denise Denniston. Fairfield IA: Fairfield Press. 1986.
- *TM: An Aid to Christian Growth* edited by Adrian B. Smith. Great Wakering, Essex, England. Mayhew McCrimmon Ltd, 1983.
- *Modern Science and Vedic Science.* Quarterly Journal available through MUM (formerly MIU) Press, Fairfield, IA.

# Appendix C

# The Three Doshas

## Section I: Doshic Questionnaire

Answer the following questions as you see yourself compared to the general population. Circle the number that most closely applies, then add up the totals where indicated.

"Zero" means the statement applies not at all.
"Five" means that it most strongly applies.

| | | | | | | |
|---|---|---|---|---|---|---|
| 1. I walk, talk, and act quickly | 0 | 1 | 2 | 3 | 4 | 5 |
| 2. I learn things quickly | 0 | 1 | 2 | 3 | 4 | 5 |
| 3. I forget things quickly | 0 | 1 | 2 | 3 | 4 | 5 |
| 4. I am spontaneous, vivacious, talkative | 0 | 1 | 2 | 3 | 4 | 5 |
| 5. I tend to be thin and easily lose weight | 0 | 1 | 2 | 3 | 4 | 5 |
| 6. I tend to get cold hands and feet | 0 | 1 | 2 | 3 | 4 | 5 |
| 7. My skin tends to get dry, especially in fall and winter | 0 | 1 | 2 | 3 | 4 | 5 |
| 8. I tend to get emotional, anxious, or worried quickly | 0 | 1 | 2 | 3 | 4 | 5 |
| 9. I dislike cold weather the most (cold, dry, and windy) | 0 | 1 | 2 | 3 | 4 | 5 |
| 10. I often have trouble making decisions | 0 | 1 | 2 | 3 | 4 | 5 |
| 11. I tend to get gas and become constipated easily | 0 | 1 | 2 | 3 | 4 | 5 |
| 12. I tend to have light, delayed, or disturbed sleep | 0 | 1 | 2 | 3 | 4 | 5 |

TOTAL VATA POINTS:    Add up all of the points
in this table  =

| | | | | | | |
|---|---|---|---|---|---|---|
| 1. I have strong digestion; I can eat anything I want, I can eat a lot | 0 | 1 | 2 | 3 | 4 | 5 |
| 2. I'm irritable or uncomfortable if my meal is delayed or missed | 0 | 1 | 2 | 3 | 4 | 5 |
| 3. I tend to perspire easily, armpits are usually wet | 0 | 1 | 2 | 3 | 4 | 5 |
| 4. I don't like hot weather, I prefer too cold to too hot | 0 | 1 | 2 | 3 | 4 | 5 |
| 5. I can become impatient and/or angry quite easily | 0 | 1 | 2 | 3 | 4 | 5 |
| 6. I tend to be orderly, exact, even a perfectionist | 0 | 1 | 2 | 3 | 4 | 5 |
| 7. I am rarely or never constipated, stools may tend to be loose | 0 | 1 | 2 | 3 | 4 | 5 |
| 8. I like cold foods and beverages | 0 | 1 | 2 | 3 | 4 | 5 |
| 9. I have a sharp intellect, and can speak clearly and sharply | 0 | 1 | 2 | 3 | 4 | 5 |
| 10. I tend to be moderate in build | 0 | 1 | 2 | 3 | 4 | 5 |
| 11. I can be hardheaded and stubborn | 0 | 1 | 2 | 3 | 4 | 5 |
| 12. My hair tends to be thin or light or early gray or balding | 0 | 1 | 2 | 3 | 4 | 5 |

TOTAL PITTA POINTS:      Add up all of the points

in this table   =

| | | | | | | |
|---|---|---|---|---|---|---|
| 1. I can skip a meal without much discomfort | 0 | 1 | 2 | 3 | 4 | 5 |
| 2. I am not easily disturbed, I have a peaceful mind | 0 | 1 | 2 | 3 | 4 | 5 |
| 3. My walk is slow and stable, my work is deliberate and easy | 0 | 1 | 2 | 3 | 4 | 5 |
| 4. I tend to get mucous, congestion, sinus, allergies, or asthma | 0 | 1 | 2 | 3 | 4 | 5 |
| 5. I tend to gain weight, become pleasingly plump | 0 | 1 | 2 | 3 | 4 | 5 |
| 6. I need at least eight hours of deep sleep per day | 0 | 1 | 2 | 3 | 4 | 5 |
| 7. I do not tend to get angry, impatient or irritated easily | 0 | 1 | 2 | 3 | 4 | 5 |
| 8. I have soft, smooth, skin | 0 | 1 | 2 | 3 | 4 | 5 |
| 9. People tell me I am sweet natured | 0 | 1 | 2 | 3 | 4 | 5 |
| 10. I'm not quick, but I have good athletic stamina | 0 | 1 | 2 | 3 | 4 | 5 |
| 11. I do not like cold damp weather | 0 | 1 | 2 | 3 | 4 | 5 |
| 12. I learn slowly, but I have an excellent memory | 0 | 1 | 2 | 3 | 4 | 5 |

TOTAL KAPHA POINTS:      Add up all of the points

in this table   =

Compare the totals for each table, Vata, Pitta, and Kapha. The resulting score is a sort of amalgam of both strength and imbalance. That's OK though, because both need to be addressed.

If one score is much higher than the others, then that is the dosha you should attend to in terms of diet and behavior. If two are higher, you should attend to those two, each in its season. For instance, if vata and pitta were high and kapha score low, then in vata season pacify vata, in pitta season pacify pitta, in kapha season don't worry about it, apparently kapha was not much of an issue. If all three scores were close, pacify each dosha in its season.

These guidelines are appropriate for basically healthy persons. If you have health problems or poor digestion or the questionnaire seems to steer you in an uncomfortable direction, your situation may be too complex for this simple tool to discern, and it really would be best to seek consultation with a professional.

## Section II: Diets Pacifying to the Doshas

The following basic diets are *pacifying* or *decreasing* to the dosha after which they are named. They should not be followed slavishly. The diet will say "favor", not "eat only"; and "reduce", not "thou shalt not eat". Also, many of us have more than one dosha predominant. Further, influences of season and of imbalance may affect our nutritional needs and desires. Strength of digestion must also be considered (particularly with the vata pacifying diet). There are a number of other diets used clinically as well. If a diet doesn't seem to suit you, or if you have health or digestive problems, consider having an evaluation by a doctor trained in Maharishi Ayur-Veda.

This book can only scratch the surface. Those interested in learning more will find these principles discussed in depth in the sixteen lesson Course on Diet, Digestion, and Nutrition offered by the Maharishi Ayur-Veda Schools nationwide.

| VATA PACIFYING DIET | | |
|---|---|---|
| Type of Food | FAVOR | REDUCE OR AVOID |
| General | sweet, sour, and salty tastes warm, unctuous and sufficient quantity of foods and drinks | pungent, bitter, and astringent tastes light, dry and cold foods and drinks |
| Grains | wheat, rice (whole); cooked oats in small quantities | barley, corn, millet, rye, buckwheat, raw oats |
| Beans, Dahl | yellow mung dahl | all, except yellow mung dahl and red lentils |
| Vegetables | white pumpkin, zucchini, okra, artichoke, asparagus, tender eggplant & radish, carrot, beetroot, sweet potato (with ghee or butter) tomato, cucumber, green papaya; small amounts of spinach | raw, leafy greens, orange pumpkin & squash, peas, potato, sprouts, mature eggplant & radish, broccoli, cauliflower, cabbage, chicory |
| Dairy | all dairy; cheese and yogurt should be soft and fresh (not aged) | aged cheeses, nonfresh yogurt |
| Sweeteners | sugar cane products small amounts of honey | cooked honey (bad for all), excess honey |
| Oils | all | none |
| Nuts | all except peanuts | peanuts |
| Seeds | small amounts | too much quantity |
| Spices & Condiments | cumin, ginger, mustard seeds, fenugreek, hing (asafoetida), cinnamon, cardamom, cloves, anis, fennel, salt, lemon juice, tamarind; small amounts of black pepper or others to taste | too much coriander seed, parsley, saffron, turmeric |
| Fruits | ripe sweet and juicy apples pears & oranges; dried fruit better soaked; sweet grapes, mango, papaya, sweet pineapple, banana, avocado, melons, plums, cherries, raisins, dates, prunes, figs, kiwi, peach, apricot | unripe or too dry guava, jambu, cashew fruit, cranberries, dried persimmon |

| PITTA PACIFYING DIET | | |
|---|---|---|
| Type of Food | FAVOR | REDUCE OR AVOID |
| General | sweet, bitter and astringent tastes not too hot foods and drinks | pungent, sour, salty tastes |
| Grains | wheat, rice, barley, oats | millet, corn, buckwheat, rye |
| Beans, Dahl | yellow mung dahl, small kidney beans, soy bean products | adjuki beans |
| Vegetables | asparagus, artichoke, white pumpkin, okra, zucchini, spinach, chicory, cauliflower, broccoli, cabbage, green beans, celery, potato, sweet potato, peas, sweet green pepper, green papaya, sprouts, lettuce, tender radish (with ghee or butter), lotus root, tender eggplant | tomato, beetroot, carrot, radish, hot peppers, raw onions |
| Dairy | ghee, milk, butter, sweet buttermilk, sweet lassi, cream, cream cheese | sour milk products, yogurt, sour cream, cheese (especially old & salty), quark, salty butter |
| Sweeteners | sugar, honey in small amounts | molasses, brown sugar, much honey |
| Oils | coconut, olive, sunflower | almond, corn, safflower, sesame |
| Nuts | coconut is OK | all, except coconut |
| Seeds | sunflower & pumpkin are OK | all, except as noted |
| Spices & Condiments | coriander, cumin, ginger (small amounts), turmeric, saffron, fennel, cinnamon, cardamom, a little lemon juice | chili pepper, cayenne, black pepper, mustard seeds, cloves, celery seeds, fenugreek |
| Fruits | grapes, pomegranate, banana, avocado, mango, coconut, melon, apples, pears, raisins, dates, figs, apricot, sweet orange, sweet pineapple, persimmon, cashew fruit, papaya (small amount), kiwi | papaya, grapefruit, olive, sour orange, peach, sour grapes, sour pineapple, berries, cranberries, prunes; tart fruits |

| KAPHA PACIFYING DIET | | |
|---|---|---|
| Type of Food | FAVOR | REDUCE OR AVOID |
| General | pungent, bitter, and astringent tastes<br>light, dry, and warm foods and drinks | sweet, sour, salty tastes<br>unctuous, cold, heavy foods, large quantities, especially at night |
| Grains | old (over one year) grains, barley, millet, corn, buckwheat, rye, oats, wheat, rice | new grains, especially wheat and rice |
| Beans, Dahl | all, except tofu | tofu (soy beans) |
| Vegetables | leafy greens, asparagus, artichoke, potato, carrot, cabbage, beetroot (small amounts), cauliflower, broccoli, celery, peas, pepper, sprouts, white pumpkin, zucchini, okra (dry roasted), green papaya, tomato, tender eggplant & radish | sweet potato, tapioca, other tubers |
| Dairy | lassi & Indian butter milk, low fat milk, small amounts of ghee and whole milk | yogurt, cream, butter; large amounts of whole milk or ghee |
| Sweeteners | honey (never cooked) | sugar cane products |
| Oils | mustard, corn, sesame, in small amounts | all, except as noted |
| Nuts | none | all |
| Seeds | sunflower, pumpkin | all, except as noted |
| Spices & Condiments | all (except salt), especially sharp pungent like pepper, ginger, etc.; lemon juice in small amount | salt |
| Fruits | pomegranate, grapes, persimmon, cranberries, raisins, figs, dates (best with honey), peaches, apples, papaya, guava, cashew fruit, jambu | avocado, banana, pineapple, oranges, melons, plums, prunes, mango, coconut, apricot |

# Appendix D

# Attributes of the Doshas and Subdoshas

In reading these tables, recall that these are generalizations, and that any dosha can give rise to any imbalance.

| THE THREE DOSHAS | | | |
|---|---|---|---|
| Dosha | Qualities of the doshas | Effect of imbalanced dosha | Effect of balanced dosha |
| **VATA** | dry and rough cold, subtle, minute light, moving clear, non-sticky coarse, brittle | dry, rough skin, constipation, cold intolerance, anxiety, worry, insomnia, underweight, noninflammatory arthritis, some fatigue, some headaches | normal elimination mental alertness exhilaration good immunity properly formed tissues sound sleep |
| **PITTA** | hot, sharp, slightly oily, some movement, flow; liquid, sour, pungent | bald, premature gray peptic ulcer, heartburn skin inflammation hostility, irritability unpleasant body heat visual problems | strong digestion lustrous complexion normal heat and thirst contentment dynamism, efficiency sharp intellect |
| **KAPHA** | cold heavy soft stable, steady sticky, slimy, viscous sweet unctuous, oily | oily skin sinus congestion mental dullness slow digestion asthma allergies | stable mind strong immunity muscular strength vitality, stamina courage, dignity, affection, generosity |

| THE SUBDOSHAS OF VATA | | | |
|---|---|---|---|
| Subdosha | Locations | Functions | Results of imbalance |
| Prana | head, chest, mouth, tongue, nose, throat | movement of all kinds, sensory perception, cognition, breath both gross and subtle | worry, insomnia, neurological & respiratory disorders, mental problems |
| Udana | chest, throat | speech, effort, energy | ear nose & throat problems speech disorders, fatigue |
| Samana | channels in stomach and intestines | movement of food in gut, supports agni and digestion | poor digestion and hunger, gas, nervous stomach, inadequate assimilation |
| Apana | colon, lower abdomen, pelvis | elimination of urine, semen, feces, menstrual flow; deliver babies | elimination problems, menstrual disorders, sexual dysfunction |
| Vyana | nervous and circulatory systems all over the body | circulation both gross and subtle | high blood pressure, circulatory problems, dysrrhythmias |

| THE SUBDOSHAS OF PITTA | | | |
|---|---|---|---|
| Subdosha | Locations | Functions | Results of imbalance |
| **Pachaka** | stomach, small intestine | digestion of food, maintenance of digestive agnis | heartburn, ulcers, irregular digestion, sour acid stomach |
| **Ranjaka** | liver, spleen, duodenum, blood | produce, purify and maintain the blood; aid digestion | anemia, jaundice, rashes, blood disorders, anger, hostility |
| **Sadhaka** | heart | fulfillment of desire, energy, passion; pumps blood too | heart disease, indecision, emotions like frustration, heartache, anger, sadness |
| **Alochaka** | visual system | vision, insight | visual problems, bloodshot eyes, any eye disorder |
| **Bradjaka** | skin | luster, color of skin; absorption through skin | all types of skin disorders |

| THE SUBDOSHAS OF KAPHA | | | |
|---|---|---|---|
| Subdosha | Locations | Functions | Results of imbalance |
| Kledaka | stomach | initiates digestion, moistens food | heavy, dull, slow digestion |
| Avalambaka | chest, heart, low back | supports heart and lumbar region | low back pain, heart or respiratory problems |
| Bodhaka | tongue, throat | perception of taste | taste bud or salivary gland disorders |
| Tarpaka | sinuses, spinal column, head | nourishment of mind, unctuousness of head, sinuses, nose, mouth | sinus congestion, heavy head, dull senses or dull outlook, cough |
| Shleshaka | joints | lubricates joints, cohesion in the body | joint diseases; watery, swollen, painful, loose joints |

# Appendix E

# Yoga Asanas, Surya Namaskar, Pranayam

Before practicing these postures, please review the principles noted at the end of chapter 17. If you have any significant health problems, it would be good to see a physician before beginning any new program. There are some precautions mentioned with many of the postures, but these are not all inclusive and do not substitute for common sense or good medical supervision.

This is a basic and preliminary set of yoga postures. Also, this is just a book. More advanced and in-depth information is available in the sixteen lesson course on Maharishi Yoga offered by the Maharishi Schools nationwide (see appendix A).

## Yoga Postures

Perform these on the floor on a rug, blanket, or mat. Breathe comfortably throughout; don't hold your breath or strain to get into these postures. The entire sequence need only take seven or eight minutes, or longer as is comfortable, twice a day.

1. TONING OF THE BODY

Sitting comfortably, using palms and fingers, gently press on the body moving always from the periphery toward the heart. Start at the top of the head, pressing and releasing, over the head, face, neck and chest. Then, again from the top of the head over the back of the head, back of the neck, around to the front of the chest.

Now tone your arms. Start by grasping your right hand with your left, press and release along the top of your right arm, across your chest, toward your heart. Now do the underside of your right arm. Repeat this on the other side, right hand grasping your left.

Put both hands on your lower abdomen and press and release, moving upward toward the heart. Now start at your low back, moving up your back, then around your flanks up toward the heart.

Go to your right foot, start at the toes, using both hands, up toward the heart. Repeat on your left leg.

### The Side Roll

Lie straight and flat on your back. Bring your knees up to your chest and grasp them with both hands. Now roll comfortably from side to side, five times each way (more if you want). Then, slowly straighten out again.

## 2. SEAT FIRMING POSE

Kneel. Sit back with your buttocks on your heels. If your knees don't tolerate that much flexion, put a pillow (or three) on your calves behind your hamstrings. Back straight, hands in your lap (right atop left, palms up); alternate kneeling and sitting back around three times, for 10--20 seconds each time.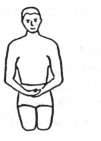

## 3. HEAD TO KNEE POSE

Sit with your legs extended straight in front of you. Keeping your right leg straight, bend your left knee with the knee out to the side (externally rotated hip), bringing your left foot into your crotch as far as it will easily go. Stretch your arms up over your head, bend forward toward your right foot. Hold for 10 to 20 seconds, relax your arms, straighten back up and relax. Repeat. Then, perform the same sequence on the other side.

### 4. SHOULDER STAND

Lie on your back with hands flat against the floor. Bend at the hips, bringing your (straight) legs up over your waist. Now, bring your hips up off the floor as your knees move a few feet in front of your face. Support your back with your hands. You are now in a half shoulder stand; you should be breathing comfortably without strain. If you choose to do the full shoulder stand, straighten your legs, point your toes toward the ceiling, take the bend out of your hips so that you make a straight line from your upper back to your toes. Hold one of these poses for few breaths.

### 5. THE PLOW POSE

From the shoulder stand, continue into this by flexing/bending at the hips, legs straight, bringing your toes toward the floor above your head. Your self-worth is not contingent upon your toes touching the floor. Extend your arms up above your head, then bend your elbows with forearms just atop your head. Hold this pose for a few breaths, easily. To leave this pose, return to a half or full shoulder stand with the hands again supporting the low back, then ease back into the supine position.

272

## 6. COBRA POSE

Lie face down with hands directly under your shoulders. Lift your chest and upper torso off the floor. Hold for a few breaths, then ease back down. Do not push up hard with your arms; it is not necessary to straighten the arms, they're just for support. Repeat once or twice.

## 7. LOCUST POSE

Still face down, hands under or next to your thighs, palms facing the ceiling, chin on the floor, raise both (straight) legs up off the floor. Hold for a few breaths, repeat once or twice. If this is too strenuous, start by raising one leg at a time.

## 8. SEATED TWISTING POSE

Sit with legs out straight in front of you. Keeping your right leg straight, bend your left knee, keep it off the floor (don't rotate your hip), keep your sole on the floor and bring your heel up toward your buttock, inside of left foot touching inside of right thigh.

Put your left palm on the floor behind you, and your right arm (elbow) on the left side of your left knee. Twist to your left, looking over your left shoulder. Don't bend your back, keep it comfortably extended vertically. Hold the pose for a few breaths. Repeat on the other side.

### 9. STANDING FORWARD BEND

Stand up, feet shoulder width apart. Lift your arms up over your head. Bend forward, bringing your fingers toward the floor. Hold for a few breaths, then stand straight up again. Repeat.

### 10. AWARENESS POSE

Lie down flat on your back, palms facing up. Relax everything. Allow the attention to go wherever in the body it is drawn. Rest for a minute or longer. Also, this pose may be performed between any of the others whenever you are inclined to do so.

Generally you will find that you will comfortably tend to exhale at the onset of poses of flexion, and inhale with extension poses. In any case, don't strain.

## Sun Salutation (Surya Namaskar)

This is a cycle of twelve postures. They are performed in a fluid sequence, synchronized with the breath, inhalation leading into extension, exhalation leading into flexion (don't strain to remember, it feels perfectly natural to do it this way). Each cycle of twelve poses takes a minute or so, less than two, each pose only lasting as long as the time between the beginnings of two successive breaths. From one to six or twelve or more cycles are done each morning.

1. SALUTATION POSITION
Stand with your palms together in front of your chest.

2. RAISED ARM POSITION
Upon inhaling, extend the arms far up and back over your head.

3. HAND FOOT POSITION
Exhaling, bend forward and down, hands toward the floor. Bend knees slightly if you need. Relax your arms, shoulders, and neck.

## 4. EQUESTRIAN POSITION

As you inhale, extend your left leg back behind you and let your left knee down to the floor. Lift your chest and look up.

## 5. MOUNTAIN POSE

Exhaling, bring your right foot back next to the left foot, hips' width apart, with your hands on the floor in front of you, hips flexed, buttocks up in the air (there's the mountain). As is comfortable, stretch your heels down to the floor.

## 6. EIGHT LIMBS POSITION

Just before you need to inhale, bring your knees to the floor and slide your body down and forward until the "eight limbs" all touch the floor: two feet, two knees, two hands, chest and chin. Hold this for only a brief second, then begin to inhale as you move to the next position....

## 7. COBRA POSITION

...Inhaling, lift the chest forward and up, gently pushing down and supporting with the hands and arms. The pelvis stays on the floor.

8. MOUNTAIN POSE

Exhaling, repeat the fifth position.

9. EQUESTRIAN POSITION

Inhaling, repeat the fourth position.

10. HAND FOOT POSITION

Exhaling, repeat the third position.

11. RAISED ARM POSITION

Inhaling, repeat the second position.

12. SALUTATION POSITION

Exhaling, repeat the first position.

This is the end of the first cycle of Surya Namaskar. Hold the salutation pose for a few breaths, then move on into your second cycle. In the next cycle, for the equestrian position, extend your **right** leg back behind you. Alternate this each cycle (it helps you keep track of which one you're doing, too). When you have finished all your cycles of sun salutes, it would be good to rest a while flat on your back in the *awareness pose* (see yoga asanas).

## Alternate Nostril Breathing (Pranayam)

This exercise has an integrating effect on the nervous and respiratory systems. It should be performed for three to five minutes twice daily ideally just before TM. There should be no straining, no holding the breath or trying to count or time the breaths.

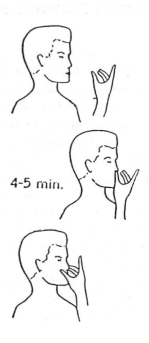

4-5 min.

Sitting comfortably, place your right hand at your nose, with your thumb alongside your right nostril and your long and ring fingers next to your left nostril. (It can be helpful to support your right elbow with your left hand.) Close your right nostril with your thumb, and easily exhale out your left nostril, then, easily inhale also through your left nostril. Switch to blocking your left nostril with your two fingers and breathe out and in through your right nostril. Continue alternating in this fashion, always beginning with exhalation, for a few minutes. If you need to breathe through the same nostril, or through the mouth for a few breaths to be comfortable, go ahead. When finished, relax your arm, rest for a few moments, and begin TM.

# Appendix F

# Further Findings in Selected Mind-Body Topics

**Author's note**: As I trust I've been clear about in the previous chapters, I chose the field of Maharishi Ayur-Veda because I became convinced that it holds the most promise for the fulfillment of the aspirations of all who wish to heal. I hope I've done a passable job in presenting to you the evidence for this conviction.

In the pages that follow, I present a review of much of the current scientific knowledge about the mind-body connection. As one might expect, some of these data have been derived from studies of procedures not within the realm of Maharishi Ayur-Veda. How much support of Natural Law these various methods enjoy, I do not know. (That's one reason why I value this longstanding tradition, because its effects are known.) I present this information not to support or advocate any of these approaches particularly, but rather to demonstrate that the psychophysiologic mechanisms which are enlivened by the Maharishi Vedic Approach to Health have already been verified by numerous scientific studies.

# Section I: Endocrine; gastrointestinal; pain; asthma; placebo effect

## Endocrine

> ... it may well be difficult to see which was the primary factor in endocrinologic diseases: psychic instability or the disturbed secretion of these endocrine organs.[1]
>
> -- Dr. Harvey Cushing, the father of modern endocrinology
> American Journal of Insanity

The above quote is from 1913. Even then, one would think they could have come up with a better title for their journal.

In the one year prior to the onset of Cushing's Syndrome (a syndrome named after Dr. Harvey Cushing), 30 people had more distressing and undesirable life events compared to controls.[2] Anger and irritable mood[3] and depression[4] have been associated with endocrinologic disorders.

Newly-diagnosed individuals with Graves Disease (or toxic diffuse goiter of the thyroid), also had more negative life events in the 12 months preceding their diagnosis and these negative life-event scores were also significantly higher than in matched controls.[5]

Treatment of hyperthyroidism has cured patients of long-standing agoraphobia.[6] Not only may hyperthyroidism induce anxiety and fearfulness but anxiety may increase vulnerability to hyperthyroidism. Generally, anger and irritable mood are found to affect vulnerability to medical illness.[3]

Major depression has been associated with a number of endocrine diseases. It is often a major and life-threatening complication of Cushing's Syndrome, but also Addison's Disease (from which President John Kennedy suffered), thyroid disease and other conditions.[3]

## Gastrointestinal

Peptic ulcer and irritable bowel were addressed in the text. Non-ulcer dyspepsia, that is indigestion and abdominal pain which is not associated with ulcer disease, has been associated with stress,[7] and with the *perception* of stress. In one study, 33 persons with dyspepsia who had normal examinations of the inside of their stomach by endoscopy and ultrasound and 33 control individuals of comparable sex, age and social class were studied. Both groups selected from 56 major life events they had experienced and rated how they perceived those events. Also, they selected from 117 items of daily stress and rated the severity of each item. The number of positive and negative events were about the same in both the patients with dyspepsia and the controls, but the patients with dyspepsia had a higher **perception** of the magnitude of negative events. Researchers concluded that psychological factors probably play a role in the generation of non-ulcer dyspepsia.[7]

## Pain

A retrospective investigation of *pre-injury* emotional trauma -- that is, looking at what the emotional status was, *prior* to the onset of their injury -- of out-of-work, blue collar individuals who had chronic back pain revealed a high rate of pre-injury emotional trauma in patients with chronic back pain. Whether that trauma lowered the pain threshold of these individuals so they more readily experienced pain, or whether the old emotional trauma itself actually predisposed them to become injured, are as yet unanswered questions.[8]

Construction workers with low back pain and neck and shoulder pain were evaluated with a psychological questionnaire. Low back pain was about one-and-a-half times more prevalent and severe back pain was about three times more prevalent when workers reporting high stress were compared to workers reporting low stress.[9]

In 80 individuals with chronic low back pain, a significant excess of adverse life events had occurred prior to the onset of back pain with no organic cause. These findings indicate that stress is involved in the onset of functional back pain.[10]

Significant stressful life events have an association with numerous types of pain. But what about the chronic, everyday stressors that you and I tend to face? Headache pain, your typical run-of-the-mill muscle contraction headache or tension headache, while not particularly associated with major negative stressful life events, is provoked by ongoing daily stressors.[11]

## Arthritis

It has been widely postulated that there is a significant psychological aspect to rheumatoid arthritis. Some studies have found that individuals with rheumatoid arthritis tend to be self-sacrificing, masochistic, inhibited, perfectionistic and retiring. In the face of these psychodynamics, the body (via the immune system) attacks itself.[12] Other studies though, have shown that there is perhaps little difference psychologically between those with rheumatoid arthritis and those without. So, it's somewhat unclear whether those particular psychological characteristics tend to provoke rheumatoid arthritis.[13]

But, it is clear that there is some linkage among the nervous system, immunity and rheumatoid arthritis. Some interesting natural experiments which have demonstrated this connection. Arthritic limbs tend to improve after the nerves to them have been cut.[14] Also, it's been found that limbs paralyzed in accidents tend to be unaffected by rheumatoid arthritis when the paralysis happens before the rheumatoid arthritis begins.

## Asthma

Episodes of asthma have been linked to periods of heightened stress and emotions.[15] The tone of the muscles around the bronchioles tends to increase in response to stress in both asthmatics and non-asthmatics, and tends to decrease in response to relaxing stimuli.[16]

The three most commonly cited precipitants of asthma in many studies in the past have been infections, allergies and allergenic exposures, and emotional stressors.[17,18,19]

## Placebo

The term placebo comes from a Latin verb which means *to please*. In the Middle Ages, the term placebo had begun to take on other meanings. Most of those meanings were negative. It was used to denote a servile flatterer. Professional mourners were hired to "sing placebos" at the deceased if there were no family members to do so. In medicine, it was first defined back in 1785 as "a commonplace method or medicine." Ten years later, by 1795, in the medical dictionary by Mothersby, the description also included the words "calculated to amuse for a time rather than for any other purpose." The next edition of the dictionary also stated explicitly that a placebo was "a make-believe medicine" devoid of effect.

# Section II: Your Heart

> My life is in the hands of any rascal who chooses to annoy and tease me.
>
> -- John Hunter

He was right. Dr. John Hunter, the great surgeon and anatomist quoted above, suffered from angina pectoris. Opposition to the appointment of his successor at St. George's Hospital so provoked him that he died of a heart attack at the board meeting.[20]

In the six months following their first heart attack, loneliness was the one significant variable among patients who suffered another heart attack or cardiac death during that time.[21]

People treated medically for their coronary artery disease were followed for up to 14-1/2 years. The most important variable for their survival was not hypertension, smoking, cholesterol or any of the other commonly recognized cardiovascular risk factors; rather, it was the presence of a spouse or a confidant.[22]

The technical term for a heart attack is **m**yocardial infarction or **MI**, for short. Myocardial means referring to heart muscle and infarction refers to the death of tissue inside a living body. So if part of the heart muscle dies inside of a person who is alive, this is called a myocardial infarction. It's usually due to blockage of what are called the *coronary arteries* which are the arteries which actually serve the heart muscle. Now, we would think the heart being full of blood should have plenty of oxygen carrying blood, but the heart, like any other muscle, has to have a blood supply. The blood which is inside it does no more good to oxygenate the heart muscle than does money in the bank make the teller rich. So, when the heart pumps blood, part of the blood that goes out through the major vessels that leave the heart goes into very specialized vessels that then go back into the heart muscle and supply the muscle itself. If these arteries become blocked by atherosclerotic plaques and deposits of fat, cholesterol and so forth, then the flow of blood is decreased, the amount of oxygen that gets to the heart muscle is decreased, and, if we become stressed and the heart muscle requires more oxygen and it can't get it, then that heart muscle will begin to complain and we can experience chest pain, called *angina pectoris*. If it becomes quite severe, then that part of the heart muscle will actually die for the lack of oxygen rich blood.

Another term for this lack of blood is called *ischemia*. You'll see in much of medical terminology that many words end in "emia": that refers to the blood (thus, anemia, ischemia, hypoglycemia, etc.). *Ischemic heart disease* then refers to heart disease where the coronary arteries are obstructed and there is a lack of blood flow to the heart muscle itself.

Let's look at those people who have already had a heart attack and how emotions affect their recovery (or lack of recovery). Also, we can consider the effects of chronic stress and long-term stress on the heart, as well as the effects of acute stress on the heart, and on recovery.

- It was noted in the beta blocker heart attack trial that there was a four-fold increase in risk of mortality after acute myocardial infarction (*acute MI*), in persons who were described as being **socially isolated** and who had high levels of life **stress**.[23]
- Another study[24] looked at this issue and confirmed that **socially-isolated** persons were 49 percent more likely to die after infarction than patients classified as not being socially isolated.
- Depression also is an independent risk factor for cardiovascular disease.[25] One group followed almost 1,200 male medical students continuously for an average of 35 years. Twenty-four of the 114 men who reported depression had at least one form of cardiovascular disease. **Depressed** men had a 68 percent higher risk of cardiovascular disease than did non-depressed men, an association which held up even when other risk factors were controlled for.
- In a study of 222 men and women hospitalized for acute MI **depression** was an important independent predictor of death during the first 18 months of follow-up. Patients with moderate or mild depression had a risk adjusted, almost five-fold higher likelihood of death compared with non-depressed MI patients.[26,26a]
- In another study, 380 patients with coronary artery disease were enrolled in a cardiac rehabilitation program. It was noted that

those with **psychological distress** on entry to the program had a three-and-a-half-fold increased risk of a subsequent cardiac event during the next two years of follow-up.[27]

- High **stress** after MI was associated with a three-fold increase in risk of cardiac mortality over five years and an approximately one-and-a-half-fold increase in risk of reinfarction over the same period of time. In contrast, highly-stressed patients who took part in a one-year program of stress monitoring and intervention did not experience any significant long-term increase in risk.[28]

- In another study of men who had had heart attacks, 21 of the 25 most pessimistic died within eight years, but, of the most optimistic, only six of 25 died in the same time.[29]

- Patients with angina pectoris who were instructed in the **purely mental technique** of Transcendental Meditation had improved exercise tolerance compared to controls who were not taught TM.[30]

- Looking at **optimism**, researchers at Duke University studied over 1,700 men and women who had undergone heart catheterization, a procedure used to check for clogged arteries. When these patients were interviewed, 14% said they doubted they would recover enough to resume their daily routines. A year later, 12% of these **pessimists** had died compared to 5% who were optimistic about getting better.[31]

What about those of us who have not had a heart attack, and don't want to get a heart attack? Does stress pose a risk to us? As it turns out, excess **fatigue** is the most prevalent precursor of sudden cardiac death.

Over thirty-three hundred males between the ages of 45 and 59 were followed for 9-1/2 years. Exhaustion was assessed by the following statement: "At the end of the day I am completely exhausted, mentally and physically." Among those who were free of coronary heart disease at the beginning of the study, 69 subjects died because of myocardial infarction.[32] The results showed that those who were exhausted had risks that were from three times to nine times increased over those who did not. These researchers argued that exhaustion before cardiac death does not necessarily reflect heart disease itself, but there is an interaction between the prolonged tension and stress, and subclinical levels of heart disease that may increase the risk of cardiac death.

Another study looked at **burnout** as a risk factor for heart disease.[33] This time 3,877 men aged 39 to 65 were followed for 4.2 years. Among the men who were free of coronary heart disease at the beginning of the study, 59 subjects experienced a heart attack during follow up. Those who answered positively to the question, "Have you ever been burned out?" when they entered the study were found to have twice the risk for myocardial infarction when the authors controlled for age, blood pressure, smoking and cholesterol.

## How Arteries Get Blocked

It's been noted that chronic stress increases *platelet aggregation*. Platelets are tiny blood cells which help blood to clot. Stress also increases *thrombus* and *embolus* formation.[34] A thrombus is a blood clot; an embolus is a clot that gets loose in the circulation. When these clots get stuck in a blood vessel, the tissue served downstream can get starved for blood, and die. (In the brain, this is a stroke.) Increased neurohormonal activity caused by stress contributes to dysfunction in the cells that line the insides of blood vessel walls. That's the first step in the *atherosclerotic* process. These abnormal cells are unable to retard platelets from adhering to the damaged blood vessel wall. Increased infiltration of lipids (fats in the blood), particularly oxidized "bad" cholesterol (LDL-ox cholesterol) into the vessel wall contribute to rapid progression of the atherosclerotic plaque.

Acute stress, on the other hand, tends to lead to what is called *coronary spasm*. The muscles of the arterial wall become very tight and constricted and inhibit the flow of blood to the heart muscle. When both atherosclerosis and spasm are put together, you can see that's a dangerous mix.

## How Arteries Get Evaluated

There are a number of ways of evaluating the decrease in blood flow to the heart: some of you may have experienced treadmill stress tests; other tests involve using ultrasound to do what's called an *echocardiogram* where sound waves are bounced off the heart and abnormalities in the motions of the wall of the heart can indicate that wall of the heart is not being adequately supplied with blood. Other techniques involve injecting into the veins radioactive material (that's not as bad as it sounds) which is preferentially taken up by heart muscle. We can see what the blood supply is to different areas in the heart by measuring the radioactive decay of those materials. The most definitive way (perhaps becoming obsolete due to new CT scan technology) of getting a look at the inside of the coronary arteries is to inject opaque dye, which shows up on x-ray, directly into those blood vessels in a process called *angiography*.

Nineteen patients with coronary artery disease were given either a placebo or a drug which blocks the effects of the stress hormones on the heart. Then they were subjected to either **mental stress** or bicycle exercise studies. The degree of ischemia was assessed by looking at abnormalities in the motion of their heart walls by echocardiography. *Mental stress-induced wall motion abnormalities occurred at a lower heart rate than exercise induced-wall motion abnormalities.* Also, the drug -- which is designed to block the effects of the hormones and such which increase the heart's demand for oxygen -- that drug did not significantly reduce the magnitude of the mental stress-induced wall motion abnormalities.[35] Further, even though that drug did tend to block blood pressure elevations generated by regular exercise, it did not block mental stress-induced blood pressure elevations.

**Hostility** as measured by a psychological hostility inventory was positively correlated with the severity of *perfusion defects*, (problems in perfusing the heart muscle with blood).[36] In patients with coronary artery disease, hostility traits are significantly correlated with the extent of daily life ischemia and with the severity of exercise-induced myocardial ischemia, as well.

**Anger** can actually be more potent than other mental stress. When patients who had coronary artery disease were subjected to exercise, arithmetic, and recall of an incident that elicited anger, anger reduced the capability of the main chamber of the heart to eject blood more than exercise or even mental stress.[37] Outbursts of anger double your risk of heart attack in the next two hours.[38]

In another study ischemia was provoked by a variety of mental stress tasks.[39]   These tasks included arithmetic calculations, reading aloud and what the researchers called "emotionally-arousing speech," which is a pleasant way of saying somebody got in there and pushed their buttons.   "Personally-relevant, emotionally-arousing speech tasks" caused more ischemia than did math and reading tasks.

Two studies have demonstrated that **anxiety** can be fatal. One study followed almost 34,000 US male health professionals, aged 42 to 77 years, for two years. It was found that those who had scored higher on a test for anxiety had increased risk of death due to coronary heart disease. And, death was due almost exclusively to *sudden cardiac death*. The risk was over six times greater for those who scored highest on the anxiety scale.[40]   Another study[41] looked at 2,271 men for over 30 years, from 1961 to 1993. Anxiety symptoms markedly increased the odds for fatal coronary heart disease. Overall, coronary heart disease fatality increased over threefold in those men who scored high on an anxiety symptom scale, and, again, the odds of **sudden death** were almost six times as much.

# Section III: Immunity and

# Psychoneuroimmunology

## Basics of immunity

The human body has the ability to resist almost all types of organisms or toxins. This capacity is called *immunity* and is mediated by our *immune system....* Let me cut to the chase: the immune system *is* connected to the nervous system, the mind, and the emotions, and is affected by the events we experience. Immune functioning can in turn be influenced for good or ill by our thoughts and emotions. For those of us who went to medical school in the 70's or earlier, this is heresy. In the pages that follow, I will describe how and why we now know this to be true.

First, let's get the big picture of the immune system.

The immune system can be divided into two large areas. The first type of immunity is called *innate immunity*. It includes the nature of our skin to resist invasion by organisms, the acid secretions in our stomach to destroy organisms that are swallowed, and other similar mechanisms. It's innate immunity that makes us virtually completely resistant to certain diseases such as some that animals get. You don't find humans getting hog cholera or cattle plague or distemper, even though the virus that kills a large number of dogs is present in our environment and we're exposed to it. (On the other hand, your dog is never going to get syphilis or mumps.) Innate immunity is wonderful, but we're not going to talk any more about it.

The second large area of immunity is going to be more our concern. This is called *acquired* immunity or *adaptive* immunity. This is the ability of the human body to develop very powerful, specific immune responses against individual invading agents such as viruses, bacteria and toxins.

Acquired immunity also can be divided into two major types. In one of these types, the body develops circulating *antibodies*. Antibodies are not cells, they are just large molecules that are capable of attacking the invading agent. This type of immunity is called *humoral* immunity. The second type of acquired immunity is called *cellular* immunity. It's achieved through the formation of large numbers of highly-specialized white blood cells, specifically different types of *lymphocytes*, that are specifically sensitized against a particular foreign agent. These *sensitized lymphocytes* have the special ability to attach to a specific foreign agent and to destroy it. This is the inherent capability of the body to distinguish between self and non-self, between foreign substances that are bad news and need to be addressed and substances which are part of the body, or belong in the neighborhood and don't need to be attacked.

Still with me? Good. Let's go a little further, and look at these cells in the blood.

Blood is basically water with some proteins, salts and other chemicals and hormones floating around in it, and cells. Almost all the cells are either red cells, white cells, or platelets. Most of the cells in the blood are red blood cells. Their job is just to carry oxygen to your tissues. The smaller cells called platelets contribute to the clotting capability of the blood. But, the workhorses of immunity are the white blood cells. Again, there are different types of white blood cells but the main players that we're going to talk about are lymphocytes.

Lymphocytes can be divided into two types. Those two types of cells are called *B cells* and *T cells*. They've been given these letters because of the way they develop. When we are tiny embryos in our mothers' wombs, we're already beginning to develop these lymphocytes and they're already beginning to become destined to specialize. T cells are responsible for cellular immunity; B cells will produce antibodies.

B cells further specialize into cells which produce different classes of antibodies. There are five major classes of antibodies that are called immunoglobulins. The classes which you might see again are immunoglobulin G, or IgG; also IgM, IgA, IgE and IgD. These antibodies are produced by the B cells in response to an attack. They are present in the blood and other body secretions such as saliva to neutralize the antigens, the invaders, when they meet them.

Let's meet the different types of T-cells and then we're about done with our immunology class. Cell mediated immunity, again, involves the direct intervention of T cells in the immune response. These lymphocytes, T cells, are further subdivided into three major subgroups. You may well have heard of these because one of them is affected by the AIDS virus. First are *killer* cells or *natural killer* cells, the second are called *helper* cells, and third, *suppressor* cells. Basically, the killer T lymphocytes bind and destroy the target cell, the helper T cells strengthen both cellular and humoral responses by the production of various hormones and chemicals which enhance that response. Suppressor T cells are thought to negatively regulate the immune response. That is, the immune response gets turned on, attacks, destroys, gets augmented and then somebody's got to turn off the switch; that's the job of the suppressor T cells. It is the helper cell or T-4 cell which is preferentially invaded and destroyed by the human immunodeficiency virus (HIV).

## The Headless Horseman

One tricky thing about these cells is that they basically have one job. In other words, if you have a certain T cell that is pro-grammed to attack a particular type of bacterium, then that's the only type of bacterium that it will attack; it will ignore all the others. Similarly, if you've got a B cell that is programmed to produce an antibody to a certain antigen or attacking virus, for instance, then that is the only antibody that B cell can produce. So you can see you have to have a lot of cells in order to do all the different jobs that are done. In fact, the body clones these cells, makes billions of them, each clone doing just one exact job.

It's thought that this is genetically determined; it's in the blue-print in all the cells of our body, our DNA, to know how to make all of these various multiples of clones to deal with all of the possible organisms and antigens that we might encounter in our journey through life. This is in part why the immune system has been called a "headless horseman," thought to be autonomous, independent of other organ systems, unaffected by our emotions. The genes pro-gram these cells. If we run into a certain type of bacterium, the lym-phocytes recognize these cells, they tell the other lymphocytes that we have been invaded by a certain type of cell which is in the mem-ory of our genes from all of the hundreds of millions of years of evo-lution through which we and our ancestors have been on this planet, and then we make the antibodies and/or the T cells to address that particular organism.[42]

I'm going into all this because there are a number of interesting studies we'll consider in these areas. Also, the whole field of modern medicine is less intimidating if you are acquainted with some of the jargon. Let's move from the basics of the immune system to discuss how we measure functioning in the immune system.

## Functional Testing

One way is just to count the total number of white blood cells or the total number of lymphocytes in blood samples. A lot of the earlier studies did only that. But it would be nice to measure their function; we'd like to examine just how the immune system reacts to various agents.

One procedure is called *T lymphocyte proliferation*, and it's just about what it says. We measure these T lymphocytes, which are responsible for cellular immunity, and we see how they *proliferate* -- how they grow -- in response to something that should make them grow. For instance, if we put a substance that causes cancer (a *mitogen*) or causes inflammation in contact with these cells either inside a human body or in a test tube we can measure how they perform.

Another commonly used functional procedure is to measure levels of antibodies. That can be a little bit complex because sometimes elevated levels of antibodies are an indication of strength of the immune system and other times elevated levels of antibodies can be interpreted as an indication of suppression of the immune system; we'll talk about that as it comes up.

Lastly, a commonly used functional measure of immunocompetence is the measurement of the natural killer cell's ability to destroy target cells.[43]

Now that you've had a stroll through the immune system and have seen how it's studied, let's look at what we've learned about it.

## Psychoneuroimmunology

We may tend to think of scientists as somewhat dispassionate and flaccid; but the scientific process can sometimes become very intense. The directions of research are sometimes argued very vigorously and with a lot of excitement. The concepts that the immune system is subject to the effects of thoughts and emotions, and that these processes can have measurable effects on our health, are often hotly argued. Some commentators have gone so far as to call the whole idea that our thoughts and emotions can have effects on our health as being "folklore."[44] Others argue that a lot of the divisions that we see in contemporary medicine and physiology are really quite arbitrary. The divisions among rheumatology and gastroenterology and neurology and psychology are put in place just by virtue of the fact that that's the way we tend to look at things. One might just as logically lump headache, asthma, irritable bowel syndrome and low back pain together under a new field of "muscle dysregulation". Immunology in particular is undergoing a revolution in terms of how that field fits itself into the paradigm of science.

There are a number of questions we would like to have answered about immune functioning and stress and health. Does stress have an effect on immunity? Do the effects that stress has on immunity have any significant impact on our health? Is there anything we can do about stress? Do the things that we can do about stress have any effect on our immunity and do those effects have any impact on our health?

If indeed it is true that the mind and emotions are intimately connected with our immune system, there are a few points that we would like to find to support such a hypothesis.

1. We should see that there is some kind of connection anatomically between the nervous system and lymphoid organs.
2. If we do something to the brain and to the nervous system we should be able to find that action influencing our immune response.
3. It would be nice to find that it's a two-way street, and that changes in our immune system are accompanied by some changes in the nervous system.
4. We should be able to find that the mediators of our immune response, particularly the lymphocytes, somehow are able to respond to signals from the nervous and endocrine systems.
5. It would only be logical that we should be able to find that these white blood cells are able to produce some sort of signal that the nervous and endocrine systems would be able to recognize.

6. We should be able to look at the tissues themselves -- immune tissues and nervous tissues -- and perhaps see how it is that they're able to communicate with one another.
7. We should be able to demonstrate that stress and conditioning somehow influence immunologic reactivity.

Let's take a walk through the field now being called *psychoneuroimmunology*: psycho for mind; neuro for nervous system; and, immunology for the immune system. This field is sometimes called *psychoneuroendocrinoimmunology*, a cumbersome term borne of the recognition that the mind, the nervous system, the endocrine system and the immune system are all intimately connected. Perhaps in years to come, these terms will have to be abandoned because it'll be recognized that the mind, the nervous system, the immune system, the endocrine system, cardiovascular, pulmonary, gastrointestinal, gynecologic, genital-urinary, musculoskeletal, indeed every system is talking to every other system. Let's consider the questions we posed earlier.

## 1. Are there anatomic connections?

Researchers have found *neurotransmitters* which are the messengers that the nervous system sends to itself -- the signals that flash between nerve cells. These neurotransmitters have been located at the junctions between nerve cells and immune cells. A junction between two nerve cells is called a *synapse*. The nerve cells don't actually touch; between each nerve cell are branches called *dendrites* which go from one nerve cell very close to the other. There's a gap between the two nerve cells and in that gap these neurotransmitters are secreted. As they leave one nerve cell they float over to the other and then influence it. The junctions between nerve cells and immune cells appear anatomically much like synapses.[45,46]

The thymus, the way-station for the processing of T lymphocytes which are responsible for cellular immunity, have nerve end fibers from the central nervous system.[47] Also, bone marrow, the cradle of the immune system, has a nerve supply.[48] Lesions in the brain have been shown to affect functioning of the bone marrow.[49] It has also been shown that nerve fibers connect to individual lymphocytes in the spleen.[50] In sum, the brain does hook up to the immune system.

## 2. Do changes in the nervous system cause changes in immunity?

Over three decades ago, in 1963, researchers showed that by creating a lesion in a certain portion of the *hypothalamus* of a rat, they were able to demonstrate decrease in formation of a certain type of antibody.[51] Other researchers[52,53] were able to show that lesions elsewhere in the hypothalamus decreased the incidence of lethal immune reactions. It has been shown as well that lymphocytes themselves change their shape in response to (the animal from which they come) being subjected to stress.[54]

Stimulating the hypothalamus in rats will lead to changes in the formation of immunoglobulins.[55] Destruction of certain parts of the brains of rabbits will lead to suppression of antibody response. (This is measured by a decrease in the autoimmune reaction which tends to follow streptococcal infection in these rabbits.) Also, it was shown that grafts which usually would be rejected by the body were retained longer in animals who had had this part of their brain injured, and that if the same part of the brain was stimulated then antibody responses were increased.[51] Also, it has been noted that cutting certain nerves leads to an increase in the severity of the expression of a disease called *myasthenia gravis*.[56] This indicates that the nervous system is not only stimulating to immune function but also can serve to have an inhibitory effect. Both cases demonstrate, though, that the nervous system directly influences the immune system.

## 3. Do changes in the immune system cause changes in the nervous system?

Injury of the immune system affects brainwaves in the hypothalamus and in the cerebral cortex, the superficial thinking part of the brain.[57,58] In fact, it's been shown that certain types of immunization will increase the firing rate of neurons in the hypothalamus.[59] This indicates that the brain is indeed paying very close attention to what's going on in the immune system.

The brain monitors the progress of immunity.[60] The hypothalamus, particularly, is involved in this process. The pituitary also, when stressed, generates a number of hormones. These hormones include ACTH, which is a hormone which stimulates the adrenal gland, and also a substance called beta endorphin, which is very much like a narcotic. These opioid narcotic-like chemicals modulate immune function.[61]

### 4. Does the immune system respond to the signals from the nervous system?

A number of neurotransmitters produced by the nervous system have specific effects in the immune system.[62,63,64] Particularly, *norepinephrine* has the effect of increasing the activity of natural killer cells. Another substance produced in the brain called serotonin tends to have the effect of decreasing the immune response to various antigens.[65,66] Also, it's been noted that these *neuropeptides* will control the migration of certain immune cells that are called *monocytes*. Neuropeptides are substances which are chains of amino acids produced by the nervous system which have particular effects on other nerve cells and now have been found to have these effects on monocytes. Monocytes are large white blood cells that also participate in cellular immunity.

### 5. Do immune cells produce substances to which the nervous system responds?

Yes. Antigenic challenges will lead to changes in steroid levels and changes in the firing rates of nerve cells in the hypothalamus.[67] Also, the lymphocytes themselves make substances that mediate immune function and are usually created by the neuroendocrine system. Lymphocytes make beta-endorphin and ACTH.[68]

Substances which are made by the immune system can be *radio labeled.* That is, we attach a radioactive atom or molecule to it, and then by using monitoring machines, tracking the level of radioactivity, we can actually follow these substances and see where they go. Substances made by the immune system will go to the brain.[69] Also, other *cytokines*, substances which have modulating effects on a number of different kinds of cells and which are released by the immune system, mediate signals which are perceived by the nervous system.[70]

### 6. Can we tell how these tissues communicate with each other?

One elegant way of trying to figure out who is talking to whom in nervous tissue and immune tissue is to evaluate these cells for the presence of certain kinds of *receptors*. The idea is not unreasonable that if a cell has a receptor on it which is designed to receive a certain molecule as a signal, then, probably it's doing exactly that. And, indeed, it has been found that immune cells have receptors to steroids, insulin, testosterone, estrogen, beta adrenergic or stimulating stress hormones, histamines, growth hormones, acetylcholine (which is a neurotransmitter) and enkephalins (which also mediate both immune response and nervous function) and a number of other different substances.[71,72] And, these substances actually have measurable effects to immune function.[73] Leading researchers in these fields are now noting that virtually every brain receptor -- every receptor site which is found on nervous tissue -- can also be found on macrophages, which are large immune cells.[74,75]

It appears that everybody is talking to everybody else. Every time you stub your toe or have a nasty thought, your immune system, your heart, your gut, your brain -- every organ that has receptors to all of these hormones and neurotransmitters that are being elaborated -- everyone is eavesdropping on everyone else. These neurotransmitters are messengers from innerspace. They are little impulses of consciousness which travel throughout the physiology and clue everybody in to the status of the organism as a whole.

### 7. Can immunity be conditioned? Is immunity influenced by our life's events?

In 1975, there was published the study that really put the field of psychoneuroimmunology on the map. This landmark research[76] demonstrated that the immune system can be *conditioned*.

Now, what does it mean to be conditioned? You may recall Mick Jagger of the Rolling Stones singing about "salivating like Pavlov's dogs". Well, Dr. Pavlov was a scientist who conditioned some dogs.  To be conditioned is to respond to a stimulus like it was something else.  In case it's unclear, let's recount again the story of Dr. Pavlov and his dogs.

Pavlov used to feed his dogs.  In anticipation of being fed, the dogs would begin to salivate.  The dogs began to associate Pavlov with the food.  Every time he would bring the food the dogs would salivate. Eventually, all he had to do was just walk in the door and the dogs would begin to salivate even if there was no food around. This is called conditioning.  A certain stimulus (the food) we understand should specifically make dogs salivate; but he conditioned the animals to respond with salivation to another, non-specific stimulus such as his walking into the room.

It had always been thought the immune system was not influenced by this effect of conditioning.  That is, the immune system responds to certain antigens.  We've talked about the clones of B cells and T cells which are thought to be genetically programmed to respond only to a streptococcus or a mumps virus or whatever.  It was thought that this system was autonomous.  You remember the analogy of the Headless Horseman.  It doesn't respond to nonspecific stimuli, it only responds to particular organisms and antigens that it specifically identifies and then attacks.

The watershed study mentioned demonstrated behaviorally-conditioned immunosuppression.  These researchers paired sweet-tasting *saccharine* along with a drug called *cyclophosphamide*, which is an immunosuppressant drug.  Just as Dr. Pavlov had conditioned his dogs by pairing his arrival with the food, these researchers conditioned rats by pairing saccharine with cyclophosphamide.  A specific agent, cyclophosphamide, has the effect of suppressing immune functioning.  The saccharine has no particular effect on immune functioning.  After these animals had been conditioned for some time, they were injected with red blood cells from sheep. Researchers then measured the antibodies to these red blood cells.  Now, the immune system of an intact rat will see that these sheep red blood cells don't belong floating around in its rat blood stream and its immune system just goes crazy and begins to make antibodies to attack them. It was found that high quantities (or *titers*, as they're called), of antibodies to the sheep blood cells were observed in rats who had not been subjected to the conditioning with the cyclophosphamide and the saccharine. Animals who were given just the immunosuppressant cyclophosphamide did not make the antibody: their immune system was suppressed. And, the interesting thing was that animals who had been conditioned, had recovered, *and then had no longer been given the cyclophosphamide but instead were given only the saccharine* also were found to be significantly immunosuppressed. This was a very eye-opening study.

It demonstrated that the immune system of this rat, which presumably has been genetically programmed through millions of years of evolution to be able to recognize and attack red blood cells from a sheep and to create a clone of cells that would generate antibodies to those sheep red blood cells now was having that immune response *weakened by a substance which should not have any effect on the immune response.* The saccharine is only having an effect because the rat had been conditioned to respond to this innocuous substance. This is the relevant point. The idea is that we can take a substance or experience which is in and of itself not significant; and yet via conditioning we can perceive it as a threat or a blessing; and, indeed, our immune system and our bodies can respond to it as if it were significant, either a threat capable of weakening us, or something supportive.

This type of research has been extended and followed up. Mice who are prone to a disease called *lupus erythematous*, which is an autoimmune disease wherein the immune system begins to attack host tissues, had less disease when treated with saccharine after the saccharine had been paired to the cyclophosphamide.[77,78] This is similar to the first study I just discussed.

It has been noted in humans that a similar conditioning protocol resulted in a need for less *cytoxan*, which is also an immune-suppressive drug, in a child with an autoimmune disease.[79]

Another way of looking at this type of phenomenon is in the setting of transplantation. In animals who had been conditioned with saccharine and cyclophosphamide, subsequent treatment with saccharine prolonged the tolerance of a skin graft that would otherwise have been rejected by the immune system.[80]

Other studies have confirmed these findings.[81] This matter of conditioning is very germane in our behavior. These studies have demonstrated that Reality, to some degree, is all about the *perception* of our experience rather than our experience itself. What we think of as being the objective reality outside of ourselves is really a function of the way we process our experience, and the way we perceive the world around us.

## Does It Matter?

Let's turn to another aspect of psychoneuroimmunology. We've seen that the nervous system and immune system are connected, that they have reciprocal relationships back and forth, that all the receptors are located on all of these various cells and that the immune system can be conditioned; but does it have noticeable effects? That is, in real life, can we anticipate that such effects of stress would have some impact on our immune system? And do different types of stress have different effects on immunity?

Initially, this was studied in animals. Rats who are placed in very crowded situations have a decrease in their humoral or antibody immunity.[82] Also, rats and other animals who are strongly stressed have a decrease as well in their cellular immunity.[83]

In animal models transplanted kidneys had enhanced survival when the organisms were stressed by one day of restraint. If you're going to have someone transplant a kidney into you, ideally, you'd like it not to make you sick. But your immune system is geared to recognize that as being foreign material and will attack it. (It's paradoxical that the clinical outcome is actually worsened by having an intact immune system.) When they stressed these animals by restraining them for one day, they found that the survival of the kidney graft was prolonged, indicating that the stress of the restraint had suppressed immune functioning.[84,85]

There is difference between *controllable* stress and *uncontrollable* stress. Animals who are subjected to an inescapable, **uncontrollable** shock had a decrease in their lymphocyte proliferation. You'll remember that lymphocyte proliferation is the ability of these white blood cells to make more white blood cells in the face of a mitogen, a chemical substance which causes white blood cells to reproduce. Those who were subjected to controllable shock -- the rats could learn how to escape this shock -- did not have a decrease in their lymphocyte proliferation.[86]

Similarly, uncontrollable stress led to a decrease in natural killer cell activity, whereas, controllable stress did not have as strong a negative effect on natural killer cell activity.[87]   Lack of control seems to make us sicker.  How to deal with these issues of control is something that I've discussed in the text of this book.

Immune proliferation is increased when people allow themselves to feel and express grief, while those who **repress** these feelings and also individuals who are **depressed**, have a decrease in immune proliferation.[88]

A number of studies in humans have demonstrated that states of mind and life events and stress will have effects on immune functioning.  These are intriguing studies and I'll spend a little bit of time talking about them.

Individuals with higher **anxiety** scores on psychological testing were less able to mount an effective immune response to immunization against Hepatitis B.[89]   As noted in the text, residents near the Three Mile Island Nuclear Power Plant (TMI) were found to have depressed immune functioning.[90]  Subjects lived from five miles to more than 80 miles away from the nuclear power plant.  It was found that none of these people had been exposed to any significant radiation but those closer to TMI had depressed immune functioning.  Specifically, they had an *increase* in antibody production to latent viruses.

## When Up is Down

This deserves a little bit of explanation because this type of study will be looked at a number of times.  I had alluded earlier that it can be somewhat confusing.  On the one hand, it's easy to understand that a *decrease* in antibody response is a sign of suppressed immune functioning; but now we're saying that an *increase* in antibody response is a sign of depressed immune functioning.  How does that happen?

There are certain *latent viruses* which can infect us: Herpes virus, Epstein-Barr virus (EBV) and cytomegalovirus (CMV), for instance.  These viruses are like chicken pox virus; after we're exposed to them they stay around in the body long after the acute illness they caused has gone away. The virus remains but our *cellular* immunity keeps it under control. It's thought that if we become stressed our cellular immunity is less efficient at keeping these viruses under control and it forces our *humoral* immunity, the B cells, to make more antibody to deal with these viruses.[91] That's why in this circumstance increased antibody to latent viruses indicates that indeed the immune system is being stressed and challenged. A meta-analysis[92] also found that antibody production to latent viruses increased with stress.

**Caretakers** of persons with Alzheimer's Disease also had decreased immune functioning, decreased antibody response (this is not to latent viruses but a decreased antibody response in general to other antigens) and also tended to be **depressed**.[93] Often, they feel like they have little control over their situation, no honorable way to free themselves from the very difficult and all consuming burden of such caretaking.

## Immunity and Cancer

Tumors are also attacked by the immune system by macrophages, the large cells that eat up the bad guys. Stress neurohormones suppress the ability of (the interferon manufactured by) the body to activate those macrophages to eat our tumor cells.[94] Severe and negative life events and difficulties are associated with recurrences of breast cancer.[95] Also, suppressed anger and changes in immunoglobulin A levels have been associated with both benign and malignant breast disease.[96] Other studies have shown that tumor growth is increased by chronic, severe stress.[97]

## Examination Stress

If you are a researcher looking to find populations of people to stress and study, one fruitful place to go is down the hall to some of the medical students. They're often a bunch of eager beavers, ready to participate in research. They're often stressed out of their minds and it's not foreign to them to have people suggest that they stick their arm out to have needles stuck in them. A number of

303

studies have looked at the effects of stress on immune functioning in students.

Researchers looked at the effects of a commonplace stressful event on *interferon* production and natural killer cell activity and numbers.[98] Interferon is a substance which the body produces to enhance its immune response, particularly to viruses. Interferon production and natural killer cell activity and numbers were decreased when subjects were stressed going through medical school examinations compared to how they had been six weeks earlier.

The percentage of activated T cells decreased while undergraduate psychology students were going through examinations,[99] compared to how they had been both before and after the examinations and compared to control students who were not being stressed by exams. Similarly, the proliferative response of these T cells to antigens and mitogens was decreased presumably due to the examinations.[100]

In addition to decreased natural killer cell activity, school examination stress has also been associated with the impaired lymphocyte proliferation response to mitogens.[101]

## Social Support and Loneliness

The concentration of immunoglobulin A in saliva in healthy undergraduate students decreased during their final exams.[102] Students who reported more adequate social support at the pre-exam period, had higher salivary IgA levels than did their peers who reported less adequate social support.[103]

Life change stress, anxiety, depression, particularly when associated with poor coping skills, have also been associated with decreased natural killer cell activity.[104]

Medical students who scored higher in a test for loneliness had significantly higher antibody titers to herpes than low loneliness subjects.[105] Again, in this context with regard to latent viruses like herpes, high antibody titers indicate degradation of immune functioning. (So, those who were lonelier had poorer immune functioning.) Similarly, natural killer cell activity in medical students declined significantly during exams[106] and those who scored highly on tests for stressful life events and loneliness had significantly lower levels of natural killer cell activity. (The need to subject our future healers to this kind of stress is controversial. That is a topic for another book, but it is food for thought.)

Loneliness has also been shown to decrease cellular immune competence in inpatient psychiatric patients.[107]

## Bereavement and Depression

Persons who have lost their spouses have decreased lymphocyte stimulation and decreased natural killer cell activity.[108,109,110] Bereaved individuals have decreases in the numbers of lymphocytes.[111] Women who have lost their husbands experience decreases in natural killer cell activity and increases in cortisol, a stress hormone which comes from the adrenal gland and which has been associated with depressed immune functioning.[112,113]

Depressed persons have decreased lymphocyte stimulation responses.[114,115] Also, the decrease in natural killer cell activity is associated with severity of depression.[116]

## Marriage and Divorce

Poor marital quality is associated with a decrease in immune functioning.[117] In persons who are divorced and who are still drawn to their ex-spouses, immune functioning is poorer. Those who are more distressed and lonelier have an increased frequency of illnesses.[118] Men who had surgery for hernia had different healing times and different immune functioning depending upon their level of social and spousal support.[119] Measures of social and marital support correlate with immune functioning, total lymphocyte counts and lymphocyte stimulation responses.[120]

## Coping Skills

Stress has been defined in a number of different ways. One definition: it is an observable event; a stressor that influences a person in a certain undesirable or harmful way. Another definition: it's not the *event* that happens to you but rather it is the *processing* of that experience. In other words, it's not what happens to you, but what you do with it that counts.

Many studies have indicated that the **degree of stress controllability** rather than the stress itself is the factor in immunosuppression. The natural killer cell activity of people with poor coping skills was significantly lower[121] than the activity of those who demonstrated good coping skills. Researchers concluded that psychosocial stress in persons with poorer coping skills may lead to decreased natural killer cell activity.

Similarly, in students, it was found that decreases in salivary IgA were not associated so much with changes in the level of stress but rather with an index of *internal locus of control.* That is, those students who felt that their stress was out of control had decreases in salivary IgA, whereas, those who felt in control of the stress in their lives, did not experience those changes.[122]

Just as we saw in rats, it turns out that controllable stress does not decrease lymphocyte stimulation response but uncontrollable stress does.[86]

## Good Times, Bad Times

Our immune response is a function of many factors, some of which are mediated by stress hormones. At first blush, the data appear to conflict. It's been found that stress hormones suppress T lymphocyte production, but they tend to enhance natural killer cell activity. This is confusing, even more so since it depends on which hormones we're talking about as well; steroids, for instance, tend to decrease natural killer cell activity.[123]

The point is that there seems to be what is called a *biphasic* response to stress hormones.[124] That is, for example, with response to "good stress" *lower* levels of beta endorphin are produced which lead to an *increase* in natural killer cell activity. Whereas, bad stress, uncontrollable stress, tends to lead to very *high* levels of beta endorphin and *decreased* levels of natural killer cell activity. It may be that the runner's high that's experienced is a manifestation of the effect of these beta endorphins which are experienced at modest levels in long-distance runners. When subjected to terrible stress, many people report that they experience some degree of disassociation from that experience. Some survivors of the death camps during the Holocaust report being beaten and tortured and yet feeling completely distanced from it and not suffering so much. Presumably, at that point, they were gaining the benefits of these very high levels of beta endorphin with their morphine-like effects. Obviously, such experiences are not desirable, from both the perspective of common sense and also from the immunologic perspective, as these high levels lead to decreased natural killer cell activity.[125]

## Clinical Outcomes

We've seen by now that stress clearly has effects on immunity, both in animal models and in humans. But, do these effects on immunity translate into clinical results? Most of us don't walk around cognizant of or caring about the level of our natural killer cell activity or whether our lymphocytes are able to generate a proliferative response to a mitogen. What we want to avoid are illnesses and diseases and discomforts.

Increased incidents of coronary artery disease as well as bacterial and viral diseases have been attributed to chronic stress.[126,127,128,129] Stress increases the frequency of naturally-occurring upper respiratory infections.[130,131] In a lab setting, stress also increased the nasal secretions in experimentally-induced upper respiratory infections.[132]

One of the best of these upper respiratory infection studies[133] was published in 1991. After completing questionnaires assessing degrees of psychological stress, 394 healthy subjects were given nasal drops containing one of five different types of respiratory viruses. An additional 26 persons were given just salt water drops. The subjects were quarantined and then monitored for the development of signs and symptoms of infection. Rates of both respiratory infection and clinically-apparent common colds increased directly with increases in the degree of psychological stress on the initial testing. Reaction rates ranged from about 74 percent to approximately 90 percent, according to levels of psychological stress and the incidents of colds ranged from 27 percent to 47 percent. Researchers concluded that psychological stress was associated with an increased risk of acute infectious respiratory illness (and this risk was attributable to increased rates of infection rather than just increased frequency of symptoms).

The importance of this study is that it demonstrated not just that stress could contribute to the development of colds but it put together a number of different links in the chain. Scientists are very touchy about this. For instance, if we can show that stress results in some effect on immune functioning and we can show in some other study that changes in immune functioning are related to a clinical disease, then it might make sense to you and me that we can say that stress contributes to that particular clinical disease. But, the scientist says, "Wait a minute. I need to show in the same study that stress will cause a clinical outcome." That's what this study demonstrated.

Another pair of studies [134,135] were performed on individuals who had malignant melanoma, a type of skin cancer. Sixty-eight persons with melanoma participated in a six-week, structured psychiatric group intervention. For the control patients, 13 of the 34 had recurrence of the cancer and ten out of 34 died. Whereas, among those who had undergone the psychiatric group intervention only seven of 34 had recurrence and three of 34 died. Baseline **coping skills** and enhancement of active behavioral coping over time were predictive of lower rates of recurrence and death even despite the fact that the experimental group tended to have a higher level of baseline distress.

Six months after the psychiatric group intervention, the subjects had increases in the percent of certain kinds of lymphocytes, including natural killer cells, along with indications of increase in natural killer cell cytotoxic activity. The conclusion of these studies is that short-term psychiatric group intervention in this population of people generated changes *both* in immune functioning *and* also changes in disease recurrence and mortality rates. Studies that supply all these links in the chain are important.

Other studies have demonstrated[136] that **stress** generated an increase in circulating epinephrine levels of stress hormone which is associated with decreases in IgA antibody *and* an increased frequency of upper respiratory infections. Also,[137] college **examinations** generated a decrease in interferon, an increase in antibody titers to Epstein-Barr virus, a decrease in T killer cell activity and increase in frequency of infectious disease. Stress in patients with Herpes Simplex virus led to a decrease in T cells. An increase in **depression** and **anger**, which also is associated with a decrease in T helper cells and depression, led to an increase in the rate of Herpes Simplex virus infection expression.[138]

As stated earlier in this text, one very telling study was performed at the United States Military Academy at West Point. This study was very well designed in that it lasted four years and was prospective, that is, looking forward in its design rather than reviewing that which had already happened. Cadets at the military academy were identified as being either susceptible to or immune to Epstein-Barr virus by the absence or presence of antibody to that virus. On entry to the study, about one-third of the cadets lacked the antibody, of whom about 20 percent became infected at sometime during the study. About one-fourth of those who seroconverted, that is, who went from being antibody negative to antibody positive, developed definite clinical and recognized infectious mononucleosis. Psychosocial factors significantly increased the risk of clinical infectious mononucleosis. These psychosocial factors included having fathers who were over-achievers, having a high level of motivation and doing relatively poorly academically. The combination of **high motivation** and **poor academic performance** interacted in predicting clinical infectious mononucleosis. On a level of common sense, one can almost predict that a young man going into the military academy with that load behind him, having over-achieving fathers, being driven both internally and probably by family to excel and then finding himself performing poorly academically -- that's enough to make anybody sick.[139]

Another study[140] found through a rigorous statistical analysis that fluctuations in **negative moods** were able to account for 14 percent of recurrences of Herpes Simplex virus. Negative mood[141] was associated with an increase in cold sores in nurses. Increased stress[142] was associated with an increase in Herpes Simplex Types 1 and 2 and a decrease in T lymphocyte function.

We've seen that **depression** can affect immune functioning; but it can also affect survival.[29] Patients who had malignancy treated with bone marrow transplantation were studied. Twelve of 13 such patients who were depressed died in less than one year. But, of 87 who were not depressed, 34 were alive after two years.

In pregnant women, those who have **less social support** and/or less control over life stress problems tend to have lower birthweight babies and an increase in obstetric complications.[143,144,145]

We've seen that **bereavement** has adverse effects on immune functioning, but does it have clinical effects? Indeed, unfortunately, it does. Bereaved men tend to die suddenly after the deaths of their wives.[146] Also, bereavement has been associated with increased morbidity (disease) in addition to increases in mortality.[147]

**Job dissatisfaction** has been associated with increased frequency of disease.[148] Studies in twins have indicated differences in rates of coronary artery disease owing to stress and job dissatisfaction.[149]

## Strange Bedfellows

I discussed earlier some of the mechanisms by which stress and cholesterol combined to damage the lining of the insides of the walls of blood vessels which can contribute to atherosclerotic plaque formation, heart disease, and heart attack. As we continue to learn, it looks more and more like the immune system is playing a very integral role in all of this.

Macrophages (*macro* meaning big and *phage* meaning to eat) tend to eat fat in the vascular *endothelium*, particularly the oxidized, damaged low-density lipoprotein (LDL, the bad stuff) component of cholesterol.[150] These activities of the macrophages, while perhaps making sense to the macrophage, actually tend to have a damaging effect on the lining of the inside wall of the blood vessel.

Also, we find out that such unrelated diseases such as peptic ulcer disease may indeed have very significant immune components. In fact, a couple of the medicines that are used in peptic ulcer disease such as cimetidine (or *tagamet*) and ranitidine (or *zantac*) seem to act not so much on acid-secreting cells in order to prevent ulcers, but rather act more on immune cells: macrophages and antibody-producing plasma cells in the stomach lining.[151] And, peptic ulcer disease turns out to be, at least in some people, an infectious disease, perhaps more prone to occur in the face of an immune inadequacy. You may have heard of the "new" bacterium, *Helicobactor pylori*, associated with peptic ulcer disease. Peptic ulcer disease, in some persons, is treated with antibiotics, an approach which would have met with howls of derision as recently as a decade ago.

An infectious component in coronary atherosclerosis is now being investigated. Researchers have found that a bacterium, *Chlamydia pneumoniae*, was present in 79% of the coronary artery walls of persons with coronary artery disease, but was present in only 4% of the vessels of people without the disease. [152]

Once again in our stressed out examination fried medical students, there were significant declines in the percentage of helper T Cells and in natural killer cell activity in blood samples obtained on the day of examinations. But, in the half of the group that had been taught relaxation, the **frequency of relaxation practice** was a significant predictor of the percentages of helper inducer cells (T helper cells) in the exam sample. The control non-relaxation group had increased self-rated distress associated with the examination, compared to no increase in distress in the relaxation group.[153]

Stress can decrease natural killer cell activity.[154] Conversely, relaxation and imagery can increase IgA levels. Even simple relaxation can increase natural killer cell activity, decrease antibody levels to Herpes Simplex virus, increase the percentage of helper to depressor cell and increase immunoglobulins.[155,156,157] Researchers have studied salivary immunoglobulin A secretion and perceived daily **mood** over numbers of weeks.[158] Subjects had higher concentrations of IgA on days when they perceived themselves to be in a positive mood, and lower concentrations when in a negative mood.

**Positive attitudes,**[159] **humor,**[160] and exposure to **uplifting films**[161] enhance immunocompetence. Salivary IgA concentration increased significantly after subjects viewed a humorous video tape and did not change significantly after they viewed a didactic or boring video tape. Students who watched a film about Mother Teresa's work were found to have an increase in salivary IgA and this was regardless of whether or not they outwardly expressed approval for the type of work Mother Teresa does.

Persons with **multiple personality disorder** have some unusual psychophysiologic phenomena, some of which relate to immune functioning.[162,163] Such persons can have different immune functioning depending on which personality happens to be running the show at the moment. For instance, one patient had an allergy to orange juice but another personality in that same patient was not allergic. The non-allergic personality could be drinking a glass of orange juice but if the allergic personality then came to the fore, an allergic reaction would ensue. If the non-allergic personality then resumed control of the individual, the allergic symptoms would abate.

# Section IV: AIDS

The particular cell affected by the HIV or Human Immunodeficiency Virus is the T4 cell (or CD4 Cell). HIV invades the cell and lives there, often unmanifest for extended periods. When it becomes more active and reproduces thousands of more viral particles, that's dangerous. The cells break open and spread these viruses throughout the blood; then the viruses have the opportunity to infect other cells. This productive state, where more viruses are produced, can be induced by **exposure to other viruses**.[164]

We've already seen that psychosocial factors are associated with evidence of reactivation of latent viruses in healthy persons, and, presumably, that same thing happens with persons with AIDS. We've seen that increases in cortisol (associated with increases in stress) decrease number and functions of these CD4 counts, which, again, are the cells which are reduced in number and function in AIDS.[165]

Hydrocortisone, a steroid hormone which is produced in the adrenal gland and is secreted in response to **stress**, has been shown to increase the expression of HIV by mononuclear cells in cell culture.[166]

The mechanism of some degree of immune impairment due to negative perception of HIV infection has been well postulated. An unhappy mood tends to generate changes in the autonomic and adrenergic nervous systems, which lead to increases in circulating norepinephrine, which lead to changes in functions of T lymphocytes, which lead to problems with immune impairment due to HIV.[167]

The numbers of T4 cells tend to plateau for three years or even longer, with no significant decrease, in 58 percent of persons who are infected with HIV.[168] A number of things can provoke these cells into falling further and fall off the plateau. Increases in numbers of **bereavement** episodes are associated with increases in levels of stress symptoms.[169] High stress levels correlate with depression and symptoms of unhappy mood or dysphoria.[170] Bereavement decreases lymphocyte response to mitogen challenges as well as decrease in natural killer cell activity. This is true in persons with

AIDS. **Depression** also decreases lymphocyte proliferative response.[171]

The number of bereavement losses and the degree of distress secondary to those losses, is predictive of HIV progression. We don't need to be reminded that this population of individuals has suffered a highly disproportionate level of losses and bereavement. These are often young people whose friends and peers have been dying around them at rates which are unnatural for persons of their years.[172]

The death of an intimate partner leads to a decrease of lymphocyte proliferative response.[173] There is a correlation between depressed mood and depressed CD4 levels even in persons who are not bereaved.[174] Depression leads to a steeper decline in CD4 levels.[175]

**Helplessness** also was a significant predictor of decreases in CD4 levels one year later.[171] **Fatalistic** men survived a shorter time.[176] Such men found themselves characterized by statements such as, "I tend to prepare myself for the worst," or "I go over in mind what I would say or do if I got AIDS." HIV positive men who are both fatalistic and bereaved tended to survive the shortest amount of time.[177]

Some glimmer of good news in all this is it has been found that active **coping** style was directly and positively associated with natural killer cell cytotoxicity.[178]

Unfortunately, stress in this population sometimes is addressed by a number of **behaviors** which can be damaging to immune functioning. Particularly among those who are fatalistic, stressed and depressed, there is a tendency to turn toward alcohol, drugs, a tendency for decrease in sleep, inadequate nutrition and increase in sexual activity.[167] Increased stressed and decreased coping ability[179] are associated with a lower total lymphocyte count in asymptomatic HIV positive men.

## No News is Bad News

The virus itself is bad enough. But even just the psychological aspect of the diagnosis of that viral infection also can have devastating effects on immune functioning. One study[180] looked at changes in immune and psychological measures as a function of **anticipation** and **reaction** to news of HIV antibody status. This population of homosexual males between the ages of 18 and 40 years seems to be walking around in a state of **dread** with corresponding degradation of immune function. Even those men who have not been diagnosed with infection of HIV tend to experience depressed natural killer cell cytotoxicity, clinical levels of anxiety, intrusive thoughts and avoidance responses. These tend to return to non-clinical baseline levels within five weeks or so after notification in both men who were notified that they were positive and those who were notified they were negative. This means that both those who were HIV positive and those who were HIV negative but didn't know their status had depressed immune functioning just in anticipation of finding out what their status was. Then, after they were told, even those who were told they were positive had some degree of relief from this immune suppression. Dread and anticipation impair lymphocyte proliferative responses[181] and are associated with higher plasma cortisol levels (cortisol, you recall, is a stress hormone).

Group therapy in HIV positive persons[182] has been helpful. Among those undergoing group therapy, there was no increase in depression after they were told of their diagnosis of HIV infection, whereas, control individuals who were informed of their HIV infection but did not have group therapy did have an increase in depression. Psychosocial intervention has been shown to modulate antibody responses to Epstein-Barr and herpes viruses in HIV-positive and at-risk gay men.[183]

## Survivors

A population of men from whom we may be well be able to learn something very important are those who have markedly decreased T cells but do well anyway. They should have many hundreds of T cells, but despite having T cells less than 50, they are and have been asymptomatic for greater than six months. What can we learn about these people?[184]

They tend to accept their HIV positive status but they do not have the perception of a death sentence. They have a sense of control. They have a sense that the future holds unmet goals for them. They have the ability to withdraw from excessive demands in order to nurture themselves. They also tend to have normal natural killer cell activity. In psychological testing, they tend to score the least on scales of meekness, bitterness and guilt. Simply put, they know how to live.

# Section V: Touch, Non-Touch, Prayer, and Attention

Massage feels good. It feels even better when administered by someone who cares for you. Massage has been looked at for its therapeutic value and has been found to have very beneficial effects.

Massage was given to 20 pre-term newborns[185] who were in a neonatal intensive care unit. Their growth, sleep, weight, behavior and developmental performance was compared with 20 control neonates who were not massaged. The massage consisted of stroking the bodies of these tiny babies (whose mean birth weight was less than three pounds), passively moving their limbs for three 15-minute periods per day, for ten days. The neonates so treated averaged a 47 percent greater weight gain per day, were more active and alert, and showed more mature orientation and range of behavior on objective tests than the control infants. Also, their hospital stay was six days shorter.

In this touching perhaps something tangible is being physically transmitted to these little babies. What we're seeing, I believe, is a manifestation also of the flow of love and consciousness that babies need just as they need calories and water. But you don't need actually to touch someone in order to have these therapeutic effects.

There is a technique called non-contact therapeutic touch (or NCTT) in which the healer's hands do not actually touch the patient. They are held a short distance from the patient's body. Typically, this procedure consists of an individual (usually a nurse) centering herself, having the intention to help the subject, moving the hands over the body part or the entire body to attune the practitioner to the subject's condition, redirecting areas felt to be tense or unhealthy by movement of the hands and sending some attention in specific areas by placing the hands 4" to 6" from the body part or, if the entire body is being attended to, over the solar plexus area.

In one study[186] of 34 patients, artificially-created surgical wounds were treated. The subjects inserted the arm with the wound through a hole in the wall, beyond which they could not see into the adjoining room. (They were told that the purpose of this was "to measure biopotentials from the surgical site.") They were not told anything about this non-contact therapeutic touch and were not told that any type of healing intervention would be taking place. The NCTT practitioner was present in the adjoining room during exposure sessions for the active treatment group of 23 patients, and the room was empty during the control periods for the other 21 patients. As the practitioner attempted to heal the wounds, she avoided any physical contact with the subjects. Over the course of some days at different stages, the wound area was traced onto transparent sheets by a physician who didn't know whether the patients were assigned to the active group or the control group; then an independent technician who was also blinded to the two groups would accurately measure the degree of healing.

The results were highly significant. By the eighth day, the wound sizes of the treated subjects showed less variation than those of the untreated subjects and were much smaller. Thirteen of the 23 treated subjects were completely healed on day 16 compared to none of the untreated group. It is important to note that since the subjects did not believe they were receiving a particular healing treatment, it is unlikely that the placebo response was involved.

In another study, patients with anxiety were treated by NCTT.[187] Thirty-seven men and 23 women hospitalized in a cardiovascular unit were randomized into experimental and control groups. The purpose of the intervention was to have a beneficial effect on the anxiety of the patients. In the treatment group the nurses performed the NCTT. In the control group, non-contact was performed but there was no therapeutic touch. That is, the nurse made no attempt to center herself, there was no intention to assist the subject, there was no attuning to the condition of the subject and no direction of energy toward the subject. The nurse was trained in making the particular movements of her hands that the non-contact therapeutic touch nurses were making, but, instead, her attention was on some arithmetic problems; subtracting from 100 by sevens and counting backwards from 240 down to zero. The total time of the intervention in both groups was five minutes. The results: significant decreases in anxiety following the non-contact therapeutic touch treatment, with significantly smaller decreases in anxiety in the control group.

Researchers have shown that the mental images of one person can have effects on the autonomic nervous system of another, that the second person may be at some distance, and even be unaware that the attempt is being made, yet the changes will still take place.[188]

This anecdote was cited by Larry Dossey, M.D. in his book Healing Words:

> As an example of the apprehension that exists in medical institutions about spiritual healing, consider a true story that originated in a large hospital. Several nurses became interested in learning therapeutic touch, a technique developed by nurse academician, Dolores Krieger, of New York University. This technique, a variation of the ancient practice of laying on of hands, has been scientifically studied in several, carefully-controlled experiments. One weekend, these nurses went away to take a course in this technique which apparently infuriated the Director of Nursing. When the nurses returned to work on Monday morning fresh from the course, they were met by a large sign on the bulletin board in the Nursing Department: THERE WILL BE NO HEALING IN THIS HOSPITAL![189]

# Prayer

> There is a type of person in whose mind God is always mixed up with vitamins.
>
> -- Manly P. Hall[190]

Prayer has been the subject of a number of scientific studies. One of them[191] was performed in the Coronary Care Unit (CCU) at San Francisco General Hospital. Three hundred ninety-three patients admitted to the CCU were randomly assigned either to a group that was prayed for by home prayer groups or to a group that was not addressed by prayer. This experiment was doubled blinded, which means that no one except the researchers knew which group the patients were in.  The prayer groups were given only the first names of their patients and a brief description of their situation. They were asked to pray each day in whatever way they understood prayer.

The patients who were prayed for had a number of interesting outcomes.  They were five times less likely to require antibiotics, and three times less likely to develop pulmonary edema (fluid backup in the lungs), which results from heart failure.  None of the prayed for patients required endotracheal intubation, a procedure in which an airway is inserted into the windpipe and attached to a ventilating machine, while twelve in the unprayed for group did require that procedure.  Also, there were fewer fatalities in the prayed for group (although this was not a significant difference, statistically).

The magnitude of these changes is significant; if a drug or surgical procedure had accomplished these, it probably would be standard therapy in coronary care units all over the country.

An organization in Oregon called Spindrift has done numerous laboratory experiments documenting the effectiveness of prayer.[192]  They have tried to distinguish between directed prayer and non-directed prayer.  In directed prayer we have in mind a specific goal.  So if I'm praying for a new bicycle under the Christmas tree, that's a directed prayer.  In non-directed prayer, our approach is less specific.  The prayer makes no attempt to direct God or the universe or nature to accomplish a specific feat.  (This is in contrast to what many practitioners these days hold to be important: that one must clearly visualize lymphocytes chewing up cancer cells or whatever particular outcome is desired.)  Simple laboratory experiments involve, for instance, growing a mold on the surface of an agar plate. Individuals would pray trying to encourage the growth of a mold on a particular area of a plate.  When directed prayer was abandoned and non-directed prayer substituted, the growth of the mold was enhanced.  The researchers concluded that healers would be more effective if they tried to be free of visualizations, associations or specific goals, replacing those with "a pure and holy qualitative consciousness of whoever or whatever the patient may be."[193]  This non-directed prayer, if it has any goal, focuses on "what's best for the organism."

In a series of germination experiments, the researcher praying did not know what was best for the seeds involved. A batch was oversoaked in water, another batch was undersoaked. Not knowing which batch was which, the practitioner couldn't pray for the undersoaked seeds to absorb water or the oversoaked seeds to get rid of water, so he used non-directed prayer, and this approach seemed to work. The oversoaked beans eliminated water, the undersoaked beans gained water; each moved in a direction that was healthy for them.[194]

Perhaps being too specific in our prayer or desire places restrictions on how it may be fulfilled. There is the story of the man of great faith caught in a flood, sitting on his roof, praying for deliverance. A boat came by to rescue him, but he declined, saying, "God will save me." The floodwaters rose. A helicopter flew over him. "Grab this line, we'll lift you off." He shook his head: "God will save me!" His house submerged, the water up to his neck, he saw the last boat. "Get in the boat or you'll drown!" they shouted. He gurgled, "God will save me...." The man drowned. Upon reaching the Pearly Gates, he asked St. Peter for an audience with God. "My Lord," he asked, "how could You let me drown? I had such faith in you!" "Why complain to Me?" God replied. "I sent two boats and a helicopter!"[195]

It appears that a key element for successful undirected prayer is a quality of *surrender* or *non-attachment*. This quality is also seen in the case reports of individuals who have experienced spontaneous remissions of cancer. Surrender is not the same as giving up; in fact, they are opposite in many ways.

It appears that human minds can influence not only other people but also machines. There have been a number of experiments at the Princeton Engineering Anomalies Research Laboratory studying the ability of people to influence the behavior of random physical events. A microelectronic Random Event Generator produces a series of binary samples at the rate of a thousand per second and then tracks the number that conformed to a regular positive or negative alternation. A person sits in front of this device, views on a display the sequence of numbers and tries to influence the output in either a positive or a negative direction, willing the machine's output up or down.

Over the years, more than a quarter of a million attempts to influence the Random Event Generator have been tested. Results clearly indicate that people can influence the machine, steering its output from randomness toward a particular pattern.

The experiments show that this act is independent of distance. Experiments have been carried out with the person influencing a machine on the other side of the world. Even more interesting is that these effects seem to be independent of time. People are able to influence the output of the device before the device is actually running. Most paradoxically, operators can also influence the machine's output after it has run. That is, the machine runs, nobody looks at the results and then the subject tries to influence its output at some later time. The results are just as strong as efforts made in the present. [196,197,198]

Experiments indicate that these past, random events are capable of being influenced mentally, even though they have already occurred and have been recorded in some way, so long as they have not been observed. Somehow our observation seems to fix the object of our attention in space and time. In a twist on these experiments, a third party observes the pre-recorded events during the interval between their generation and the session in which the mental influence is attempted. Results suggest that this pre-observation may prevent or obstruct the mental influence on past events. Most interesting, the ability of observation to "fix the past" has been tested in cases when not only humans but even dogs and goldfish were the observers! [199,200]

Is it possible that this ability of our mind to affect events remote in both space and time might play havoc with scientific experimentation? Indeed, it is suggested in some studies [201] that a physician's beliefs can alter the results of these double-blind studies.

The idea of a *double blind* is that the attitude of the physician and the attitude of the patient are irrelevant because neither of them know what the patient is taking. These studies showed that even in double-blind settings certain drugs prove to be significantly more powerful than the placebo but only for the physician who believed in it, even though the physician and the patient didn't know who was taking what. Somehow the effectiveness of the drug over the placebo was correlated with the physician's mindset. Somehow the belief and the attitude of the physician can penetrate these double-blind conditions and change the action of the drug.[202]

A researcher concluded[203] "studies with a wide variety of treatments have conclusively affirmed that the administering physician or researcher is not independent of the results in double-blind treatment effectiveness studies...as a general rule, the double blind cannot any longer be assumed to guarantee the exclusion of the non-specific effects of the treatment, especially when the actual treatment has a weak or variable effect."

We've already seen the ability of prayer and attention to affect molds, which certainly would be independent of a placebo effect since presumably a mold does not know what you're thinking about it. A number of other studies are mentioned and synopsized in the book Healing Words. They are intriguing, so I'll mention just five of them.

- Ten subjects tried to inhibit the growth of fungus cultures in the laboratory through conscious intent by concentrating on them for 15 minutes from a distance of approximately a yard and a half. The cultures were then incubated for several more hours and 151 out of 194 showed retarded growth.[204]
- In a replication of this study, one group of subjects demonstrated the same effect in 16 out of 16 trials while stationed from one to 15 miles away from the fungus cultures.[205]
- Sixty subjects who were not known to have any particular healing abilities were able both to impede and stimulate significantly the growth of cultures of bacteria.[206]
- In a similar experiment, two healers held a bottle of water in their hands for 30 minutes. Samples of the water were then added to solutions of yeast cells in test tubes. Metabolic activity of the yeast was significantly increased in the yeast cultures who were given the "treated" water in four out of five tests.[207]
- Sixty volunteers with no known healing abilities were asked to alter the genetic ability of a strain of bacterium. Subjects tried to influence nine test tubes of the bacterial cultures: three to increase a certain type of mutation; three to decrease a certain type of mutation; and, three tubes uninfluenced as controls. Results

indicated that the bacteria indeed mutated in the directions desired by the subject volunteers.[208]

We've seen that how we speak and what we think can influence others; can cause both beneficial and deleterious effects in other persons; that these effects can take place even without the other person knowing about them; that they can take place removed in time and removed in space. Our minds can influence mutations in bacteria and the growth of fungi. The influence of our minds can go back in time to change random events that have been generated by machines. There doesn't seem to be much that is beyond the capability of our minds to accomplish.

But what is the utility of this bewildering array of information? First, these findings force us to acknowledge that our linear Newtonian world view is incomplete; not wrong, just incomplete. Next, we must develop hypotheses and models that can account for these outcomes. I submit that the framework offered by Vedic science, confirmed by modern physics, and described in the text of this book, does just that. I am not aware of any other understanding that is comprehensive and coherent enough to explain the mechanics of all these phenomena.

Fortunately, we live in a time when this knowledge and understanding is not only available for our intellectual and scientific satisfaction, but is also codified and applicable as the Maharishi Vedic Approach to Health.

# Appendix G

# The Discovery of Veda and Vedic Literature

# in Human Physiology

| Qualities of Consciousness | Vedic Literature | Corresponding anatomical area |
|---|---|---|
| holistic | Rk Veda | The whole physiology |
| flowing wakefulness | Sama Veda | Sensory systems |
| dynamic and creative | Yajur-Veda | Processing systems |
| reverberating wholeness | Atharva Veda | Motor systems |
| established in itself | Sthapatya Veda | Anatomy |
| invincible and progressive | Dhanur-Veda | Immune system biochemistry |
| integrating and harmonizing | Gandharva-Veda | Cycles and rhythms pacemaker cells |

| Qualities of Consciousness | Vedic Literature | Corresponding anatomical area |
|---|---|---|
| **Vedangas** | | |
| expression | Shiksha | Autonomic ganglia |
| transformation | Kalp | Limbic system |
| expansion | Vyakaran | Hypothalamus |
| self-referral | Nirukt | Pituitary gland |
| measuring and quantifying | Chhand | Neurotransmitters neurohormones |
| all-knowing | Jyotish | Basal ganglia, cerebral cortex cranial nerves, brain stem |
| **Upangas** | | |
| decisive and distinguishing | Nyaya | Thalamus |
| specific | Vaisheshik | Cerebellum |
| enumerating | Samkhya | Types of neuronal activity |
| unifying | Yoga | Association fibers |
| analysing | Karma Mimansa | Twelve divisions of central nervous system (CNS) |
| I-ness or Being | Vedant | Integrated functioning of CNS |

| Qualities of Consciousness | Vedic Literature | Corresponding anatomical area |
|---|---|---|
| **Brahmanas** | | |
| memory | Smirti | Memory systems and reflexes |
| ancient and eternal | Puran | Great intermediate net |
| blossoming of Totality | Itihas | Voluntary motor and sensory projections |
| structuring | Brahmana | Descending tracts of CNS |
| stirring | Aranyak | Fasciculi proprii |
| transcendental and self-referral | Upanishad | Ascending tracts of CNS |
| **Ayur-Veda** | | |
| holding together, nourishing and supporting | Charak | Mesodermal tissues and organs |
| balancing | Sushrut | Endodermal tissues and organs |
| communicating and eloquent | Vagbhatt | Ectodermal tissues and organs |
| enlightening | Bhava-Prakash | Cell nucleus |
| synthesizing | Sharngadhar | Cytoplasm and cytoskeleton |
| detecting and recognizing | Madhav Nidan | Cell membrane |

| Qualities of Consciousness | Vedic Literature | Corresponding anatomical area |
|---|---|---|

### Pratishakyas

| Qualities of Consciousness | Vedic Literature | Corresponding anatomical area |
|---|---|---|
| all-pervading | Rk Veda Pratishakya | Plexiform layer horizontal communications |
| silencing, sharing and spreading | Shukl-Yajur-Veda Pratishakya | Corticocortical fibers |
| omnipresent | Krishn-Yajur-Veda Pratishakya (Taittiriya) | Commisural and corticocortical fibers |
| unmanifesting the parts but manifesting the whole | Sama Veda Pratishakya (Pushpa Sutram) | Thalamocortical fibers |
| unfolding | Atharva Veda Pratishakya | Cortico-striate, -tectal, -spinal fibers |
| dissolving | Atharva Veda Pratishakya (Chaturadhyayi) | Corticothalamic corticoclaustral fibers |

# Appendix H

# References

**Chapter 1**

1. Brantley PJ, Dietz LS, McKnight GT, et al. Convergence between the daily stress inventory and endocrine measures of stress. J Consult Clin Psychol 1988;56(4):549-51.
2. Sutherland JE. The link between stress and illness. Postgraduate Medicine 1991;89(1):159-164.
3. Holmes TH, Rahe RH. The Social Readjustment Rating Scale. J Psychosom Res 1967;11(2):213-8.
4. Petrich J, Holmes TH. Life change and onset of illness. Med Clin North Am 1977;61(4):825-38.


**Chapter 2**

1. Prochaska JO, DiClemente CC. Stages of change in the modification of problem behaviors. In, Progress in Behavior Modification. Sycamore IL. Sycamore Press. 1992.
2. Maharishi. Bhagavad-Gita. p12.
3. Wallace RK. The physiological effects of Transcendental Meditation: a proposed fourth major state of consciousness. 1970 UCLA PhD thesis. Reprinted in Collected Papers, op cit. 1:43-78.
4. Dillbeck MC, Orme-Johnson DW. Physiological differences between Transcendental Meditation and rest.American Psychologist 1987;42:879-881.
5. Wallace RK. Physiological effects of Transcendental Meditation. Science 1970;167:1751-1754.
6. Wallace RK, Benson H, Wilson AF. A wakeful hypometabolic state. Am J Physiol 1971;221:795-799.
7. Collected Papers, op cit Vols. 1-5.
8. Daniels D. Comparison of the Transcendental Meditation technique to various relaxation procedures. Collected Papers, op cit. 2:864-868.


**Chapter 3**

1. Eppley KR, Abrams AI, Shear J. Differential effects of relaxation techniques on trait anxiety: a meta-analysis. J Clin Psychol 1989;45(6):957-974.
2. Jevning R, Wilson AF, Smith WR, Morton ME. Redistribution of blood flow in acute hypometabloic behavior. Am J Physiol 1978;235(1):R89-R92.
3. Jevning R, Wilson AF, O'Halloran JP. Muscle and skin blood flow and metabolism during states of decreased activation. Physiology and Behavior 1982;29(2):343-348.

4. Jevning R, Wilson AF. Behavioral increase of cerebral blood flow. The Physiologist 1978;21:60.

5. Jevning R, Wilson AF, Smith WR. The Transcendental Meditation technique, adrenocortical activity, and implications for stress. Experentia 1978;34:618-619.

6. Bevan AJW. Endocrine changes in Transcendental Meditation. Clin Exp Pharm Physiol 1980;7:75-76.

7. Subrahmanyam S, Porkodi K. Neurohumoral correlates of Transcendental Meditation. J Biomed 1980;1:73-88.

8. Orme-Johnson DW, Haynes CT. EEG phase coherence, pure consciousness, creativity, and TM-Sidhi experiences. Int J Neurosci 1981;13:211-217.

9. Dillbeck MC, Bronson EC. Short-term longitudinal effects of the Transcendental Meditation technique on EEG power and coherence. Int J Neurosci 1981;14:147-151.

10. Dillbeck MC, Orme-Johnson DW, Wallace RK. Frontal EEG coherence, H-reflex recovery, concept learning, and the TM-Sidhi program. Int J Neurosci 1981;15:151-157.

11. Shafii M, Lavely R, Jaffe R. Meditation and marijuana. Am J Psychiatry 1974;131(1):60-63.

12. Aron EN, Aron R. The patterns of reduction of drug and alcohol use among Transcendental Meditation participants. Bulletin of the Society of Psychologists in Addictive Behaviors 1983;2(1):28-33.

13. Royer A. In, Self Recovery: Treating Addictions Using Transcendental Meditation and Maharishi Ayur-Veda. Alexander CN, O'Connell DF, editors. Harrington Park Press, New York. 1994:221-239.

14. Alexander CN, editor. Higher States of Human Development: Perspectives on Adult Growth. New York. Oxford University Press 1990;286-341.

15. Journal of Social Behavior and Personality 1991;6:189-247.

16. Dissertation Abstracts International 1975;36:4361A-4362A.

17. Perceptual and Motor Skills 1974;39:1031-1034.

18. Perceptual and Motor Skills 1987;65:613-614.

19. Dissertation Abstracts International 1977;38:3351A.

20. Journal of Personality and Individual Differences 1991;12:1105-1116.

21. Perceptual and Motor Skills 1986;62:731-738.

22. British Journal of Educational Psychology 1985;55:164-166.

23. Education 1986;107:49-54.

24. Cooper MJ, Aygen MM. Effect of Transcendental Meditation on serum cholesterol and blood pressure. Harefuah ( J Israel Med Assoc ) 1978;95(1):1-2.

25. Cooper MJ, Aygen MM. Transcendental Meditation in the management of cholesterolemia. J Human Stress 1979;5(4):24-27.

26. Wallace RK, Dillbeck M, Jacobe E, Harrington B. The effects of the Transcendental Meditation and TM-Sidhi program on the aging process. Int J Neurosci 1982;16:53-58.

27. Glaser JL, Brind JL, Vogelman JH, Eisner MJ, Dillbeck MC, Wallace RK, Chopra D, Orentreich N. Elevated serum dehydroepiandosterone sulfate levels in practitioners of the Transcendental Meditation (TM) and TM-Sidhi Program. J Behav Med 1986;15(4):327-334.

28. Orme-Johnson D. Medical care utilization and the Transcendental Meditation program. Psychosom Med 1987;49(5):493-507.

29. Herron RE. The impact of Transcendental Meditation practice on medical expenditures. Dissertation Abstracts International 1993;53(12):4219A.

30. Herron RE, Hillis SL, Mandarino JV, Orme-Johnson DW, Walton KG. The impact of the Transcendental Meditation program on government payments to physicians in Quebec. American Journal of Health Promotion 1996;10(3):208-216.

31. Schneider R, Staggers F, Alexander CN, Sheppard W, Rainforth M, Kondwani K, Smith S, King CG. A randomized controlled trial of stress reduction for hypertension in older African-Americans. Hypertension 1995;26(5):820-827.

32. Schneider R, et al. Hypertension 1996;28(2).

33. Herron RE, Schneider RH, Mandarino JV, Alexander CN, Walton KG. Cost-effective hypertension management: comparison of drug therapies with an alternative program. American Journal of Managed Care 1996;2:427-437.

34. Zamarra JW, Schneider R, Besseghini I, Robinson DK, Salerno JW. Usefulness of the Transcendental Meditation program in the treatment of patients with coronary artery disease. American Journal of Cardiology 1996;77:867-870.

35. Hayward CD, Piscopo J, Santos AD. Physiological effects of Benson's relaxation response during submaximal aerobic exercise in coronary artery disease patients. J Cardiol Rehabil 1987;7:534-539.

36. Alexander CN, Chandler HM, Langer EJ, Newman RI, Davies JL. Transcendental Meditation, mindfulness, and longevity: an experimental study with the elderly. J Personality Soc Psychol 1989;57:950-964.

37. Alexander CN, Barnes V, Schneider R, Langer EJ, Newman RI, Chandler HM, Davies JL, Rainforth M. A randomized controlled trial of stress reduction on cardiovacular and all-cause mortality in the elderly: results of 8 year and 15 year follow-ups

## Chapter 4

1. Rees B. Lisa: a student's notebook. The New Physician 1978;27(10):23-26.

2. Holmes NE, Blethen SL, Weldon VV. Somatomedin C response to growth hormone in psychosocial growth retardation. Am J Med Sci 1984;288(2):86-88.

3. Albanese A, Hamill G, Jones J, Skuse D, et al. Reversibility of physiological growth hormone secretion in children with psychosocial dwarfism. Clin Endocrinol (Oxf) 1994;40(5):687-692.

4. Alpers DH. Functional gastrointestinal disorders. Hosp Pract (Off) 1983;18(4):139-153.

5. Cassileth BR, Drossman DA. Psychosocial factors in gastrointestinal illness. Psychother Psychosom 1993;59(3-4):131-143.

6. Cobb S, Rose R. Hypertension, peptic ulcer, and diabetes in air traffic controllers. JAMA 1973;224(4):489-492.

7. Clouse RE. Anxiety and gastrointestinal illness. Psychiatr Clin North Am 1988;11(2):399-417.

8. Whitehead WE, Crowell MD, Robinson JC, Heller BR, Schuster MM. Effects of stressful life events on bowel symptoms: subjects with irritable syndrome compared with subjects without bowel dysfunction. Gut 1992;33(6):825-830.

9. Williams RB, Barefoot JC, Califf RM, Haney TL, Saunders WB, Pryor DB, Tlatky MA, Siegler IC, Mark DB. Prognostic importance of social and economic resources among medically treated patients with angiographically documented coronary artery disease. JAMA 1992;267:520-524.

10. Case RB, Moss AJ, Case N, McDermott M, Eberly S. Living alone after myocardial infarction. Impact on prognosis. JAMA 1992;267:515-519.

11. Frasure-Smith N. In-hospital symptoms of psychological distress as predictors of long term outcome after myocardial infarction in men. Am J Cardiol 1991;67(2):121-127.

12. Rozanski A, Krantz DS, Bairey CN. Ventricular responses to mental stress testing in patients with coronary artery disease. Pathophysiological implications. Circulation 1991;83(4 suppl):II137-144.

13. Krantz DS, Helmers KF, Bairey CN, Nebel LE, et al. Cardiovacular reactivity and mental stress-induced myocardial ischemia in patients with coronary artery disease. Psychosom Med 1991;53(1):1-12.

14. Wei Jiang, et al. Mental stress-induced myocardial ischemia and cardiac events. JAMA 1996;275(21):1651-1656.

15. Friedman M, Rosenman RH, Carroll V. Changes in the serum cholesterol and blood clotting time in men subjected to cyclic variation of occupational stress. Circulation 1958;17:852-861.

16. Eliot RS. Relationship of emotional stress to the heart. Heart Dis Stoke 1993;2:243-246.

17. Markovitz J, et al. Psychological predictors of hypertension in the Framingham study: is there tension in hypertension? JAMA 1993;270(20):2439-2443.

18. Kawachi I, Colditz GA, Ascherio A, Rimm EB, et al. Prospective study of phobic anxiety and risk of coronary heart disease in men. Circulation 1994;89(5):1992-1997.

19. Kawachi I, Sparrow D, Vokonas PS, Weiss ST. Symptoms of anxiety and risk of coronary heart disease. The Normative Aging Study. Circulation 1994;90(5):2225-2229.

20. Mittleman M. Cited by Boschert S in Family Practice News 15 April 1996; page 8.

21. Williams RB, Barefoot JC, Shekelle RB. The health consequences of hostility. In, Anger and Hostility in Cardiovascular and Behavioral Disorders. Hemisphere Publishing Corp 1985:173-185.

22. Mittleman MA, Maclure M, Sherwood JB, et al. Triggering of acute myocardial infarction by episodes of anger. Circulation 1995:92:1720-1725.

23. Miller LH, Smith AD. Boston University. Cited by: Masters M. Stress and the family physician. Calif Fam Phys Jan/Feb 1994:9-11.

24. Solomon GF, Amkraut AA. Emotions, immunity and disease. In, Emotions in Health and Illness: Theoretical and Research Foundations. New York: Grune & Stratton. 1983;167-186.

25. Zozulia AA, Patsakova EK, Kost NV. Reaction between methionine enkephalin and human lymphocytes. Akad Med Nauh SSSR 1982;1:28-32.

26. Cantor H, Gershon RK. Immunological circuits. Cellular compositions. Fed Proc 1979;39:2058-2064.

27. Helderman JH, Strom TB. Specific binding site on T and B lymphocytes as a marker of cell activation. Nature 1978;274:62-63.

28. Pert CB. The wisdom of the receptors: Neuropeptides, the emotions, and bodymind. Advances 1986;3(3):8-16.

29. Ader R, Cohen N. Behaviorally conditioned immunosupression. Psychosomatic Medicine 1975;37:333.

30. Laudenslager ML, Ryan SM, Drugar RC, Hysen RE, Maier SF. Coping and immunosuppression: inescapable but not escapable shock suppresses lymphocyte proliferation. Science 1983;221:568-570.

31. Kemeny M. Mind, emotions and the immune system. Presentation at annual conference of Institute of Noetic Sciences, Arlington, VA; June 1993.

32. Hatch MC, Wallenstein S, Beyea J, Nieves JW, Susser M. Cancer rates after the Three Mile Island nuclear accident and proximity of residence to the plant. Am J Pub Health 1991;81:719-724.

33. Kubitz KA, Peavey BS, Moore BS. The effect of daily hassles on humoral immunity: An interaction moderated by locus of control. Biofeedback and Self-Regulation 1986;11(2):115-123.

34. Kasl SV, Evans AS, Niederman JC. Psychosocial risk factors in the development of infectious mononucleosis. Psychosom Med 1979;41:445.

35. Braun BG. Neurophysiologic changes in multiple personality due to integration: a preliminary report. Am J Clin Hypn 1983;26(2):84-92.

36. Braun BG. Psychophysiologic phenomena in multiple personality and hypnosis. Am J Clin Hypn 1983;26(2):124-137.

37. Fauci AS. AIDS: Immunopathogenic mechanisms and research strategies. Clin Res 1987;35:503-510.

38. Ritchie AW, Oswald I, Micklem HS, et al. Circadian variation of lymphocyte subpopulations: A study with monoclonal antibodies. BMJ 1983;286:1773-1775.

39. Coates TJ, McKusick L, Kuno R, et al. Stress reduction training changed number of sexual partners but not immune function in men with HIV. Am J Pub Health 1989;79:885-887.

40. Solomon GF, Temoshok L, O'Leary A, Zich J. An intensive psychoimmunologic study of long-surviving persons with AIDS. Ann NY Acad Sci 1987;496:647-655.

41. Fauci A. Quoted in Patient Care 15 May 1995:22.

**Chapter 5**

1. Dillon KM, Minchoff B, Baker KH. Positive emotional states and enhancement of the immune system. Int J Psychiatr Med 1985-86;15:13-18.
2. Berk LS, Tan SA, Nehlsen-Cannarella SL, et al. Humor associated laughter decreases cortisol and increases spontaneous lymphocyte blastogenesis. Clin Res 1988;36:435A.
3. McClelland DC, Kirshnit C. The effect of motivational arousal through films on salivary immunoglobulin A. Psychol Health 1988;2:31-52.
4. Kobosa SC, Maddi SR, Kahn S. Hardiness and health: A prospective study. J Personality Soc Psychol 1982;42:168-177.
5. Cousins N. Head First: The Biology of Bones. NY. EP Dutton. 1989.
6. Seligman MEP. Learned Optimism. NY. Knopf. 1991.
7. Seachrist L. Spontaneous cancer remissions spark questions {news}. JNCI 1993;85(23):1892-1895.
8. Den Otter W. Immune surveillance and natural resistance: an evaluation. Cancer Immunol Immunother 1986;21(2):85-92.
9. Shekelle RB, Raynor WJ, Ostfeld Am, et al. Psychological depression and 17-year risk of death from cancer. Psychosom Med 1981;43:117-125.
10. Persky VW, Kempthorne-Rawson J, Shekelle RB. Personality and risk of cancer: 20-year followup of the Western Electric study. Psychosom Med 1987;49:435-449.
11. Zonderman AB, Costa PT, McCrae RR. Depression as a risk for cancer mobidity and mortality in a nationally representative sample. JAMA 1989;262(9):1191-1195.
12. LeShan L. An emotional life-history pattern associated with neoplastic disease. Ann NY Acad Sci 1966;125:780-793.
13. Levy SM, Herberman RB, Maluish AM, et al. Prognostic risk assessment in primary breast cancer by behavioral and immunologic parameters. Health Psychol 1985;4:99-113.
14. Levy SM, Herberman RB, Lippman M, D'Angelo T. Correlation of stress factors with sustained depression of natural killer cell activity and predicted prognosis in patients with breast cancer. J Clin Oncol 1987;5:348-353.
15. Levy SM, Herberman RB, Whiteside T, et al. Perceived social support and tumor estrogen/progesterone receptor status as predictors of natural killer cell activity in breast cancer patients. Psychosom Med 1990;52:73-85.
16. Grossarth-Maticek R, Eysenck HJ. Length of survival and lymphocyte percentage in women with mammary cancer as a function of psychotherapy. Psychol Rep 1989;65:315-321.
17. Fawzy FI, Kemeny ME, Fawzy NW, et al. A structured psychiatric intervention for cancer patients. II. Changes over time in immunological measures. Arch Gen Psychiatry 1990;47:729-735.
18. Basso AM, Depiante-Depaoli M, Molina VA. Chronic variable stress facilitates tumoral growth: reversal by imipramine administration. Life Sci 1992;50:1789-1796.

19. Hatch MC, Wallenstein S, Beyea J, Nieves JW, Susser M. Cancer rates after the Three Mile Island nuclear accident and proximity of residence to the plant. Am J Pub Health 1991;81:719-724.

20. Cox T, Mackay C. Psychosocial factors and psychophysiological mechanisms in the aetiology and development of cancers. Soc Sci Med 1982;16(4):381-396.

21. Kiecolt-Glaser JK, Stephens RE, Lipetz PD, Speicher CE, Glaser R. Distress and DNA repair in human lymphocytes. J Behav Med 1985;8(4):311-320.

22. Spiegel D, Kraemer HC, Bloom JR, et al. Effect of psychosocial treatment on survival of patients with metastatic breast cancer. Lancet 1989;2:888-891.

23. Schulz R, Bookwala J, Knapp JE, et al. Pessimism, age, and cancer mortality. Psychol Aging 1996;11:304-309.

**Chapter 6**

1. Carrese JA, Rhodes LA. Western bioethics on the Navaho reservation. JAMA 1995;274:826-829.

2. Klopfer B. Psychological variables in human cancer. J Projective Techniques 1957;21:331-340.

3. Turner JA, Deyo RA, Loeser JD, Von Korff M, Fordyce WE. The importance of placebo effects in pain treatment and research. JAMA 1994;271(20):1609-1614.

4. Cobb LA, Thomas GI, Dillard DH, Merendino KA, Bruce RA. An evaluation of internal-mammary-artery-ligation by a double-blind technic. NEJM 1959;260:1115-1118.

5. Dimond EG, Kittle CF, Crockett JE. Comparison of internal mammary ligation and sham operation for angina pectoris. Am J Cardiol 1960;5:483-486.

6. Spiro HM. Doctors, Patients, and Placeboes. New Haven, Conn. Yale U Press. 1986.

7. Trousseau A. Quoted in NEJM 1984;311(6):413-414.

8. Lasagna L, Laties VG, Dohan JL. Further studies on the 'pharmacology' of placebo administration. J Clin Invest 1958;37:533-537.

9. Blackwell B, Bloomfield SS, Buncher CR. Demonstration to medical students of placebo responses and non-drug factors. Lancet 1972;1:1279-1282.

10. Buckalew LW, Coffield KE. An investigation of drug expectancy as a function of capsule color and size and preparation form. J Clin Psychopharmacol 1982;2:245-248.

11. Gowdey CW. A guide to the pharmacology of placebos. Can Med Assoc J 1983;128:921-925.

12. Shapira K, et al. Study on the effects of tablet colour in the treatment of anxiety states. BMJ 1970;2:446-449.

13. Kline D. The power of the placebo. Hippocrates 1988;May/June:24-26.

14. Luparello T, Leist N, Lourie CH, Sweet P. The interaction of psychologic stimuli and pharmacologic agents on airway reactivity in asthmatic subjects. Psychosom Med 1970;32:509-513.

15. Shapiro AK, Shapiro E. Patient-provider relationships and the placebo effect. In, Behavioral Health: A Handbook of Health Enhancement and Disease Prevention. NY. Wiley-Interscience 1984:371-383.

16. Wolf S, Pinsky RH. Effects of placebo administration and occurrence of toxic reactions. JAMA 1954:155.

17. Pogge RC. The toxic placebo, I: side and toxic effects reported during the administration of placebo medicines. Med Times 1963;91:1-6.

18. Lasagna L. The placebo effect. J Allergy Clin Immunol 1986;78(#1 part 2):161-165.

19. Vinar O. Dependence on a placebo: a case report. Br J Psych 1969;115:1189.

20. Mintz I. A note on the addictive personality: addiction to placebos. Am J Psychiatr 1977;134:3.

21. Thomas KB. General practice consultations: is there any point in being positive? BMJ 1987;294:1200-1202.

22. Buchholz WM. West J Med. Cited by: Cousins N. Head First: The Biology of Hope. NY. EP Dutton. 1989:99.

23. Quoted by: Skelly F. Cancer and the mind. Am Med News 17 Jun 1991:29-34.

**Chapter 7**

1. Strauss MB. NEJM 1960;262:805.

2. Key TH. A short cut to metaphysics. Punch 14 July 1855.

3. Chapter 13 verse 2.

**Chapter 8**

1. British Medical Journal. 1991;303:798-799.

2. Field MJ, Lohr KN. Guidelines for clinical practice. Institute of Medicine. Washington D.C.: National Academy Press 1992:34.

3. Ornish D, Brown SE, Scherwitz LW, Billings JH, et al. Can lifestyle changes reverse coronary heart disease? The Lifestyle Heart Trial. Lancet 1990;336(8707):129-133.

4. Orme-Johnson D. Medical care utilization and the Transcendental Meditation program. Psychosom Med 1987;49(5):493-507.

5. JAMA. 1994;272:1851-1857.

6. JAMA. 1995;274:29-34.

7. Archives of Internal Medicine. 1995;155:1949-1956.

8. Abstracted by Barry Charles MD from Harrison's Principles of Internal Medicine.

9. Sharma RK, Dash B. Agnivesa's Caraka Samhita. Translation and critical exposition. Varanasi, India. Chowkhamba Sanskrit Series Office. 1983. Most of the portions cited in the next few chapters will be found in Sutrasthana, chapters VII and XXX, and in Vimanastanam, chapter 5.

**Chapter 9**

1. Sharma RK, Dash B. Agnivesa's Caraka Samhita. Translation and critical exposition. Varanasi, India. Chowkhamba Sanskrit Series Office. 1983. Most of the

portions cited in the next few chapters will be found in Sutrasthana, chapters VII and XXX, and in Vimanastanam, chapter 5.

2. Williams RJ. Biochemical Individuality. 1956; New York: John Wiley & Sons Inc.

3. Hagelin J. Is Consciousness the Unified Field? A Field Theorist's Perspective. Modern Science & Vedic Science 1987;1(1):29-87.

4. Hagelin J. Restructuring Physics from its Foundation in Light of Maharishi's Vedic Science. Modern Science and Vedic Science 1989;3(1):3-72.

**Chapter 10**

1. Maharishi Mahesh Yogi. The Science of Being and Art of Living. Copyright 1963. Maharishi International University Press. Livingston Manor , New York. Ninth printing, 1976. Hardback. Page 182.

2. Sharma RK, Dash B. Agnivesa's Caraka Samhita. Translation and critical exposition. Varanasi, India. Chowkhamba Sanskrit Series Office. 1983.    Most of the portions cited in the next few chapters will be found in Sutrasthana, chapters VII and XXX, and in Vimanastanam, chapter 5.

3. Bhishagratna KK. Sushruta Samhita. Translated and edited. Varanasi, India. Chowkhamba Sanskrit Series Office. 1981. Sarira Sthanam, chapter 9.

4. Maharishi Mahesh Yogi. On the Bhagavad-Gita: A New Translation and Commentary Chapters 1-6. Copyright 1967. Penguin Books, New York, NY. Ninth printing, 1979. Softcover. Page 227.

5. Maharishi. Bhagavad-Gita. Chapter2 verse38 page114.

6. Eliot RS. Coronary artery disease: biobehavioral factors. Circulation1986;76(Suppl I):110I-111.

7. Rosenman RH, Friedman M. Coronary heart disease in the Western Collaborative Group study. JAMA 1975;233(8):872-877.

8. Williams RB Jr. Refining the type A hypothesis: emergence of the hostility complex. Am J Cardiol 1987;60(18):27-32J.

9. Williams RB Jr., Haney TL, Lee KL, Kong Y-H, Blumenthal JA, Whalen RE. Type A behavior, hostility, and coronary atherosclerosis. Psychosom Med 1980;42(6):539-549.

10. Barefoot JC, Dahlstrom WG, Williams RB. Hostility, coronary heart disease incidence, and total mortality: A 25 year follow-up study of 225 physicians. Psychosom Med 1983;45(1):59-63.

11. Goodman M. Mayo Clinic Proceedings 1996;71:729-734.

12. Mittleman MA, Maclure M, Sherwood JB, et al. Triggering of acute myocardial infarction by episodes of anger. Circulation 1995;92:1720-1725.

13. Maharishi. Bhagavad-Gita. Page 236.

14. Ibid. p 163.

15. Ibid. p 46.

16. Ibid. ch 5  v 23

17. Ibid. p369-370.

18. Denollet J, et al. Personality as an independent predictor of long term mortality in patients with coronary heart disease. Lancet 1996;347:417-421.

**Chapter 12**

1. Maharishi. Bhagavad-Gita. ch 3 v 35 p 233.
2. Collected Papers: Scientific Research on Maharishi's Transcendental Meditation and TM Sidhi Programs. Volumes 1-5. MIU (now MUM) Press; Fairfield, Iowa.
3. Maharishi. Bhagavad-Gita. p369-370.
4. This is described in detail in Maharishi's translation of the Bhagavad Gita, as well as in the 33 videotape lesson Science of Creative Intelligence course offered at Maharishi Vedic Universities and Transcendental Meditation centers (see Appendix A).
5. Maharishi. Bhagavad-Gita. ch 3 v 33.
6. Ibid. Ch 3 v29 p224.
7. Ibid. p231-232.
8. Ibid. Ch 2 v 33.
9. Ibid. p109-110.
10. Ibid. Ch 4 v 17.
11. Haynes SG, Feinleib M. Women, work, and coronary heart disease: prospective findings from the Framingham heart study. Am J Pub Health 1980;70:133-141.
12. Hibbard JH, Pope CR. Effect of domestic and occupational roles on morbidity and mortality. Soc Sci Med 1991;32:805-811.
13. Kritz-Silverstein D, Wingard DL, Barrett-Connor E. Employment status and heart disease risk factors in middle-aged women: the Rancho Bernardo study. Am J Pub Health 1992;82:215-219.
14. Maharishi. From a videotaped lecture.
15. Freud S. Civilization and its discontents. In: Strachey J (ed.) The standard edition of the complete psychological works of Sigmund Freud, vol 20. London: Hogarth, 1959.
16. Levin JS, Vanderpool HY. Is frequent religious attendance really conducive to better health? Toward an epidemiology of religion. Soc Sci Med 1987;24:589-600.
17. Dossey L. Healing Words. San Francisco. Harper. 1993:252-253.
18. Larson DB, Larson SS. Religious commitment and health: valuing the relationship. Second Opinion: Health, Faith, and Ethics 1991;17(1):26-40.
19. Craigie FC Jr, Larson DB, Liu IY. References to religion in The Journal of Family Practice: Dimensions and valence of spirituality. J Fam Pract 1990;30(4):477-480.
20. Maharishi. Bhagavad-Gita ch4 v38 p313.
21. Ibid. Ch6 v32 p449.

**Chapter 13**

1. Carrese JA, Rhodes LA. Western bioethics on the Navaho reservation. JAMA 1995;274:826-829.

2. Hackett TP, Rosenbaum JE. Emotion, psychiatric disorders, and the heart. In, Braunwald E, Heart Disease: A Textbook of Cardiovascular Medicine. Philadelphia. WB Saunders. 1980:1923-1943.

3. Beecher HK. Pain in men wounded in battle. Ann Surg 1946;123:96-105.

4. Dossey, Healing Words. p30-32.

5. Maharishi. Bhagavad-Gita ch 2 vv 20,23-25.

6. Ibid. ch 2 v 47.

7. Gospel according to John 9:1-3. King James version.

8. Dossey, Healing Words. p19-21.

9. Maharishi.. Science of Being and Art of Living. p229.


**Chapter 14**

1. Rush B. Lectures on the practice of physic, I, No. 31.

2. Caraka Samhita, op cit.

3. Maharishi. Bhagavad-Gita. p 160.

4. Wysocki AB. The effect of intermittent noise exposure on excisional wound healing in albino rats. In: American Nursing Association. International Nursing Research Conference Abstracts. 1987:459.

5. Redding JS, Hargest TS, Minsky SH. How noisy is intensive care? Critical Care Med 1977;5:275.

6. Hansell HN. The behavioral effects of noise on man.: The patient with "intensive care unit psychosis." Heart and Lung. 1984;13(1):59-65.

7. Snyder-Halpern R. The effect of critical care unit noise on patient sleep cycles. Critical Care Quarterly 1985;7:41-50.

8. Minckley BB. A study of noise and its relationship to patient discomfort in the recovery room. Nurs Res 1968;17:247-251.

9. Amario A, Lopez-Calderon A, Jolin T, Balasch J. Responses of anterior pituitary hormones to chronic stress. Neurosci Biobehav Rev 1986;10(3):245-250.

10. Monjan AA, Collector MI. Stress-induced modulation of the immune response. Science 1977;196:307-308.

11. Liley A. The fetus as a personality. Austr N Zeal J Psychiatry 1972;6:99-105.

12. Clements M. Observations on certain aspects of neonatal behavior in response to auditory stimuli. presented at Fifth Annual Congress of Psychosomatic Ob Gyn.Rome 1977.

13. Held R. Plasticity in sensory-motor systems. Scientific American 1965;213(5):84-94.


**Chapter 15**

1. Caraka Samhita, op cit. Su. 27;3.

2. Ibid. Vi 5;23.

3. Ibid. Su. 28;41.
4. Maharishi. Bhagavad-Gita. p 128.

**Chapter 16**
1. Charaka Samhita, Su. 27;349.
2. Ibid. Su. 27;350.
3. Ibid. Vi. 1;24.

**Chapter 17**
1. Liskowsky DR. Biological rhythms and shift work. JAMA 1992;268(21):3047.
2. Occup Med 1990;5:273-299.
3. Scand J Work Environ Health 1989;15:165-179.
4. Time magazine, 17 Dec 1990.
5. Wirz-Justice A. Circadian rhythms in mammalian neurotransmitter receptors. Prog Neurobiol 1987;29(3):219-259.
6. Decousus HA, Croze M, Levi FA, Jaubert JG, et al. Circadian changes in anticoagulant effect of heparin infused at a constant rate. Br Med J 1985;290(6465):341-344.
7. Petit E, Milano G, Levi F, Thyss A, et al. Circadian rhythm-varying plasma concentration of 5-fluorouracil during a five-day continuos venous infusion at a constant rate in cancer patients. Cancer Res 1988;48(6):1676-1679.
8. Levi F. [Chronobiology and cancer]. Pathol Biol 1987;35(6):960-968.
9. Lamberg L. Timing may be everything for diagnostics, drug therapy. American Medical News. March 4, 1996:16-19.
10. Phillips DP, King EW. Death takes a holiday: mortality surrounding major social occasions. Lancet 1988;2(8613):728-732.
11. Phillips DP, Smith DG. Postponement of death until symbolically meaningful occasions. JAMA 1990;263(14):695.
12. Breslow L, Enstrom JE. Persistance of health habits and their relationship to mortality. Prev Med 1980;9:469-483.
13. Palmblad J, Petrini B, Wasserman J, Akerstedt T. Lymphocyte and granulocyte reactions during sleep deprivation. Psychosom Med 1979;41(4):273-277.
14. Adam K, Oswal I. Sleep helps healing. Br Med J 1984;289:1400-1401.
15. Palmblad J, et al. Stressor exposure and immunological response in man: interferon-producing capacity and phagocytosis. J Psychosom Res 1976;20:193-199.
16. Paffenberger RS Jr, Hyde RT, Wing AL, Hsieh CC. Physical activity, all-cause mortality, and longevity of college alumni. NEJM 1986;314(10):605-613.
17. Blair SN, Kohl HW 3rd, Paffenberger RS Jr, Clark DG, et al. Physical fitness and all-cause mortality. A prospective study of healthy men and women. JAMA 1990;263(15):2047-2048.
18. Arraiz GA, Wigle DT, Mao Y. Risk assessment of physical activity and physical fitness in the Canada Health Survey mortality folow-up study. J Clin Epidemiol 1992;45(4):419-428.

19. Lee IM, Paffenberger RS Jr. Physical activity and its relation to cancer risk: a prospective study of college alumni. Med Sci Sports Exerc 1994;26(7);831-837.

20. Giovanucci E, Ascherio A, Rimm EB, Colditz GA. Physical activity, obesity, and risk for colon cancer and adenoma in men. Ann Intern Med 1995;122(5):327-334.

21. Leon AS, Connett J. Physical activity and 10.5 year mortality in the Multiple Risk Factor Intervention Trial (MRFIT). Int J Epidemiol 1991;20(3):690-697.


**Chapter 18**

1. Sharma HM, et al. Pharmacol Biochem Behav 1990;35:767-773.

2. Sharma HM, et al. J Res Edu Ind Med 1991;10(3):1-8.

   Sharma HM, et al Am Physiol Soc & Am Soc Pharmacol Exp Therapeutics 1988:A121 (Abstracts).

3. Patel VK, et al. Nutr Res 1992;12:667-676.

4. Sharma HM, et al. Antineoplastic properties of Maharishi-4 against DMBA-induced mammary tumors in rats. Pharmacol Biochem Behav 1990;35:767-773.

5. Johnston BH, et al. Pharmacologist 1991;3:39.

6. Prasad KN, et al. Neuropharmacology 1992;31:599-607.

7. Sharma HM, et al. Clin Ter Cardiovasc 1989;8:227-230.

8. Sharma HM,et al. J Res Edu Ind Med 1991;10(1):1-8.

9. Dileepan KN, et al. Biochem Arch 1990;6:267-274.

10. Maharishi Mahesh Yogi. In a lecture, March 1987.

11. Schneider RH, Cavanaugh KL, Kasture HS, Rothenberg S, Averbach R, Robinson D, Wallace RK. Health promotion with a traditional system of natural health care: Maharishi Ayur-Veda. J Soc Behav Personality 1990;5(3):1-27.

12. Sharma HM. Freedom from Disease. Veda Publishing. Toronto, Ontario, Canada. 1993;285-287.

13. Waldshutz R. Physiological and psychological changes associated with an Ayurvedic purification treatment. Ph.D. Thesis, University of Freiberg, Germany. 1988.


**Chapter 19**

1. Maharishi. Bhagavad-Gita. p 63.

2. Dillbeck MC, Landrith 3rd G, Orme-Johnson DW. The Transcendental Meditation program and crime rate change in a sample of forty-eight cities. J Crime & Justice 1981;4:25-45.

3. Dillbeck MC, et al. Maharishi's global ideal society campaign: improved quality of life in Rhode Island through the Transcendental Meditation and TM-Sidhi program. op cit: Collected Papers 1989;4:2521-2531.

4. Orme-Johnson DW, Alexander CN, Davies JL, Chandler HM, Larimore WE. International peace project in the Middle East: the effects of the Maharishi Technology of the Unified Field. J Conflict Resolution 1988;32(4):776-812.

5. Dissertation Abstracts International 1988;49:2381A.

6. J Mind Behav 1987;8:67-104.

7. op cit: Collected Papers Vol 2-5.

8. Data on file, Institute of Science, Technology and Public Policy, 1000 N. 4th St. Fairfield, IA 52557. Submitted for publication.

**Chapter 20**

1. Woo B, Woo B, Cook EF, Weisberg M, Goldman L. Screening procedures in the asymptomatic adult: comparison of physicians' recommendations, patients' desires, published guidelines, and actual practice. JAMA 1985;254:1480-1484.

2. Scutchfield FD, Hartman KT. Physicians and preventive medicine. JAMA 1995;273(14):1150-1151.

3. Shugars, et al. Arch Fam Med 1994;3:951.

4. US Public Health Service. Healthy People 2000: National Health Promotion and Disease Prevention Objectives. Washington, DC: US Dept Health and Human Services; 1991. Publication PHS 91-50212.

5. Orme-Johnson D. Medical care utilization and the Transcendental Meditation program. Psychosom Med 1987;49(5):493-507.

6. Bleick CR, Abrams AI. The Transcendental Meditation program and criminal recidivism in California. J Criminal Justice 1987;15:211-230.

7. Dillbeck MC, Abrams AI. The application of the Transcendental Meditation program to corrections. Int J Comparative & Applied Criminal Justice 1987;11:111-132.

8. Japanese Journal of Industrial Health 1990;32:656.

9. Japanese Journal of Public Health 1990;37:729.

10. Journal of the Iowa Academy of Science 1989;96:A2.

11. Academy of Management Journal 1974;17:362-368.

12. Education 1986;107:49-54.

13. Personality and Individual Differences 1991;12:1105-1116.

14. Gelderloos P. Psychological health and development of students at Maharishi International University: a controlled longitudinal study. Modern Science and Vedic Science 1987;1(4):471-487.

15. Alexander CN, et al. Growth of higher stages of consciousness: Maharishi's Vedic Psychology of human development. In, Higher Stages of Human Development: Perspectives on Adult Growth. New York; Oxford University Press 1990.

16. J Soc Behav & Personality 1991;6:189-247.

17. Education 1989;109:302-304.

18. Modern Science and Vedic Science 1987;1:433-468.

19. Hutchings R. Treating Addictions. The Source Dec 94-Jan 95:21.

20. Self Recovery: Treating Addictions Using Transcendental Meditation and Maharishi Ayur-Veda. Alexander CN, O'Connell DF, editors. Harrington Park Press, New York. 1994.

**Appendix A**

1. Maharishi. Thirty Years Around the World: Dawn of the Age of Enlightenment. MIU Press. Page 567.

**Appendix F**

1. Cushing H. Psychic disturbances associated with the ductless glands. American Journal of Insanity 1913;69:965-990.

2. Sonino N, Fava GA, Grandi S, et al. Stressful life events in the pathogenesis of Cushing's syndrome. Clin Endocrinol 1988:29;617-623.

3. Fava GA, Sonino N, Morphy MA. Major depression associated with endocrine disease. Psychiatric Developments 1987;4:321-348.

4. Mastrogiacomo I, Fava M, Fava GA. Correlations between psychologic symptoms in hyperprolactinemic amenorrhea. Neuroendocrinology Letters 1983;5:117-122.

5. Winsa B, Adami HO, Bergstrom R, Gamstedt A, et al. Stressful life events and Graves' disease. Lancet 1991; 338(8781):1474-1479.

6. Emanuele MA, Brooks MH, Gordon DL, et al. Agoraphobia and hyperthyroidism. Am J Med 1989;86:484-486.

7. Hui WM, Shui LP, Lam SK. The perception of life events and daily stress in nonulcer dyspepsia. Am J Gastroenterol 1991;86(3):292-296.

8. Blair JA, Blair RS, Rueckert P. Pre-injury emotional trauma and chronic back pain. An unexpected finding. Spine 1994;19(10):1144-1147.

9. Holmstrom EB, Lindell J, Moritz U. Low back and neck/shoulder pain in construction workers: occupational workload and psychosocial risk factors. Part 1: Relationship to low back pain. Spine 1992;17(6):663-671.

10. Craufurd DI, Creed F, Jayson MI. Life events and psychosocial disturbance in patients with low-back pain. Spine 1990;15(6):490-494.

11. Holm JE, Holroyd KA, Hursey KG, et al. The role of stress in recurrent tension headache. Headache 1986;26(4):160-167.

12. Cassileth BR, Lusk EJ, Strouse TB, et al. Psychological status in chronic illness: a comparative analysis of six diagnostic groups. N Engl J Med 1984;311:506-511.

13. Crown S, Crown JM, Fleming A. Aspects of the psychology and epidemiology of rheumatoid disease. Psychol Med 1975;5:291-299.

14. Silverman AJ. Rheumatoid arthritis, in Comprehensive Textbook of Psychiatry, 4th edition. Baltimore, Williams and Wilkins, 1985, pp 1185-1198.

15. Lehrer PM, Isenberg S, Hochron SM. Asthma and emotion: a review. J Asthma 1993;30(1):5-21.

16. Kotses H, Hindi-Alexander M, Creer TL. A reinterpretation of psychologically induced airways changes. J Asthma 1989;26(1):53-63.

17. Moran M. Psychological factors affecting pulmonary and rheumatologic diseases. Psychosomatics 1991;32(1):14-23.

18. Weiner H. Psychobiology and human disease. New York, Elsevier, 1977.

19. Tunsater A. Emotions and asthma, II. Eur J Respir Dis [Suppl] 1984;136:131-7.

20. In, Familiar Medical Quotations. Maurice Strauss, editor. Little, Brown & Co. Boston.1968:19.

21. Case RB, Moss AJ, Case N, McDermott M, Eberly S. Living alone after myocardial infarction. Impact on prognosis. JAMA 1992;267:515-519.

22. Williams RB, Barefoot JC, Califf RM, Haney TL, Saunders WB, Pryor DB, Tlatky MA, Siegler IC, Mark DB. Prognostic importance of social and economic resources among medically treated patients with angiographically documented coronary artery disease. JAMA 1992;267:520-524.

23. The beta-blocker heart attack trial. Beta-Blocker Heart Attack Study Group. JAMA 1981;246(18):2073-2074

24. Jenkinson CM, Madeley RJ, Mitchell JR, Turner ID. The influence of psychosocial factors on survival after myocardial infarction. Public Health 1993;107(5):305-317.

25. Ford DE. Cited in Modern Medicine 1995;63:23.

26. Frasure-Smith N, Lesperance F, Talajic M. Depression following myocardial infarction. Impact on 6 month survival. JAMA 1993;270(15):1819-1825.

26a. Frasure-Smith N, Lesperance F, Talajic M. Depression and 18 month prognosis after myocardial infarction. Circulation 1995;91:999-1005.

27. Cited in Family Practice News 1994;24:1.

28. Frasure-Smith N. In-hospital symptoms of psychological distress as predictors of long term outcome after myocardial infarction in men. Am J Cardiol 1991;67(2):121-127.

29. Strain J, of Mount Sinai Hospital NYC. Cited in Bottom Line/Personal newsletter 30 July 1992.

30. Zamarra JW, Besseghini I, Wittenberg S. The effects of the Transcendental Meditation program on the exercise performance of patients with angina pectoris. 1975. In, Scientific Research on the Transcendental Meditation Program Collected Papers. MERU Press. Livingston Manor, NY. 1977;1:270-278.

31. Mark D, of Duke University, cited by Associated Press.

32. Appels A, Otten F. Exhaustion as a precursor of cardiac death. Br J Clin Psychol 1992;31(pt 3):351-356.

33. Appels A, Schouten E. Burnout as a risk factor for coronary heart disease. Behav Med 1991;17(2):53-59.

34. Sutherland JE. The link between stress and illness. Postgraduate Medicine 1991;89(1):159-164.

35. Bairey CN, Krantz DS, DeQuattro V, Berman DS, Rozanski A. Effect of beta-blockade on heart rate-related ischemia during mental stress. J Am Coll Cardiol 1991;17(6):1388-1395.

36. Helmers KF, Krantz DS, Howell RH, Klein J, et al. Hostility and myocardial ischemia in coronary artery disease patients: evaluation by gender and ischemic index. Psychosom Med 1993;55(1):29-36.

37. Williams RB, Barefoot JC, Shekelle RB. The health consequences of hostility. In, Anger and Hostility in Cardiovascular and Behavioral Disorders. Hemisphere Publishing Corp 1985:173-185.

38. Mittleman MA, Maclure M, Sherwood JB, et al. Triggering of acute myocardial infarction by episodes of anger. Circulation 1995:92:1720-1725.

39. Gupta R, Gupta KD. Induction of myocardial ischemia by mental stress in coronary heart disease. J Assoc Physicians India 1993;41(2):75-78.

40. Kawachi I, Colditz GA, Ascherio A, Rimm EB, et al. Prospective study of phobic anxiety and risk of coronary heart disease in men. Circulation 1994;89(5):1992-1997.

41. Kawachi I, Sparrow D, Vokonas PS, Weiss ST. Symptoms of anxiety and risk of coronary heart disease. The Normative Aging Study. Circulation 1994;90(5):2225-2229.

42. Guyton AC. Textbook of Medical Physiology. WB Saunders Co. Philadelphia. Fifth Edition 1976:77-87.

43. Houldin AD, Lev E, Prystowsky MB, Redei E, Lowery BJ. Psychoneuroimmunology: A review of the literature. Holistic Nurs Pract 1991;5(4):10-21.

44. Angell M. Disease as a reflection of the psyche. NEJM 1985;312(24):1570-1572.

45. Felten DL, Felten SY. Sympathetic noradrenergic innervation of the immune organs. Behav Immun 1988;2:293-300.

46. Bulloch K, Moore RY. Innervation of the thymus gland by brain stem and spinal cord in mouse and rat. Am J Anat 1981;162:157-166.

47. Spector NH. Anatomic and physiologic connections between the central nervous and the immune systems (neuroimmunomodulation). In Immunoregulation. New York: Plenum Press 1983.

48. Calvo W. The innervation of the bone marrow in laboratory animals. Am J Anat 1968;123:315.

49. Baciu I. La regulation nerveuse et humorale di l'erythropoiese. J Physiol (Paris) 1962;54:441.

50. Moran MG. Psychological factors affecting pulmonary and rheumatologic diseases. Psychosomatics 1991;32(1):14-23.

51. Korneva EA, Khai LM. The effect of the destruction of areas within the hypothalamic region on the process of immunogenesis. Sechkenov Physiol J USSR 1963;49:52-62.

52. Luparello TJ, Stein M, Park CD. Effect of hypothalamic lesions on rat anaphylaxis. Am J Physiol 1964;207:911-914.

53. Szentivanyi A, Filipp G. Anaphylaxis and the nervous system. Ann Allergy 1958;16:143-151.

54. Dougherty TF, Frank JA. The qualitative and quantitative responses of blood lymphocytes to stress. J Lab Clin Med 1953;42:160-169.

55. Fessel WJ, Forsythe RF. Hypothalamic role in control of gamma globulin levels. Arth Rheum 1963;6:770.

56. Angeletti RH, Hickey WF. A neuroendocrine marker in tissues of the immune system. Science 1985;230:89-90.

57. Blalock JE, Smith EM. A complete regulatory loop between the immune and neuroendocrine systems. Federation Proceedings (Bethesda MD) 1985;44:108-111.

58. Dafny N, Dougherty P, Pellis NR. The effect of immunosupression and opiates upon the visual evoked responses of cortical and subcortical structures. Society for Neuroscience Abstracts 1985;11:907.

59. Besedovsky HO, Del Rey A, Sorkin E, Da Prada M, Kieler HH. Immunoregulation mediated by the sympathetic nervous system. Cell Immunol 1979;48:346.

60. Dunn AJ. Nervous system-immune system interactions: An overview. Journal Receptor Research 1988;8(1-4):598-607.

61. Fischer EG. Opioid peptides modulate immune functions. A review. Immunopharmacology Immunotoxicology 1988;10(3):265-326.

62. Keller SF, Weiss JM, Schleiffer SJ, Miller NE, Stein M. Stress-induced suppression of immunity in adrenalectomized rats. Science 1983;221:1301-1304.

63. Locke S, Kraus K, Kutz I, Edbril S, Phillips K, Benson H. Altered natural killer cell activity during norepinephrine infusion in humans. First International Workshop on Neuroimmunomodulation. 27 Nov 1984.

64. Hadden JW. Cyclic nucleotides and related mechanisms in immune regulation: a mini review. In Immunoregulation 1983;201-230.

65. Devoino LV, Eremina OF, Ilyutchenok R, Yu. The role of the hypothalamo-pituitary system in the mechanism of action of reserpine and 5-hydroxytryptophan on antibody production. Neuropharm 1970;9:67-72.

66. Devoino LV, Ilyutchenok R, Yu. Influence of some drugs on the immune response. II. Effects of serotonin, 5-hydroxytryptophan, reserpine and iproniazid on delayed hypersensitivity. Eur J Pharm 1968;4:449-456.

67. Besedovsky H, Sorkin E, Felix D, Haas H. Hypothalamic changes during immune response. Eur J Immunol 1977;7:323-325.

68. Smith EM, Blalock JE. Human lymphocyte production of corticotropin and endorphin like substances: association with leukocyte interferon. Proc Natl Acad Sci USA 1981;78:7530-7534.

69. Besedovsky HO, Del Rey A, Sorkin E, Da Prada M, Burri R, Honneger C. The immune response evokes changes in brain noradrenergic neurons. Science 1983;221:564-565.

70. Ader R. On the clinical relevance of psychoneuroimmunology. Clinical Immunology and Immunopathology 1992;64(1):6-8.

71. Solomon GF, Amkraut AA. Emotions, immunity and disease. In, Emotions in Health and Illness: Theoretical and Research Foundations. New York: Grune & Stratton. 1983;167-186.

72. Zozulia AA, Patsakova EK, Kost NV. Reaction between methionine enkephalin and human lymphocytes. Akad Med Nauh SSSR 1982;1:28-32.

73. Cantor H, Gershon RK. Immunological circuits. Cellular compositions. Fed Proc 1979;39:2058-2064.

74. Helderman JH, Strom TB. Specific binding site on T and B lymphocytes as a marker of cell activation. Nature 1978;274:62-63.

75. Pert CB. The wisdom of the receptors: Neuropeptides, the emotions, and bodymind. Advances 1986;3(3):8-16.

76. Ader R, Cohen N. Behaviorally conditioned immunosupression. Psychosomatic Medicine 1975;37:333.

77. Ader R, Cohen N. The influence of conditioning on immune responses. In, Psychoneuroimmunology 2nd Ed. Academic Press, New York 1991;611-646.

78. Ader R, Cohen N. Behaviorally conditioned immunosuppression and murine systemic lupus erythematosus. Science 1982;214:1534-1536.

79. Olness K, Ader R. Conditioning as an adjunct in the pharmacotherapy of lupus erythematosus: A case report. J Dev Behav Pediatr 1992.

80. Gorczynski RM, Kennedy M, Ciampi A. Conditioned enhancement of skin allografts in mice. Brain Behav Immun 1990;4:85-92.

81. Metal'nikov S, Chorine V. The role of conditioned reflexes in immunity. Ann Inst Pasteur 1926;40:893-900.

82. Solomon GF. Stress and antibody response in rats. Int Arch Allergy 1969;35:97-104.

83. Amkraut AA, Solomon GF, Kasper P, Perdue A. Effect of stress on the graft versus host response. Adv Exper Med Biol 1973;29:267-274.

84. Kort WJ, VanDongen JJ, Westbrook DL. The effect of stress on the survival of grafted organs. Microchirurgie 1976;1:21-23.

85. Kort WJ, Wejima JM, Westbrook DL. Effect of stress and dietary fatty acids on allograft in the rat. Eur Surg Res 1979;11:434-444.

86. Laudenslager ML, Ryan SM, Drugar RC, Hysen RE, Maier SF. Coping and immunosuppression: inescapable but not escapable shock suppresses lymphocyte proliferation. Science 1983;221:568-570.

87. Maier SF, Laudenslager MI, Ryan SM. Stressor controllability, immune function and endogenous opiates. Unpublished manuscript cited in Advances 1985:2(1):6-19.

88. Kemeny M. Mind, emotions and the immune system. Presentation at annual conference of Institute of Noetic Sciences, Arlington, VA; June 1993.

89. Jabaaij L, Grosheide P, Heijtink R, Duivenvoorden H, Ballieux R, Vingerhoets A. Influence of perceived psychological stress and distress on antibody response to low dose rDNA hepatitis B vaccine. J Psychosom Res 1993;37(4):361-369.

90. Hatch MC, Wallenstein S, Beyea J, Nieves JW, Susser M. Cancer rates after the Three Mile Island nuclear accident and proximity of residence to the plant. Am J Pub Health 1991;81:719-724.

91. McKinnon W, Weisse CS, Reynolds CP, Bowles CA, Baum A. Chronic stress, leukocyte subpopulations and humoral response to latent viruses. Health Psychol 1989;8:389-402.

92. Van Rood Y, Bogaards M, Goulmy E, van Houwelingen H. The effects of stress and relaxation on the in vitro immune response in man: A meta-analytic study. J Behav Med 1992;16(2):163-181.

93. Kiecolt-Glaser JK, Glaser R, Dyer C, Shuttleworth EC, Ogrocki P, Speicher CE. Chonic stress and immune function in family caregivers of Alzheimer's disease victims. Psychosomatic Medicine 1987;49:523-535.

94. Koff WC, Dunegan MA. Modulation of macrophage-mediated tumoricidal activity by neuropeptides and neurohormones. J Immunol 1985;135:350-354.

95. Ramirez AJ, Craig TKJ, Watson JP, et al. Stress and relapse of breast cancer. BMJ 1989;298:291-293.

96. Pettingale KW, Greer S, Tee DEH. Serum IgA and emotional expression in breast cancer patients. J Psychosom Res 1977;21:395-399.

97. Basso AM, Depiante-Depaoli M, Molina VA. Chronic variable stress facilitates tumoral growth: reversal by imipramine administration. Life Sci 1992;50:1789-1796.

98. Glaser R, Rice J, Speicher CE, Stout JC, Kiecolt-Glaser JK. Stress depresses interferon production by leukocytes concomitant with a decrease in NK cell activity. Behavioral Neuroscience 1986b;100:675.

99. Halversen R, Vassend O. Effect of examination stress on some cellular immunity functions. J Psychosom Res 1987;31:693.

100. Vassend O, Halversen R. Personality, examination stress and serum concentration of immunoglobulins. Scand J Psychol 1987;28:233-241.

101. Dorian BJ, Keystone E, Garfinkle PE, Brown GM. Aberrations in lymphocyte subpopulations and functions during psychological stress. Clin Exp Immunol 1982;50:132-138.

102. Jemmott JB, Magloire K. Academic stress, social support, and secretory immunoglobulin A. Journal of Personality and Social Psychology 1988;55:803-808.

103. Jemmott JB, Borysenko M, Chapman R, Borysenko JZ, McClelland DC, Meyer D, Benson H. Academic stress, power motivation, and decrease in secretion rate of salivary secretory immunoglobulin A. Lancet 1983;1:1400-1402.

104. Locke SE, Kraus L, Leserman J, Hurst MW, Heise LS, Williams RM. Life change stress, psychiatric symptoms, and natural killer cell activity. Psychosom Med 1984;46:441-453.

105. Glaser R, Kiecolt-Glaser JK, Speicher CE, Holiday JR. Stress, loneliness, and change in herpes virus latency. J Behav Med 1985a;8:249.

106. Kiecolt-Glaser JK, Garner W, Speicher CE, Penn GM, Holliday J, Glaser R. Psychosocial modifiers of immunocompetence in medical students. Psychosom Med 1984;46:7-14.

107. Kiecolt-Glaser JK, Ricker D, Messick G, Speicher CE, Garner W, Glaser R. Urinary cortsol, cellular immunocompetency and loneliness in psychiatric inpatients. Psychosom Med 1984;46:15-24.

108. Bartrop RW, Lockhurst E, Lazarus L, Kiloh LG, Penny R. Depressed lymphocyte function after bereavement. Lancet 1977;1:834-836.

109. Schliefer SL, Keller SE, Camerino M, Thomton JC, Stein M. Suppression of lymphocyte stimulation following bereavement. JAMA 1983;250:374-377.

110. Linn MW, Linn BS, Jensen J. Stressful events, dysphoric mood, and immune responsiveness. Psychol Rep 1984:54:219-222.

111. Stein M, Keller S, Schleifer S. Stress and immunomodulation: The role of depression and neuroendocrine function. J Immunol 1985;135:827s-833s.

112. Irwin M, Daniels M, Risch SC, Bloom ET, Weiner H. Plasma cortisol and natural killer cell activity during bereavement. Biological Psychiatry 1988;24:173-178.

113. Irwin M, Daniels M, Smith TL, et al. Impaired natural killer cell activity during bereavement. Brain Behav Immun 1987;1:98-104.

114. Cappel R, Gregorie F, Thiry L, Sprechers S. Antibody and cell-mediated immunity to herpes simplex virus in psychotic depression. J Clin Psychiatry 1978;39:266-268.

115. Darko DF, Rose J, Gillin JC, et al. Peripheral white blood cells and HPA axis neurohormones in major depression. Int J Neurosci 1989;45:153-159.

116. Irwin M, Daniels M, Bloom ET, Smith TL, Weiner H. Life events, depressive symptoms, and immune function. Am J Psychiatry 1987;144(4):437-441.

117. Kiecolt-Glaser JK, Fisher L, Ogrocki P, Stout JC, Speicher CE, Glaser R. Marital quality, marital disruption, and immune function. Psychosom Med 1987a;49:13-35.

118. Kiecolt-Glaser JK, Kennedy S, Malkoff S, Fisher L, Speicher CE, Glaser R. Marital discord and immunty in males. Psychosom Med 1988;50:213-229.

119. Linn B, Linn M, Klimas N. Effects of psychophysical stress on surgical outcome. Psychosom Med 1988;50:230-245.

120. Thomas PD, Goodwin JM, Goodwin JS. Effect of social support on stress-related changes in cholesterol level, uric acid level, and immune function in an elderly sample. Am J Psychiatry 1985;142(6):735-737.

121. Schlesinter M, Yodfat Y. Effect of psychosocial stress on natural killer cell activity. Canc Det Prev 1988;12:9-14.

122. Kubitz KA, Peavey BS, Moore BS. The effect of daily hassles on humoral immunity: An interaction moderated by locus of control. Biofeedback and Self-Regulation 1986;11(2):115-123.

123. Risenberg DE. Can mind affect body defenses against disease? Nascent specialty offers a host of tantalizing clues. JAMA 1986;256:313-317.

124. Esterling B, Rabin BS. Stress-induced alteration of T-lymphocyte subsets and humoral immunity in mice. Behav Neurosci 1987;101:115-118.

125. Selye H. History and present status of the stress concept. In, Handbook of Stress: Theoretical and Clinical Aspects. New York. Free Press 1982.

126. Alfredsson L, Karasek R, Theorell T. Myocardial infarction risk and psychosocial work environment: An analysis of the male Swedish working force. Swed Soc Sci Med 1982;16:463-467.

127. Brenner MH. Mortality and the national economy. Lancet 1979;ii:568-573.

128. Koller M. Health risks associated with shift work. An example of the time-contingent effects of long term stress. Int Arch Occup Environ Health 1983;53:59-75.

129. Smith MJ, Colligan MJ. Health and safety consequences of shift work in the food processing industry. Ergonomics 1982;25:133-144.

130. Clover RD, Abell T, Becker LA, Crawford S, Ramsey CN. Family functioning and stress as predictors of influenza B infection. J Fam Pract 1989;28:535-539.

131. Graham NM, Douglas RM, Ryan P. Stress and acute respiratory infection. Am J Epidemiol 1986;124:389-401.

132. Broadbent DE, Broadbent MHP, Phillpotts RJ, Wallace J. Some further studies on the prediction of experimental colds in volunteers by psychological factors. J Psychosom Res 1984;28:511-523.

133. Cohen S, Tyrrell DA, Smith AP. Psychological stress and susceptibility to the common cold. NEJM 1991;325(9):606-612.

134. Fawzy FI, Kemeny ME, Fawzy NW, Elashoff R, Morton D, Cousins N, Fahey JL. A structured psychiatric intervention for cancer patients. II. Changes over time in immunologic measures. Arch Gen Psych 1990;47:729-735.

135. Fawzy FI, Fawzy NW, Hyun CS, Elashoff R, Guthrie D, Fahey JL, Morton DL. Malignant melanoma: Effects of an early structured psychiatric intervention, coping, and affective state on recurrence and survival six years later. Arch Gen Psychiatry 1993;50:681-689.

136. McClelland C, Floor E, Davidson RJ, Saron C. Stressed power motivation, sympathetic activation, immune functioning and illness. J Human Stress 1980;6(2):11-19.

137. Glaser R, Rice J, Sheridan J, et al. Stress related immune suppression: Health implications. Brain, Behavior, and Immunity 1987;1:7-20.

138. Pennebaker JW, Kiecolt-Glaser JK, Glaser R. Disclosure of traumas and immune function: Health implications for psychotherapy. J Consult Clin Psychol 1988;56(2):239-245.

139. Kasl SV, Evans AS, Niederman JC. Psychosocial risk factors in the development of infectious mononucleosis. Psychosom Med 1979;41:445.

140. Katcher AH, Brightman V, Lubovsky L, Ship I. Prediction of incidence of recurrent herpes labialis and systemic illness. Psychological measurements. J Dent Res 1973;52:49.

141. Friedman E, Katcher AH, Brightman VJ. Incidence of recurrent herpes labialis and upper respiratory infection: A prospective study of the influence of biologic, social and psychologic predictors. Oral Surgery 1977;43:873.

142. Schmidt DD, Zyzanski S, Ellner J, Kumar ML, Arno J. Stress as a precipitating factor in subjects with recurrent herpes labialis. J Fam Pract 1985;20:359-366.

143. Nuckolls KB, Cassel J, Kaplan BH. Psychosocial assets, life crisis, and the prognosis of pregnancy. Am J Epi 1972;95:431-441.

144. Morris NM, Udry JR, Chase CL. Reduction of low birth weight birth rates by the prevention of unwanted pregnancies. Am J Pub Health 1973;3(11):935-938.

145. Norbeck JS, Tilden VP. Life stress, social support, and emotional disequilibrium in complications of. pregnancy: A prospective, multivariate study. J Health Soc Behav 1983;24(3):30-46

146. Calabrese Jr, Kling MA, Gold PW. Alterations in immunocompetence during stress, bereavement, and depression: focus on neuroendocrine regulation. Am J Psychiatry 1987;144(9):1123-1134.

147. Helsing KJ, Szklo M, Comstock GW. Factors associated with mortality after widowhood. Am J Pub Health 1981;71(8):802-809.

148. Rose RM, Jenkins CD, Hurst MW. Air traffic controller health change study: Aprospective investigation of physical, psychological and work related changes (Contract No. DOT-FA737WA-3211). 1978; Boston U School of Med. Cited in Who Gets Sick? by Blair Justice.

149. Liljefors I, Rahe RH. An identical twin study of psychosocial factors in coronary artery disease in Sweden. Psychosom Med 1970;32:523-542.

150. Dzau VJ. Atherosclerosis and hypertension: mechanisms and interrelationships. J Cardiovasc Pharmacol 1990;15(suppl 5):S59-S64.

151. Solomon GF. Whither psychoneuroimmunology? A new era of immunology, of psychosomatic medicine, and of neuroscience. Brain Behav Immun 1993;7:352-366.

152. Muhlestein JB, Hammond EH, Carlquist JF, et al. Increased incidence of *Chlamydia* species within the coronary arteries of patients with symptomatic atherosclerotic versus other forms of cardiovascular disease. J Am Coll Cardiology 1996;27:1555-1561.

153. Kiecolt-Glaser JK, Glaser R, Strain EC, Stout JC, et al. Modulation of cellular immunity in medical students. J Behav Med 1986;9(1):5-21.

154. Levy S, Herberman R, Lippman M, D'Angelo T. Correlation of stress factors with sustained depression of NK cell activity and predicted prognosis in patients with breast cancer. J Clin Oncol 1987;5:348-353.

155. Janowski ML, Kugler J. Relaxation, imagery and neuroimmunomodulation. Ann NY Acad Sci 1987;496:722-730.

156. Kiecolt-Glaser JK, Glaser R, Williger D, et al. Psychosocial enhancement of immunocompetence in a geriatric population. Health Psychol 1985;4:25-41.

157. Green RG, Green ML. Relaxation increases salivary immunoglobulin A. Psychol Rep 1987;61:623-629.

158. Stone AA, Valdimarsdottir H, Jandorf L, Cox DS, Neale JM. Evidence that secretory IgA antibody is associated with daily mood. J Personality Soc Psychol 1987;52(5):988-993.

159. Dillon KM, Minchoff B, Baker KH. Positive emotional states and enhancement of the immune system. Int J Psychiatr Med 1985-86;15:13-18.

160. Berk LS, Tan SA, Nehlsen-Cannarella SL, et al. Humor associated laughter decreases cortisol and increases spontaneous lymphocyte blastogenesis. Clin Res 1988;36:435A.

161. McClelland DC, Kirshnit C. The effect of motivational arousal through films on salivary immunoglobulin A. Psychol Health 1988;2:31-52.

162. Braun BG. Neurophysiologic changes in multiple personality due to integration: a preliminary report. Am J Clin Hypn 1983;26(2):84-92.

163. Braun BG. Psychophysiologic phenomena in multiple personality and hypnosis. Am J Clin Hypn 1983;26(2):124-137.

164. Fauci AS. AIDS: Immunopathogenic mechanisms and research strategies. Clin Res 1987;35:503-510.

165. Ritchie AW, Oswald I, Micklem HS, et al. Circadian variation of lymphocyte subpopulations: A study with monoclonal antibodies. BMJ 1983;286:1773-1775.

166. Markham PD, Salahuddin SZ, Veren K, et al. Hydrocortsone and some other hormones enhance the expression of HTLV-III. Int J Cancer 1986;37:67-72.

167. Kemeny ME. Psychoneuroneuroimmunology of HIV infection. Psychiatr Clin Nor Am 1994;17(1):55-68.

168. Detels R, English PA, Giorgi JV, et al. Patterns of CD4+ cell changes after HIV-1 infection indicate the existence of a co-determinant of AIDS. J Acquir Immune Defic Syndr 1988;1:390-395.

169. Martin JL. Psychological consequences of AIDS-related bereavement among gay men. J Consult Clin Psychol 1988;56:856-862.

170. Ostrow DG, Monjan A, Joseph J, et al. HIV-related symptoms and psychological functioning in a cohort of homosexual men. Am J Psychiatry 1992;146:739-741.

171. Perry S, Fishman B, Jacobsberg L, et al. Relationships over 1 year between lymphocyte subsets and psychosocial variables among adults with infection by human immunodeficiency virus. Arch Gen Psychiatry 1992;49:396-401.

172. Coates TJ, McKusick L, Kuno R, et al. Stress reduction training changed number of sexual partners but not immune function in men with HIV. Am J Pub Health 1989;79:885-887.

173. Kemeny ME, Weiner H, Duran R, et al. Immune system changes following the death of a partner in HIV positive gay men. In press; cited in ref # 116.

174. Kemeny ME, Weiner H, Taylor SE, et al. Repeated bereavement, depressed mood, and immune parameters in HIV seropositive and seronegative gay men. Health Psychol 1994;13:14 -24.

175. Kemeny ME, Duran R, Taylor S, et al. Chronic depression predicts CD4 decline over a five year period in HIV seropositive men. Paper presented at the Sixth International Conference on AIDS, San Francisco, June 1990.

176. Reed GM, Kemeny ME, Taylor SE,et al. "Realistic" acceptance as a predictor of decreased decreased survival time in gay men with AIDS. Health Psychol. In press; cited in ref # 116.

177. Kemeny ME, Reed GM, Taylor SE, et al. Negative HIV-specific expectancies predict immunologic evidence of HIV progression. Submitted; cited in ref # 152.

178. Goodkin K, Blaney NT, Feaster D, Fletcher MA, et al. Active coping style is associated with natural killer cell cytotoxicity in asymptomatic HIV-1 seropositve homosexual men. J Psychosom Res 1992;36:635-650.

179. Parillo JE, Fauci AS. Mechanisms of glucocorticoid action on immune processes. Annu Rev Pharmacol Toxicol 1979;19:179-201.

180. Ironson G, LaPerriere A, Antoni M, O'Hearn P, et al. Changes in immune and psychological measures as a function of anticipation and reaction to news of HIV-1 antibody status. Psychosom Med 1990;52(3):247-270.

181. Antoni MH, August S, LaPerriere A, Baggett HL, et al. Psychological and neuro-endocrine measures related to functional immune changes in anticpation of HIV-1 serostatus notification. Psychosom Med 1990;52(5):496-510.

182. Antoni MH, Baggett L, Laperriere A, et al. Cognitive behavioral stress mangement intervention buffers distress responses and immunologic changes following notification of HIV-1 seropositivity. J Consult Clin Psychol 1991;59:906-915.

183. Esterling BA, Antoni MH, Schneiderman N, et al. Psychosocial modulation of antibody to Epstein-Barr viral capsid antigen and human herpesvirus Type-6 in HIV-1 infected and at-risk gay men. Psychosom Med 1992;54:354-371.

184. Solomon GF, Temoshok L, O'Leary A, Zich J. An intensive psychoimmunologic study of long-surviving persons with AIDS. Ann NY Acad Sci 1987;496:647-655.

185. Field TM, Schanberg SM, Scafidi F, Bauer CR, et al. Tactile/kinesthetic stimulation effects on preterm neonates. Peds 1986;77(5):654-658.

186. Wirth DP. The effect of non-contact therapeutic touch on the healing of full thickness dermal wounds. Subtle Energies 1(1):1-20. Cited by Larry Dossey in Healing Words.

187. Quinn JF. Therapeutic touch as energy exchange: testing the theory. Adv Nurs Sci 1984;Jan:42-49.

188. Braud WG, Schlitz M. Consciousness interactions with remote biological systems: anomolous intentionality effects. Subtle Energies 1992;2(1):1-46. Cited in Healing Words.

189. Braud WG, Schlitz M. Cited in Healing Words, 186-187.

190. Cited by Dossey L., in Healing Words San Francisco. Harper. 1993:33.

191. Byrd RC. Positive therapeutic effects of intercessory prayer in a coronary care unit population. South Med J 1988;81(7):826-829.

192. Cited by Dossey L., in Healing Words; Spindrift Inc., PO Box 3995, Salem OR 97302-0995.

193. Owen R. Qualitative Research: The Early Years. Salem OR. Grayhaven Books. 1988:22-23.

194. Ibid. p89.

195. Told to me by Lupe Moore.

196. Dossey L. Healing Words. p113

197. Radin D, Nelson R. Consciousness-related effects in random physical systems. Foundations of Physics 1989;19:1499-1514.

198. Braud WG, Schlitz M. Time displaced effects? In, Consciousness interactions with remote biological systems: anomolous intentionality effects. Subtle Energies 1992;2(1):1-46.

199. Schmidt H. Superposition of PK effects by man and dog. In, Research in Parapsychology 1983. Metuchen, NJ. Scarecrow Press. 1984:96-98.

200. Schmidt H. Human PK effort on pre-recorded random events previously observed by goldfish. In, Research in Parapsychology 1985. Metuchen, NJ. Scarecrow Press. 1986:18-21.

201. Uhlenhuth EH, Cantor A, Neustadt O, Payson HE. The symptomatic relief of anxiety with meprobamate, phenobarbital and placebo. Am J Psychiatr 1959;115:905-910.

202. Uhlenhuth EH, Rickels K, Fisher S, Park LC, Lipman RS, Mock J. Drug, doctor's verbal attitude and clinical setting in the symptomatic response to pharmacotherapy. Psychopharmacologia 1966;9:392-418.

203. Solvin J. Mental Healing. In, Advances in Parapsychological Research, Volume 4. Jefferson NC. McFarland and Co. 1984:55-56.

204. Barry J. General and comparative study of the psychokinetic effect on a fungus culture. J Parapsychol 1968;32:237-243.

205. Tedder W, Monty M. Exploration of long distance PK: a conceptual replication of the influence on a biological system. Research in Parapsychology 1980. 1981;90-93.

206. Nash CB. Psychokinetic control of bacterial growth. J Am Society Psychical Res 1982;51:217-221.

207. Grad B. A telekinetic effect on plant growth: III. Stimulating and inhibiting effects. Research brief presented to the Seventh Annual Convention of the Parapsychological Association, Oxford U, 1964.

208. Nash CB. Test of psychokinetic control of bacterial mutation. J Am Society Psychical Res 1984;78(2):145-152.

# INDEX